TITLED PUBLISHED
BY
PRESS PUBLICATION
A SUBSIDIARY OF HISTORIC PUBLISHING
©2017

Africa and the American Negro

Addresses and Proceedings of the Congress on Africa: Held under the Auspices of the Stewart Missionary Foundation for Africa of Gammon Theological Seminary in Connection with the Cotton States and International Exposition December 13-15, 1895.

Edited by
J. W. E. Bowen

[1855-1933]

Southeast View of the Campus of Gammon Theological Seminary; Gammon Hall, Library and President's residence

AFRICA and the
AMERICAN NEGRO . . .

ADDRESSES AND PROCEEDINGS

OF THE

CONGRESS ON AFRICA

HELD UNDER THE AUSPICES OF THE

Stewart Missionary Foundation for Africa

OF

Gammon Theological Seminary

IN CONNECTION WITH

THE COTTON STATES AND INTERNATIONAL EXPOSITION

DECEMBER 13-15, 1895

Edited by Prof. J. W. E. Bowen, Ph.D., D.D., Secretary of the Congress

ATLANTA
GAMMON THEOLOGICAL SEMINARY
1896

AFRICA and the AMERICAN NEGRO ...

ADDRESSES AND PROCEEDINGS
OF THE
CONGRESS ON AFRICA

HELD UNDER THE AUSPICES OF THE
Stewart Missionary Foundation for Africa
OF
Gammon Theological Seminary

IN CONNECTION WITH
THE COTTON STATES AND
INTERNATIONAL EXPOSITION

DECEMBER 13-15, 1895

Edited by
Prof. J. W. E. Bowen, Ph.D., D.D., Secretary of the Congress

ATLANTA
GAMMON THEOLOGICAL SEMINARY
1896

PRESS OF
THE FRANKLIN PRINTING AND PUBLISHING CO.,
ATLANTA, GA.
1896

WILBUR P. THIRKIELD, D.D.
President of the Congress on Africa
President of Gammon Theological Seminary from its Foundation in 1883 to the
Present

Contents

PART I
AFRICA: THE CONTINENT; ITS PEOPLES, THEIR CIVILIZATION
AND EVANGELIZATION

PART II
THE AMERICAN NEGRO: HIS RELATION TO THE CIVILIZATION
AND REDEMPTION OF AFRICA

BISHOP ISAAC W. JOYCE, D.D., LL.D.
Of the Methodist Episcopal Church; Chancellor of the U.S. Grant University

INTRODUCTION

A congress on Africa! Why not?

What land is more entitled to our best thought, or more deserving the most helpful service we can render? Where the country with a history of more romantic interest, or one whose peoples have had a more varied experience or presented more serious problems for the study of mankind? Men, whose names are among the greatest in history, have been its explorers, and the students of its languages and of its dialects. It is so rich in soils and in minerals as to excite the greed of the world, and the nations of the earth have contended with each other for a division of its treasures. In the interests of commerce the steamers of the merchant princes navigate its waters, and the markets of the world are open to its products. A literature on Africa, rich in every way, has been created by scholarly men, who have made the most heroic sacrifices that they might acquaint the world with the present greatness and future possibilities of "The Dark Continent." These men, and others such as they, will continue to enrich with the best equipments those who wish to wisely study the many phases of the growing questions in relation to Africa. This Congress was surely in the order of Divine Providence. God uses men in the development of His plans. In this instance it was His servant, the Rev. W. F. Stewart, through the agency of whose consecrated wealth this "Missionary Foundation" was established, and the holding of this congress was made possible. Men of scholarship, and imbued with the spirit of Christ, deeply interested in the evangelization of Africa, came together from various parts of the United States and other countries, and presented well prepared papers on the subjects which had been assigned them. The discussions which followed revealed mental grasps of the subjects and the hearty interest of the speakers in the principles underlying the whole question. From the beginning of the congress to its close the audiences were large and the interest very great.

The utmost harmony prevailed in all the deliberations, and this volume, which is the result of the congress, is an evidence of the oneness of spirit that was at all times manifest, and also of the fervent conviction that pervaded all hearts that the Church of the Lord Jesus Christ ought to arise and go forth and evangelize Africa, thus obeying the command of the Lord to "Go into all the world."

That she is able to do this there can be no question; that it is her duty to do this, all will agree; but will she do this great work? Our faith answers: *Yes.* The establishment of this Missionary Foundation is a strong testimony that the Holy Spirit is drawing the thoughts and hearts of the servants of God to the ever-crying needs of "The Dark Continent," and a careful reading of the pages of this book will make impressions which will strengthen the testimony in favor of this truth. It would be well, from time to time in the coming years, for those in charge of this great interest to hold other congresses of like character and purpose with this one, and thus widen and intensify the influence of "The Stewart Missionary Foundation for Africa," in its association with Gammon Theological Seminary. Thus in all the years to come the names of Stewart and of Gammon would be blended in the thoughts and love of all good men, and the wealth they consecrated to the enlargement of the Kingdom of Christ among men would be multiplied many times in power for good and increased in influence for righteousness through all time, even unto the end of the world.

ISAAC W. JOYCE

Chattanooga, Tenn.

REV. WM. F. STEWART, A. M.

Establisher of the Stewart Missionary Foundation for Africa in Gammon Theological Seminary; For Fifty-Two Years member of the Ohio, then of the Rock River, Conference of the Methodist Episcopal Church; For many years one of the Trustees of the Northwestern University of Chicago.

REV. WM. F. STEWART, A. M.
Establisher of the Stewart Missionary Foundation for Africa in Gammon Theological Seminary; For Fifty-Two Years member of the Ohio, then of the Rock River, Conference of the Methodist Episcopal Church; For many years one of the Trustees of the Northwestern University of Chicago.

The Stewart Missionary Foundation for Africa and the Purpose of the Congress

BY
PROF. E. L. PARKS, D.D.
GAMMON THEOLOGICAL SEMINARY

This Foundation is in the interest, especially among American Negroes, of missionary work for Africa. It has been established by Rev. W. F. Stewart, A. M., of the Rock River Conference of the Methodist Episcopal Church. It is the outgrowth of many years of thought in the consecration of a large portion of his property. In a letter in the early part of the correspondence leading to the establishment of the Foundation, Mr. Stewart thus comprehensively states the purpose of the Foundation:

"My hope is that it may become *a center* for the diffusion of missionary intelligence, the development of missionary enthusiasm, the increase of missionary offerings and through sanctified and trained missionaries hasten obedience to the great commission to 'preach the gospel to every creature.' In addition to the direct work of the recitation room, I have contemplated other educating means that would reach our schools and missions and the whole membership of the church."

Mr. Stewart has set aside for the endowment of the Foundation a group of farms in Central Illinois, comprising in all some six hundred acres. The whole tract is tile-drained in a systematic and thorough manner, so as to make every acre of it first-class tillable land.

In placing this Foundation in connection with Gammon Theological Seminary, Mr. Stewart unites it with a largely endowed institution, which is central and at the head, in theological education, of one of the greatest systems of schools for the Negro in America. The Foundation fills an important place in the very purpose for which the Seminary was established. All the forces of the Seminary are used to reduplicate the influence of the Foundation. There is not only a remarkable parallel in the work of Mr. Gammon and Mr. Stewart, but the fundamental thought which was back of their work is also in perfect accord. This clearly appears in the following, which shows also that Elijah H. Gammon was our prophet, as well as the founder of the Seminary. As early as August, 1887, he wrote:

"I believe it most thoroughly, as Ethiopia stretches out her hands to God, help must come through your school. Who but you can furnish the thousands of missionaries for Africa? You may as well attempt to understand and comprehend the astronomy of the heavens as the possibilities of your school."

The work of the Foundation has been inaugurated by offering prizes for

essays and orations on Africa as a missionary field, the obligation of the American Negro to missionary work in Africa and kindred themes, and for missionary hymns. The object of offering these prizes is to encourage thought and investigation, spread intelligence and stimulate personal and property consecration among the American Negroes for missionary work in Africa. These prizes are offered, among the colored people, to the students of all the schools of the Freedmen's Aid and Southern Education Society, and to all the local churches of the Methodist Episcopal Church. Correspondence, to secure the prompt cooperation of all interested, is invited.

The Foundation is also gathering a special library on Africa. The nucleus already has been pronounced, by expert judges, one of the best in the country in the general field of African exploration and missionary work. The Foundation is also collecting an African museum. This collection already includes a large number of specimens of African handiwork in wood, iron, brass, cloth, grass, etc., which reveal very clearly the native genius and artistic skill of the untutored African. In addition to the above, out of a list of five hundred or more stereopticon slides, there have been selected about two hundred superior views for use in the stereopticon of the Seminary. These native fabrics and curios, as well as the stereopticon slides, will be used in the schools and churches to illustrate the products, industries and scenery of Africa, and the conditions and life of its peoples. These are only the beginnings of the collections of books and illustrative material on Africa and its peoples, which it is hoped will be made among the greatest of their kind in this country. They are deposited in the practically fire-proof library building of the Seminary. Donations are invited.

As a very important means in carrying out the purpose of Mr. Stewart in establishing the Foundation, as stated in the foregoing, the President of the Seminary, with the coöperation of the Faculty, suggested to Mr. Stewart the feasibility of a congress on Africa. Mr. Stewart heartily approved the plan. Through Mr. I. Garland Penn, Chief Commissioner of the Negro Exhibit, it was made one of the auxiliary congresses of the Cotton States and International Exposition at Atlanta.

In all the plans of the congress the Faculty of the Seminary kept in view the general purpose of the Foundation, the promotion of the interests, especially among American Negroes, of missionary work for Africa. The industrial, intellectual, moral and spiritual progress of the colored people in America is a prophecy, both of what they will become and will do for the redemption of their fatherland, and also of what the native African is capable of becoming. For this reason, it was thought wise to include in the program addresses and papers on the American Negro, by the side of those on African exploration, native peoples, languages and religion, and the opportunity, means for the promotion, and progress of civilization and of missions in Africa.

PART I

AFRICA: THE CONTINENT; ITS PEOPLES, THEIR CIVILIZATION AND EVANGELIZATION

Opening Remarks

BY
PREST. W. P. THIRKIELD, D.D.
GAMMON THEOLOGICAL SEMINARY

It is a most grateful task that falls to me, as President of this Congress, to welcome you, as delegates and friends, to the first Congress on Africa ever held in the South. This great audience at the opening session emphasizes the interest of the people in the program prepared for this occasion.

This Christian Congress indicates that God is stretching forth his hands to Ethiopia--to that "Dark Continent" which, through long and dolorous ages, has been vainly stretching forth its hands unto God.

While light is breaking in upon its darkness, the hand that blights and curses is not yet lifted. In other centuries the curse was the *stealing of Africans from Africa.* Now, it is the game among European nations of "shut your eyes and grab" in their efforts to *steal Africa from the Africans.* But God is yet in that world. Not in vain has its two hundred millions stretched forth their hands to Him. He causeth the wrath of man to praise Him. Even through the greed and wars of nations, in their selfish partition of Africa, He shall yet "save many people alive."

This Congress comes to take its place in the ever-widening plans of God for Africa. It should now be said that the original intention of the projectors of the congress was to hold it, as announced, during April, 1896. On account of the Cotton States and International Exposition, it was decided, as late as September, that the date should be changed, so as to reach and influence a larger number of people from all parts of the nation and of the world. This has necessitated some change in our plans. We congratulate ourselves, however, that we are able to present a program of such value and importance, and that the speakers, representing three continents, are now present, with two exceptions. Dr. Blyden is detained in London by serious illness. These places on the program are to be well filled, respectively, by a venerable and honored missionary with forty years experience in Zululand behind him, and by a special delegate from the American Colonization Society.

This Congress will have a large, practical tendency. It has definite aims in view. Problems of the most serious interest are before us. This nation is, in a peculiar sense, under bonds to Africa. It must come to see its duty. It must be stirred by an outlook upon its immense opportunity. We aim, therefore, to give the public clearer views of Africa and of the African movement. From a survey of the knowledge and experience gained in the last twenty-five years we should be able to deduce general principles and definite plans that may influence future work in the line of commercial, industrial, civilizing, and redeeming effort.

One of the vital and urgent problems before us is the relation of the American Negro to the civilization and redemption of his Fatherland. God's hand must be recognized in his presence in America. This is now the home and heritage of these American born of the colored race. Here he will stay. But the forefinger of that same Hand that brought him hither points the way to Africa for the tens, the hundreds, and, in future years, to the thousands who shall be agents of God in the redemption of the Dark Continent. It will appear that the call is not for the weak, the poor, the ignorant of the race. Such may only relapse into barbarism. But Africa now needs the best brain, and the best heart, the finest moral fiber, and the most skilled genius and power that the American Negro can furnish for her civilization and redemption.

To give light on these problems is the definite aim of this Congress. You shall have presented to you the latest and most accurate information on Africa; you shall have set forth clearly by word, by maps, and by illustrative slides, the land and people as they are; the life, character, customs of the natives; their tribal relations, and languages; the progress of discovery and occupation; the latest work of geographers; the march of civilization; the partition of Africa; the achievements of missions; the difficulties and drawbacks of missionary effort, and the outlook of missions for the nineteenth century.

We may congratulate ourselves that on our program there are speakers representing three continents; that we are to hear venerable and heroic missionaries who have labored from one to two score years in Africa; travelers who have penetrated the dark regions of Africa; Africanists of world-wide fame; scholars who have made original discoveries in the languages and in the religious beliefs of the people; natives of that last and most interesting of the continents, who bring the knowledge of personal life and experience, and whose presence and words furnish the strongest appeal for the civilization and redemption of their people.

I take pleasure in turning over the chairmanship of this session to Bishop I. W. Joyce, of Chattanooga, who will present to you His Excellency Governor Atkinson, of Georgia, from whom we shall have the address of welcome for this Empire Commonwealth.

Address of Welcome

BY
HIS EXCELLENCY, THE HON. W. Y. ATKINSON
GOVERNOR OF GEORGIA

[The following is a condensed report of the Governor's address, giving his most memorable sentences, as they were taken down at the time.]

Fellow citizens:

It is entirely proper that Georgia should take a leading part in a work of this character. Her first settlers were from the oppressed. They were actuated by a spirit of philanthropy which would lead their settlement to be a blessing to mankind, including Africa. Though pressed with many official duties, I am here to attest my interest, as the Governor of the State and as an individual, in this work.

A mysterious Providence has been over us. Slavery cannot be justified. But may not God have intended that you, who are the descendants of those whom slavery brought to this country, should pray and work for the redemption of your fatherland?

There is no higher duty resting upon the Governor of the State of Georgia than to advance the education of the people of the State without regard to color. If any doubt that the colored man can be educated existed, it has all been dispelled by my attending the commencements of the colleges of the State for the colored people. It is natural, proper, noble to look beyond yourselves and your country to save the people of your fatherland. No government, no society, can settle whether you should return to reside in Africa. You are free, independent citizens, and you must decide for yourselves, on the principles of your duty and your interest, whether you will reside in Georgia or in Africa. But in saving men and women from sin, degradation and hell, it is sometimes necessary to forego and forget interests. The great are not alone those who shine in high places. There are great souls careless of reputation among men and who are seeking only the approval of God.

So long as the colored man remains in Georgia, so far as is in my power, I shall see to it that he is fairly and justly treated--that he receives his rights. The Anglo-Saxon cannot defend the honor and reputation of his race by injustice to his fellow-man.

Do your duty, and for results trust in God.

Letter of Greeting and Commendation

BY
THE HON. E. W. BLYDEN, LL.D.
LIBERIAN MINISTER TO THE COURT OF ST. JAMES

28 Nov., 1895
, 3 Coleman Street, London, E. C.

Dear Dr. Thirkield:

You will regret to learn that I have been very ill since I left America, having taken a severe cold on the steamer coming over, where there was no heating apparatus in operation, and I could only keep warm in my berth by wearing my overcoat.

The "Congress on Africa" at this time is most opportune, when all the world is looking to that continent as a field for political, commercial and philanthropic effort. I hope that the results of the congress upon the Negro population of your country will be such as to lead them to take greater practical interest in the land of their fathers.

There will be, within the next few years, mighty developments on that continent. The British government are taking most active interest in the exploitation and building up of regions which have been for generations scenes of warfare and carnage. Such is the enthusiasm here for opening Africa, that when it was learned, only a few days ago, that the so-called King of Ashantee was placing obstacles in the way of England's efforts to bring that country within the pale of civilization, a magnificent expedition was organized at once, consisting of the flower of the British army, and dispatched to the scene. Two of the British princes have joined the expedition, which is intended not so much to fight as to convince the refractory chief of Coomassie, and all others like him, how utterly useless it is to attempt to cling to the hoary and pernicious superstitions of the past, and oppose efforts for the amelioration of the condition of their people.

Nothing is clearer to my mind than that it is the duty of a superior civilization to assist--not to exterminate--in the elevation of the inferior or backward populations of the earth, and your congress, I trust, will be one of the Providential agencies in the promotion of the magnificent work of Africa's regeneration.

Believe me, dear Dr. Thirkield, yours faithfully,

EDWARD WILMOT BLYDEN

Letter on the Importance of Knowledge of Africa

BY
CYRUS C. ADAMS
EDITOR *New York Sun*

The colossal work of twenty-five years has proved that the African native, in his own home, must be the foremost agent in reclaiming his continent. This century, having established the broad lines upon which the work must proceed, bequeaths to coming generations the privilege of helping the African to attain his full stature and development.

The most powerful motives, philanthropic and selfish, incite and will sustain this work; for the world needs Africa, and knows, to-day, that mankind will never profit by a tithe of her resources until the strength of Africa's millions, intellectual, moral and physical, are added to productive energy; and further, that the African's capacity for the development so essential for his own good and the world's, is being, year by year, most conclusively demonstrated.

All friends of Africa should scrutinize every phase of the work, as it goes on, so that the sentiment of civilized nations may be voiced in powerful and effective protest if intelligence, patience, humanity and justice do not shape all policies relating to Africa and her peoples.

CYRUS C. ADAMS

HELI CHATELAIN

African Philologist; Organizer of the Philafrican Liberator's League; Editor of African Terms and Names in the Standard Dictionary, and in the Century Dictionary of Names; Author of " Folk-Tales of Angola." Grammar of Kimbundu; "Comparative Grammar and Vocabularies; " Bantu Notes ; " and late African Traveler, Missionary and United States Commercial Agent at St. Paul DeLoanda

HELI CHATELAIN

African Philologist; Organizer of the Philafrican Liberator's League; Editor of African Terms and Names in the Standard Dictionary, and in the Century Dictionary of Names; Author of "Folk-Tales of Angola," Grammar of Kimbundu; "Comparative Grammar and Vocabularies; "Bantu Notes;" and late African Traveler, Missionary and United States Commercial Agent at St. Paul DeLoanda

A Bird's-Eye View of African Tribes and Languages

BY
HELI CHATELAIN,
AFRICAN TRAVELER AND PHILOLOGIST; AUTHOR OF "FOLK-TALES OF ANGOLA"

Our knowledge of African tribes and languages is still very imperfect. Every specialist who undertakes to study any single tribe or language is soon impressed with the fact that the little information he can get hold of, either in print and manuscript, or by correspondence and conversation, is far from being scientifically accurate or worthy of implicit confidence.

The outline of African ethnography and philology given in this paper is simply a resume of a critical study of the available material, and therefore no more infallible than this.

If we first consider the races represented in Africa, we find conflicting classifications and contradictory descriptions among scientific men, while in books of travel and periodical literature the wildest confusion of names is indulged in.

Some scientists hold that all native Africans belong to one racial stock with numerous ramifications.

This view is founded on the strong resemblances and common features which are observed in all populations of the Dark Continent. It brings out certain truths which it is well to retain, but the theory is far from proved.

Others insist on a certain number of races with clean cut characteristics and demarcations. They make us realize more the differences than the resemblances between the great sections of African population.

In English literature, taken generally, Dr. Cust's linguistic map of Africa made on Friedrich Muller's plan, has been taken, or mistaken, for an ethnologic map; and his linguistic divisions, which are useful if rightly understood, have been used by hasty readers and writers as a kind of standard classification of African races.

For practical purposes, it seems best to divide African tribes, according to the prevalent tinge of their skin, into white, black and brown races. In the Sudan, the brown, with all the intermediary shades between white and black, seems due to a mixture of white and black. The geographical position of these brown tribes between the white and black, the mixed nature of their languages, as well as historical data, renders this double origin almost more than probable.

While the confusion of linguistic and ethnologic names is sadly misleading, it must be confessed that the linguistic work is exceedingly valuable for ethnographic identification. There remains the great fact, that apart from political influences, great classes or families of languages correspond to great races, and that there is a parallel affinity between linguistic and ethnologic divisions.

THE WHITE RACE

Beginning with representatives of the white race, we first notice the *Arabs,* whose language and features are Semitic. They entered Africa from Arabia in four or five migrations, all in historical times. The most important branch invaded North Africa through the isthmus of Suez and conquered all Northern Africa, implanting everywhere Moslem culture and the Arabic language. That wave of Mohammedan conquest, passing over North Africa, wiped out the Christian religion, but failed to tread out the Hamitic languages, or to efface the ethnologic features, of the subjected tribes. The present states of Morocco, Tunis, Tripoli and Egypt are the remains of that conquest of Islam. The Egyptians, who were Hamitic Christians, gradually lost their language, and to a large extent, their Christian religion, but retained the racial features of the Hamites.

A second branch of Arabic Semites crossed the Red Sea and settled in the mountains of Abyssinia. The old Ethiopic and the modern Amhara and Tigre, languages of Semitic type, were wedged into Hamitic languages, but failed to supersede them. As to the racial features of the Semitic invaders, they were largely lost by inter-marriage.

In the Egyptian Sudan is found a third branch of Semites, leading a nomadic life. They also crossed the Red Sea.

From Muscat and the South-East corner of Arabia came a fourth branch, which founded settlements all along the East-Coast of Africa. In recent times they have gone from Zanzibar to the Great Lakes, and far into the Kongo Basin.

Although Moslem religion and culture are superior to African heathenism, it must be admitted that the Arabs have been a curse to Africa. We can be justly thankful that their political power is on the wane, and its final destruction inevitable. The Mohammedan religion, which has been introduced and upheld largely by the sword and the rifle of the Arabs, must necessarily suffer from the overthrow of Arab supremacy; and the final enforcement of European rule will be the signal for a wholesale desertion of a religion which has affected the externals more than the hearts and consciences of its African adepts.

The pure Arabs have never been numerically strong in Africa. They form only a fraction of the Mohammedan population speaking or understanding Arabic. Therefore, even if the Arabs and their religion finally disappear from the continent, their beautiful language is likely to remain in Egypt and all Northern Africa.

The Hamites are also considered as belonging to the white race. But in reality the white type with fair hair and blue eyes is only met with among a few tribes of Berbers. These blue-eyed Berbers were sometimes believed to be descendants of the German Vandals or more ancient immigrants from Europe, but the present tendency is rather to view them as of pure Hamitic stock. The bulk of the Africans speaking the Hamitic languages are more or less colored, and many Galla and Somal come nearer the negro than the white type.

Most writers believe that the Hamites, like the Semites, passed into Africa from Asia, but in prehistoric times. The ancient Egyptians were Hamites, and are supposed to have closed the march of Hamitic migration into Africa.

Moses says that "the sons of Ham were *Cush,* and *Mizraim,* and *Phut,* and *Canaan,*" and the present scientific division of the Hamites still rests on the genealogic table of Moses.

Mizraim was Egypt, the present Lower Egypt. There, was developed the first great civilization. From Egypt came the Libyans, who spread over North Africa, the oases of the great desert, and even to the Canary Islands. The Christian descendants of the ancient Egyptians are the *Kopts.* The descendants of the Libyans are the *Berbers.*

The ancient Carthaginians, though speaking a Semitic language, were also originally Hamites of the Punic branch.

Cush represents the inhabitants of Abyssinia and Upper Egypt,.known to the Greeks and Romans as Ethiopians. This term Ethiopian comprehended also the Negroes; but the Egyptians, who were in immediate contact with both, had a special name for the Negroes, calling them nahasi.

The *Phut* of Moses and the Puna of the Egyptians were probably the red-brown people of both coasts of the Red Sea and Indian Ocean, about the gulf of Aden. Vestiges of Hamitic tribes have recently been found in Southern Arabia. Probably the modern Somal and Galla are the descendants of the ancient Puna, from whom the Egyptians obtained incense, gold, ivory and Negro slaves.

The *Berbers,* though whites by race, and cousins of the Egyptians and Carthaginians, have never united into a powerful nation nor developed a culture decidedly superior to that of the Negroes south of the Sahara. Some inhabit the oases Siwa and Djala and parts of Tripoli and Tunis. Those of Algeria and Morocco are descended of the Roman Numidians and are frequently called Moors. In Algeria they number about two millions, of whom seven hundred and fifty thousand speak only Berber dialects, while the other one and a quarter million speak either Arabic, in addition to Berber, or Arabic alone. The Zouaves of the French army are a tribe of Berbers, inhabiting the sea-board between Algiers and Constantine. In Morocco the famous Rif pirates are Berber by race and language, and the Berber dialects Mazirgh and Shluh are still spoken from the Mediterranean to the Atlantic coast, opposite the Canary Islands.

The extensive, but arid region between Algeria and the northern bend of the Niger is inhabited by the Berber tribe of the Imoshagh, whom the Arabs call the Tuárek. Their Hamitic language is the Tamashek. Although favored with an original system of writing, in which many inscriptions have been preserved, the Imoshagh have failed to produce a national literature.

In the Nile Valley, between the Red Sea and the river, from lower Egypt to Abyssinia, the Bedja or Bisharin have upheld to this day Hamitic speech and type. The four principal tribes, the Ababde, Hadendoa, Beni-Amir and Hallenga, speak each a dialect of its own. Commonly they are known as Nubians, but this name is more properly applied to their neighbors on the banks of the Nile, who are of Negro extraction and who speak a language of nigritic structure. The Bisharin are pastoral and nomadic. They have all adopted Islam, and followed the Mahdi in his revolt.

The Danakil or Dankali, between Massawa and Obokh, are Hamitic and Pagan, but claim to be Arabs and Mohammedans. Their principal dialects are Saho and Afar.

Between the gulf of Aden and the equator, the eastern Horn of Africa is in the possession of the numerous tribes of Somals who are Hamitic by language and by descent, and Mohammedan by faith. In the North they are mixed with Arab blood, and with Negro blood in the South. Owing to this they vary much in color and form. Naturally jovial and sociable, they are fiercely opposed to foreign intrusion, and cordially hate their neighbors and kinsmen, the heathen Oroma or Galla. They tend their herds of camels, horses, oxen and sheep, while their limited agriculture is left to domestic slaves.

The *Galla,* whose number is estimated at 3,000,000, and who dwell between the Juba river and Albert Nyanza, are so called by their enemies, the Somal. They call themselves Oroma or Ilmorna, that is, "men." In race mixed Hamitic and Negro, in language and customs purely Hamitic, in religion partly Christian, partly Mohammedan, but mostly heathen, they are brave, intelligent, and industrious. Their government is largely republican, and they keep no slaves. The royal families of Uganda and Karagwe were originally Gallas of the Huma tribe.

Both Galla and Somal have preserved their languages remarkably pure from foreign loan-words; so much so that more archaic and primitive forms are found in them than even in hieroglyphic Egyptian.

The Egyptian, Berber and Cushitic languages which we have just considered are all so homogeneous in structure and word-store that they evidently form one family, derived from one mother-tongue.

In religion the Hamites are mostly Mohammedan. About one-quarter of a million Kopts in Egypt and several tribes in Abyssinia are Christians, 50,000 Falasha are Jews, and a portion of the Galla as also several tribes in or about Abyssinia are heathen.

Everywhere, except in lower Egypt, the Hamites are rather nomadic and pastoral, broken up in petty tribes, and jealous of their tribal independence.

No race, perhaps, is at the present time so little evangelized by Protestant missions.

BROWN RACES

Brown races are found in the Sudan, in southwest Africa and in Madagascar. They have nothing in common except the color. Nor is their brown color of the same tinge, some being light brown, others dark brown.

The brown people of the Sudan are probably a mixture of Hamites and Negroes; the Hottentots, Bushmen and Pygmies differ from the other brown peoples of Africa in structure, stature and physiognomy; and the brown Malagassy of the eastern and central portion of the great Island of Madagascar are Malays who have likely immigrated from Sumatra; at least linguistic affinity seems to indicate this.

It is in the ethnographic and linguistic classification of the Sudan tribes that we meet the greatest difficulties. Owing to the mixed character of racial and linguistic features different authors class the same tribe with the Hamites or with the Negroes, with the Berbers or with the Somal, or constitute it with other tribes into new groups, sub-divisions or families.

The *Fulbe* or *Fulahs* are scattered through the Sudan from Senegal to Wadai, and south to Adamawa. They are reddish brown, with straight nose and curly hair. Some differ but little from the Berbers while others look almost like negroes. Their language is remarkable for its peculiar initial formations. It can boast of a considerable literature written in Arabic character. By faith the Fulbe are Mohommedan, but not fanatical. Pastoral, like most Hamites, they are warlike, intelligent and industrious, ruling over negro tribes in Futa-Jallon, Kaarta, Segu, Massina, Gando, Sokoto, Adamawa. Around Lake Tshad, in Bornu, Baghirmi and Wadai, they are too weak in numbers to assume command. It was in the beginning of this century that they revolutionized the Sudan, founding under Otman dan Fodio their great kingdoms, which are not yet on the wane. They, and many of their negro subjects, are by no means savages or barbarians. Their populous cities are well built and evince an advanced stage of Moslem culture. Recently their territory has been included in the French, British and German spheres of influence. According to A. W. Schleicher they are a branch of the Somal; and would thus have traversed the whole continent in its greatest width.

The gap between the eastern Fulah around Lake Tshad and their cousins, the Galla and Somal, is largely filled by the Nyam-Nyam and Mombuttu, the Masai and the Kuafi, whose physique and languages show also an intermediate position between Hamites and Negroes.

Fried. Müller has joined to the language of the Nyam-Nyam or Azande those of five neighboring tribes: the Kredj, the Golo, the Amadi, the Mangbatu and the Abarambo, and constituted them into an Equatorial Family. Their territory is practically the only one in Africa which is not yet assigned to one or more European powers. It has also remained perfectly virgin of any misionary enterprise on the part of Christians. But it will not remain so long, since the discoveries of Van Gèle and others have made it accessible through the Kongo and its mighty northern affluent, the Mobanghi.

The Nyam-Nyam or Azande are said to number about two millions. They come very near the negro type in color and hair, but many peculiarities show a mixed origin. They are clever workers, hunters and musicians, but indulge in cannibalism.

The great and progressive nation of the Fang between the Gaboon and the Nyam-Nyam speak a very corrupt form of Bantu speech, and have many points of contact with the Azande.

The Masai and Kuafi, between Lake Victoria and the snow-capped peaks of Kenia and Kilimanjaro, have wedged themselves in among Bantu tribes as far south as the latitude of Zanzibar and the mouth of the Kongo. The fact that trustworthy witnesses class them physically with the Hamites and with the negroes, and that linguists are equally at variance concerning their language is strong evidence in favor of the theory that they are of mixed Hamitic and Bantu-Negro origin. They have a peculiar social organization. The young and able-bodied men lead a military life in camps, keeping the women in common, while the old men, women and children inhabit the villages and tend the cattle. The language is connected with that of the negro Bari.

The Nubahs of the Nile Valley, between Dongola and Assuan, were probably once pure negroes like their cousins, the Hill-Nubahs; but long intercourse with neighboring Hamites has so far altered their type that they are often confounded with these. The language, however, has preserved more distinct traces of their origin.

The Hottentots, or Khoi-Khoi, occupying the arid southwestern portion of Africa, are a brown people with very peculiar characteristics. They have all the distinctive features of the Negro, even exaggerated, but their color is much lighter, their stature inferior, while their straight and large forehead dwarfed nose, tapering chin and plentiful wrinkles give them a physiognomy atonce distinguishable from that of the negro. Their language reminds one by the formation of genders of the Hamitic family, while the classification of nouns savors of Bantu affinity and the numerous musical tones added to monosyllibic tendency are like an echo of Chinese parentage. What is most striking to a stranger is the clicks which are produced with tongue, palate and lips. Are the Hottentots bastards of the Bantu-Negroes with prehistoric Punas of Hamitic stock who worked the gold mines of Mashona-land and left the ruins of Zimbabie? Or are they descended from miscegenation with south-eastern Asiatics of the Chinese type who preceded the Malays of Madagascar in their far westward voyage, or were these three elements blended with Bushman blood?

The next twenty or thirty years will no doubt furnish material that will help decide this question with a probability not far removed from certainty.

The Hottentots are pastoral, and fairly intelligent. They have adopted Cape Dutch in the Cape Colony, while the Nama of German Southwest-Africa, have largely retained their own language. It is estimated that 350,000 Namas between the Orange and Kunene rivers, and 30,000 Hill-Damaras of Negro race, still speak Khoikhoi. A large proportion of the Hottentots is Christianized.

The *Bushmen,* or San, of South Africa, belong to the same race as the Pygmies or dwarfs of the Central African and equatorial forests. Their stature varies between four and five feet. Their physical appearance and their language show affinity with the Hottentots, but the relationship is very remote. The San language is poorer in morphology than the Khoikhoi, but richer in clicks. The Bushmen, like the Pygmies, are exceedingly timid, and hover, as Helots, on the skirts of Bantu settlements, which they supply with game. The Hottentots, on the contrary, are pastoral, independent, and even aggressive. They are the terror of less audacious and less advanced Bantu tribes. Perhaps no savage people on earth excell the Bushmen as hunters; and their rock-paintings show decided artistic aptitude.

Both Hottentots and Bushmen are not numerous enough to resist, independently, the absorbing influence of their Bantu and European neighbors.

The Pygmies of Central and Equatorial Africa form, most probably, one ethnic class with the Bushmen of South Africa. Their language, however, is not yet sufficiently known to warrant the expression of an opinion as to kinship with San. They are hunters and fishermen, living in temporary grass huts of bee-hive shape, and keep no domestic animals save chickens. Though culturally on the lowest scale, they are said to possess many virtues; and may, under the regenerating influence of the Gospel, develop some sterling qualities and attain pre-eminence in certain specialties.

Ba-rwa, Ba-twa, Ba-kwa, Ba-chwa is the common name of the Bushmen and Pygmies from one end of the Bantu field to the other, and should, in the form Ba-twa, be applied to the whole race or class. They have been noticed north of the Zambesi, at the head of Lake Nyassa, in the Nguru mountains near Zanzibar, on the Lulua, on the Sankuru and in the horse-shoe bend of the Kongo, in the Kuango valley, in French Kongo, on the Aruwimi, on the Blue Nile, and in Abyssinia.

THE NEGRO RACE

The field that is left to our consideration after we have disposed of the white Hamites of North Africa, the mixed brown peoples of the Sudan, the Malays of Madagascar, the Hottentots of South Africa, the Bushmen and the Pygmies, is all occupied by the Negro race, which forms the bulk of the African population, and fully deserves to be called the African race *par excellence.* The Hamites and semi-Hamites are mostly scattered in loose bands through the arid stretches of North Africa. Their unproductive soil, their nomadic habits, and their Mohammedan fanaticism preclude any rapid development of their countries and any phenomenal rise in civilization.

Nearly all the land occupied by the Negro race is rich in minerals and in fertile soil; it is watered by abundant rains and numerous rivers. The tropical sun matures in the same field two or three yearly crops of fruits, vegetables, and cereals, which in the temperate zone yield only once a year. The Negro is agricultural, commercial and industrial, of a peaceful and teachable disposition. In the Pagan state he has no religious creed to oppose to Christianity. If this religion and civilization had been presented to him free from man-stealing, commercial cheating, rum-poisoning, and blood-shedding exploration, from voracious land-grabbing and wholesale village-burning, the end of this century might have witnessed a rush of thousands into the bosom of the Christian church, a colossal demand for civilized manufactures, and torrents of tropical produce flowing northward to Europe and westward to America. But it is useless to expect ideal perfection from man, or to worry over what cannot be altered. Let us be thankful for the progress in knowledge, in politics, in religion, and, chief of all, in methods, as compared with similar movements in the past.

When I speak of the Negro race in Africa I include the so-called Bantu, who are probably, in race as well as in language, the purest stock of the black-skinned and woolly-haired variety of mankind. The distinction of Bantu and Negro races is a myth. The Negroes of Upper Guinea and the Sudan form one compact and homogeneous race with the Bantu of the Kongo Basin; their physical, mental and moral characteristics, their religious views, their folk-lore, and their social order is one and the same. The Negroes south of the equator, the so-called Bantu, speak languages ruled by a common grammar and possessing a common word-store, thus forming one great family of languages; while the Negroes north of the equator, that is in the Sudan and Upper Guinea, speak languages which have retained more or less grammatical forms of Bantu grammar and word roots of

Bantu origin, but these ruins are overgrown by a rank and wild vegetation which it will take philology a long time to penetrate. It is, however, easy in some of the better known languages spoken by Sudan Negroes to discover traces of distinctly Hamitic influence.

The physical characteristics of the black or Negro race are: A large and strong skeleton, long and thick skull, projecting jaws, skin from dark brown to black, woolly hair, thick lips, flat nose and wide nostrils. The typical color of the race is not coal black but the dark brown of a horse chestnut. Observation shows that the darkest specimens are found on the borders, where Negroes have been in contact with lighter races, while in the population of the Kongo Basin, which has been almost completely free from mixture, the dark-brown type prevails.

If we begin our survey of Negro tribes in the North, we first notice the Teda or Tibbu, who hold a large tract of the Sahara desert, north of Lake Tshad, in the very heart of the Hamitic field. No wonder that owing to this position, both the race and the language have paid rich tribute to the Hamitic surroundings.

From Senegambia to Lake Tshad, we have seen that the Negroes are mostly ruled by Fulah conquerors, who have founded great sultanates, which have swallowed up the native Negro kingdoms and their names.

In Wadai, east of Lake Tshad, the government is still in the hands of Negroes, who have maintained their independence against Arabs and Fulahs, thanks to their Mohammedan fanaticism. Wadai even exercises a sort of sovereignty over the neighboring kingdom of Baghirmi, where the bulk of the population is also Negro.

In Bornu, the government is Fulah, and the Negro population strongly mixed with Imoshagh and Arabs, all professing the Mohammedan religion. In Sokoto, the population is Hausa, who are Negroes, but slightly mixed with Hamites. They are the most promising nation of the Sudan, and their language will probably manage to compete with Arabic and English over the vast area between Lake Tshad and the Niger. It is among the one hundred millions of Sudanese that Islam is still making important progress; and there at least it seems to raise the heathen to a higher plane of life.

The peoples of Upper Guinea are mostly heathen, but widely honeycombed by Christian missions.

The Wolofs of French Senegambia, near St. Louis, are very black, well built, less prognathic than Negroes generally, and their language differs considerably from that of their neighbors.

Around *Sierra Leone* we find the Susu, Temne, and Mende tribes. Their languages have so much of Bantu structure that they deserve to be called semi-Bantu. In *Liberia,* we notice the Vei, made famous by the original syllabic character invented by one of their tribesmen; and also the athletic and hard-working Kru-men, one of the most promising nations of the west coast.

On the pestilential Gold and Slave coasts, the Ephe, the Ga, and the Tshi speaking people, including the once important kingdoms of Asante and Dahome, are being thoroughly evangelized by the heroic workers of the Basel and Wesleyan missions.

In the Lower Niger basin, the Yariba, the Nupe, the Ibo and the Efik, all speaking languages with crippled remains of Bantu grammar, are rapidly emerging out of the cruel rites of heathenism, and rising into prosperous Christian communities.

At Kamerun we strike the great field of the Bantu languages, which is considerably larger than Europe. It is the field which the explorations of Livingstone, Stanley, De Brazza. Wissmann and Holub have brought so prominently before the public, and which the powers of Christendom have taken under a partly national and partly international protectorate.

The Bantu, or Negroes south of the equator, are in some respects the most remarkable section of mankind. Separated from the rest of the world by wide oceans, virgin forests and the Sahara Desert, they have been less than any other race subject to foreign influences. No strange blood has altered their physical constitution; no foreign languages have permanently mangled the structure and the word-store of their principal forms of speech; no outside religion has seriously affected their conceptions of God, the spiritual, the animal and the natural worlds. Now they are receiving Christianity and the highest civilization the world has ever known, by methods which, however crude, inconsiderate and unjust they may appear fifty years hence, are yet far superior to all that our most sanguine forefathers could have anticipated.

In the supplement to his "Languages of Africa" Dr. Cust counts 450 African languages, with over 150 dialects. The Sudan languages number 212, and their dialects 56. The Bantu languages are estimated at 180, their dialects at 60.

With regard to the Sudan languages I will not express an opinion, as they are not in my special line; but concerning the Bantu languages, which are my special field, I am glad to be able to make the comforting statement that if we reverse the statement, and say that there are 60 languages and 180 dialects, we are much nearer the truth.

As a boy, in my native land, I studied a big book giving specimens of about 70 dialects. Now, 60 of these 70 dialects covered only a small part of three language fields, German, French and Italian. Of the African dialects, we are far from knowing all, even by name; but of the languages, we know by name a great many more than really exist.

Let me illustrate this by a few authentic examples. On the testimony of travelers and grammarians, Dr. Cust gives within the boundaries of the one Kimbundu, or Angola language, seven distinct languages. Now, these seven languages are simply dialects, and not all at that, of the language in which I am founding a Christian literature. The same process of reduction is repeated wherever sufficient material is obtained to compare the different dialects, which, until compared, seemed to deserve a separate place as languages.

Thus, in the region between Tanganyika, Bangweolo and the confluence of the Lulua and Kassai, were placed peoples with different names, the Moluas, the Barua, the Baluba, and the Bashilange, besides a number of others. My friend Dr. Summers labored two years at one end of this field, among the Bashilange, and gathered valuable linguistic material which he bequeathed to me. At the other end of the field, in Garenganze, another friend, the missionary Swan, also learned the language and published a vocabulary with a few chapters of a gospel. By comparing these materials collected at a distance of about 600 miles, I was surprised to find that it was the same language, and that the natives gave it the same name. At the same time I had opportunities to consult a Belgian explorer who had traversed the region comprised between those two extreme points, and also native Angolans who had accompanied him on his expedition. Their testimony confirmed my discovery. Further comparative study revealed the fact that other dialects are comprehended within the boundaries of this great Luba language, and that Luganda, at the north end of Lake Victoria, has practically the same grammatical structure.[*]

* See Heli Chatelain, "Bantu Notes and Vocabularies," Nos. I. and II.

During my second stay at Loanda I collected a vocabulary of U-iaka, the language of the Ma-iaka, or Ma-iakala. On my return to America I discovered, by comparison, that U-iaka was practically the same as Ki-teke, in which Dr. Sims of Stanley Pool had published a gospel and a vocabulary. Further research disclosed the fact that several other tribes, the Northern Mbamba, the Buma, the Mbete and the Tsaia speak dialects of the same language. Still further investigation into the physical appearance and the customs of these tribes showed them to be identic in all points in which they differ from their neighbors speaking other languages. These facts combined proved that between the equator and the 8° South latitude there is a cluster of tribes speaking the same language and having the same customs; forming, therefore, one great nation.[*]

* See "Bantu Notes," No. III.

This nation the powers assembled at Berlin in 1885 have, without knowing it, and without the nation's knowledge, divided between France, the Kongo State and Portugal, France getting the lion's share.

The discovery of this Ba-teke nation also enabled me to solve two or three historical riddles which had puzzled Africanists and still puzzle those who have not read my article on the Ma-iaka. The other Bantu nations and languages of some importance all deserve to be dwelt on at some length, but the time limit is inexorable, and I must dispose of them with a few words.

In the German Kamerun, the Dualla language is being officially taught in excellent government schools and in the stations of the Basel missions.

In French Kongo, or Gabun, the Mpongwe tribe is dying out, being superseded by the aggressive Fang. These speak a Bantu or rather semi-Bantu language. The Benga, on the sea-coast, rejoice in a considerable Christian literature, published by American Presbyterians.

The Kongo nation, with its sub-tribes, the Luangu, Buende, Sundi, Solongo, Ndembu, Hungu and Pangu, is evangelized by seven or eight Protestant missionary societies, in addition to the thrice centenarian work of the Catholic church.

In the semi-civilized portion of Angola the natives are joining hands and blending with the Portuguese colonists, thus preparing the creation of a powerful nationality.

In the highland of Angola the Ovi-mbundu of Bailundu and Bihe bring the produce from the head streams of the mighty Kongo to the seaport of Benguella, where they barter it for cloth and rum, and also for fire-arms and powder, which enable the Ma-kioko to continue their audacious slave raids. These Ma-kioko, one of the finest looking tribes of interior Africa, with long plaited beards, have made an end of the once powerful empire of Lunda, reducing into slavery subjects of their former suzerain, the great Muatyamvo. If published vocabularies are correct, the Kioko tribe speaks practically the same language as the Ambuella, around the western headwaters of the Zambesi river, and so we would have here again one great nation and language instead of a number of unconnected tribes and dialects.

The cattle herding Ova-herero, in German South Africa, so long the victims of the periodic raids of the Hottentots, begin to breathe and raise their heads since the German troops have finally put down the Nama chieftain Witboy.

In the Upper Zambesi valley the Barotse under Lewanika seem to respond at last to the appeals of their apostles, Missionary Coillard and his colleagues.

The Zulus, the Kaffirs, the Bechuana, the Batonga, the Matebele, the Mashona and the Ba-nyai, all south of the Zambesi, are important Bantu nations, who are coming more and more into public view as their territories are invaded by the gold hunters, land-grabbers, and by the messengers of the evangel of peace and holiness.

In Portuguese Mozambique, between the Rovuma and Zambesi rivers, the great nation of the Ma-kua, including the Lomve, Metu, Ibo and Angoche sub-tribes, sees its territory gradually invaded by the whites who secure concessions from the Portuguese.

The Wa-yao, the Ma-konde, and the Manganga, around Lake Nyassa, enjoy the protection of British and German authorities against the Maviti and the Arab raiders. Scottish, English, and German-Moravian missionaries teach thousands of their young people, while the Africa Lakes Company and an Industrial Mission employ thousands of strong hands in their commercial and agricultural undertakings.

The tribes of German East Africa, among whom the Wa-Zaramo, Wa Zeguha, Wa-Sagara, Wa-Gogo, Wa Hehe, and Wa-Nyamwezi are the principal, speak all languages so closely related to that of Zanzibar, the Ki-Suahili, that the latter may finally become the literary language of all that vast region.

All readers of the daily papers and of missionary journals have become familiar with the story of U-ganda. The wonderful changes which have there taken place since 1872, when the first missionary party entered the country, and which have transformed that semi-Pagan and semi-Mohamedan country and people into a semi-Protestant and semi-Catholic Christian nation more progressive and more promising than some sections of the Italian, Spanish, and Portuguese nations, those changes, I say, are prophetic of what is about to happen among all the great Bantu nations we have passed in review.

If my opinion about the future were asked, I should not hesitate to declare my conviction that within one hundred years all Bantu-land will contain more than 500,000,000 inhabitants, will equal Europe in civilization, will be united in a great United States of Central Africa under a new and improved edition of our American Constitution, will both speak and write a common language, the mother-tongue of all Bantu dialects, as revived by scholars and enriched with the best developments of its daughters, and will produce master-pieces of literature, science, and art, vying with all the best that Europe and America will then be able to bring forth.

ORISHETUKEH FADUMA, B. D.
Native of the Yoruba Tribe, West Africa; Educated in Sierra Leone, London, and in Yale University

ORISHETUKEH FADUMA, B. D.
Native of the Yoruba Tribe, West Africa; Educated in Sierra Leone, London, and
in Yale University

Religious Beliefs of the Yoruba People in West Africa

BY
ORISHATUKEH FADUMA, B. D. West Africa

We are now at a period in the world's history when the religions of Pagan nations are studied with a view to find out whether there is any point of contact between them and the more developed forms of religion; what are their beginnings; who were the prime leaders of their religious thought; and what changes have taken place since their existence. There are observances in the ritual of Israel found in the rituals of Egypt and Chaldea, nations by far older than the Hebrews. There is something, therefore, in common with Judaism and the ethnic religions which preceded it, and which surrounded it. Christianity is an evolution of Judaism, yet so evolved that it becomes a new religion. Mahommedanism is a corruption of Judaism, a mingling of monotheism with Arab heathenism. Max Müller, Rawlinson, Sayce, and others have contributed not a little to the study of heathen beliefs. The observations of anthropologists and ethnologists are helping us to get at facts, and draw conclusions which otherwise would be impossible. For the present we shall be satisfied with the presentation of facts, as they are not large enough to warrant us in making large deductions.

To some of the beliefs of the Yoruba people I wish to call your attention. These people are known under four names: Yoruba, Yariba, Aku, and Oku. They live in West Central Africa, having Lagos as their seaport town. Of all West African tribes the Yoruba people are preeminently agricultural and commercial. As a commercial people, their lives are not spent in seclusion, but they come in contact with many native and foreign people. They have a native civilization which combines both the native and the Mohammedan elements. The ubiquitous Arab has somewhat modified his civil as well as religious life, but has not stamped it out of existence. They are by no means a savage, but are a semi-civilized people.

The Yoruba people, like the Athenians of old, are given to much reverence. Reverence to traditions, reverence to ancestors, reverence to the gods and spirits, is interwoven with their beliefs. If it were connected with a belief which questions before it is practiced, the Yorubas would be a highly religious people. But when reverence is merely the result of custom, then men worship they know not what, and that which ought to be sacred in religion becomes painfully superstitious. When I speak of the Yorubas as very religious, I mean that they are very superstitious. Notwithstanding this, it is important to study their system of belief, or construct one if it has not been done. The study of religion in all its forms ought to be important to the student of comparative religion. The genesis and development of religious belief, the stagnant condition of some religions and the apparent or real growth of others, the underlying principles which run through all and manifest themselves in what are termed the phenomena of religion, are subjects demanding a careful study. To make such a study profitable requires a sympathetic as well as an educated mind.

In studying the pagan system of the Yorubas, we shall find the three stages observed in the evolution of religion. They are Fetichism, Nature worship, and Prophecy or Divination.

1. Fetichism, the lowest, is practical, though not exclusively so. A fetich may be any object in which the god or gods convey their powers either to protect or defend the possessor. It is worn around the neck and waist, on the arms and wrists, on the ankles, or inserted into the hair. It is often concealed by an outer covering made of cloth or leather sewed tightly together. Human hair, finger nails, refuse of animals and men, precious stones, roots of trees, relics of the dead, in fact almost anything may be used. To the traveler it is a convenient *vade mecum,* for it is portable. It therefore takes the place of the idol and may be worn around the neck of the holder. It is a kind of a god in times of emergency. It brings good luck to the individual who wears it, and protects him from injury. It guards him against the attack of witches and the malevolence of personal and private foes. The hunter ties it near the muzzle or nipple of his gun, and it is thought to make him aim straight at his victim. What, in ordinary civilized life, would be considered a trained and skilled marksman, would be attributed to the charm or fetich. In all such cases it is some spirit whose power is felt through the charm, which is its medium. The favor or disfavor of heaven is communicated through the material medium called fetich.

2. In *Nature worship,* we have the image of a god made out of stone or wood. The god has the form and features of a person. It is generally an ill-shapen image, but this is probably due to the primitive state in which art is. It belongs to a high stage of civilization to produce the work of a Phidias, a Praxiteles, or a Polycletus. Yet Greek art had quite as humble beginning. Side by side with this nature worship is fetichism, so that one is at a loss to say whether the former is

really an evolution from the latter. The worshipper of images has also a fetich which may be about his person even when he is in the act of worshipping his image.

3. Along with fetichism and idolatry is developed a system of priestcraft which may be at one time esoteric, and at another time exoteric. A man may make his own fetich, but when difficulties of a peculiar kind arise, the trained hand is sought. It is the man whose chief employment is to make fetiches, who knows the nature of diseases, foretells the future, and is in closer touch with the god or gods. Such a man has a powerful influence in the community; he is a physician of rare ability, a herbalist of repute, and a magician. He is sought by the high and low, consulted in family disappointments, and at the King's Court. His advice is taken, and he is dreaded by all.

The Yoruba gods are many. There is a god of war, like the Roman Mars or the Ares of the Greeks, who leads armies to victory and to whom human victims are offered. There is *Shango,* the god of thunder, whose priests are white-robed. He is like the Jupiter Tonans of the Romans. When he thunders and sends forth his lightning upon the dwellings of men, his priests are sought after to appease his wrath. There is a god who, like Ceres, controls agriculture, to whom the first fruits of the field are offered. Over the sea presides the water-god, who, like Neptune, calms the stormy seas and puts to flight the storm clouds. There are gods of the mountains, valleys and hills; gods of the market and pathways, household gods the peculiar treasures of individual families, and gods of the nation. There are several names by which the gods are known, but above them all is *Olodumare,* the supreme king both of gods and men, who assigns a sphere of influence to each of the local gods. He holds precisely the same relations to the gods as Jupiter held in the Roman pantheon, or Zeus in the Greek. The existence of these gods seems to be an arrangement by which the supreme God is helped to rule the country. Since the native worshipper cannot see the supreme god who is hid somewhere in the clouds, his nature demands the presence of one to whom he can appeal in cases of need, some one who can be seen by the naked eye. The necessity therefore arises for the fabrication of an object which would be a symbol of the Supreme God. It is a remarkable, though crude, expression of the people's need of an agent who shall come between them and their God, an agent who is not clothed with spirituality, but who can be seen and touched. To this visible obiect his needs are made known. Through all ethnic religions such an agent is found. In Christianity we have a solution of this need, and the truest expression in the living, the personal, visible, and tangible Christ, who is God clothed in flesh, and the mediator between God and man. Through the ages men have been groping in the dark, seeking, if haply, they may find such a Christ.

The Yoruba worships the objects of nature above him. The moon is one of them. Constant reflection on its movements sharpens his intellect. He is a good calculator. He tells his age by the number of moons he has seen. To him the moon is a harbinger of joy or sorrow; he supplicates it when it appears in its new crescent robe to avert all evils of the new month. Throughout the system of image worship, what appears first as a symbol of the God, is now confounded with, and worshipped as God. The distinction between them is lost, so that if there is a monotheism in the system, is lost in polytheism. God, as spirit, is lost and absorbed in God as matter.

Of the origin of the human race, the Yorubas have a very faint conception. The first pair sprang from that section of Yoruba country known as Iffe (Iffeh).

Of the future life they have some conception. The doctrine of the transmigration of souls is prevalent. The spirit of a good man is changed at death to some good being or animal, while that of a bad man is transformed to a ferocious animal or an evil spirit. Ancestors may be born again in the world. The children, called *Abiku,* that is, children who die prematurely, are said to return to life at the next birth of its mother, if at this birth the child also dies prematurely. At the death of one, messages are sent in tears and songs to dead relatives and friends. Feasts are observed and sacrifices offered to the dead. On the third day after burial, an early morning sacrifice of meal and oil is made at the grave of the deceased, and his spirit is supposed to eat a portion of it. On the seventh day after burial there is a feast preceded by a morning sacrifice, in which the spirit of the deceased and the spirits of ancestors partake. After this feast and sacrifice, the spirit of the deceased is supposed to leave the old home and take interest in the welfare of surviving friends.

The whole system of Yoruba worship is steeped in spirit worship. Spirits are found everywhere. They are the controllers of diseases. When a child suffers from convulsions it is because he sees a spirit which frightens him. The medicine man, therefore, washes his eyes with a solution prepared from the bark of a medicinal plant. There are spirits which exert evil influence in the world. These may be seen, and are called *egbere* (aygbayray). They are of diminutive stature; they leave their graves at midnight and return to them before daybreak. Sheep-riding is their delight. They are the cause of the destruction of sheep by disease.

The medicine man is often called to drive them away by shooting at them, or supplying individuals who are spirit-frightened with a charm or fetich as a protection. There are also good spirits. These exert good influence in the world, and protect men from danger, and appear to them in dreams. If there is sorrow at the grave of the departed it is relieved after the seventh day, when a feast of rejoicing follows, and by the knowledge of the fact that the spirit of the deceased has gone to join those of his ancestors. There is a kind of spirit telegraphy by which the present and the future are connected.

The sacrificial system of the Yorubas has nothing peculiar. It has the same characteristics found in other systems of pagan religions. The one who offers sacrifice may be the father of the family in ordinary cases. In peculiar and trying circumstances a trained hand is sought. The medicine man is qualified by years of training for the post. The offices of doctor and sacrificer are invariably combined under the same individual. Sacrifice has a *raison d'etre.* It is, first of all, prophylactic. Men feel the pain of diseases, they know that evil spirits surround them and are seeking their destruction, they are aware of personal foes who are bent on their destruction; they are, therefore, compelled to sacrifice to a God and ask for his protection. The idea of communing with the gods is not a prominent one, though it is found in the system. What stands in bold relief is the feeling of deliverance and salvation from outward, not inward, evils. No one ever thinks of praying to the gods for strength to overcome personal feelings and to resist temptations. When one is surrounded by evil, or has escaped some calamity, the god is approached and his protection sought, or he is thanked for averting a calamity. Sacrifice is a prophylactic, as well as a thank-offering.

The religion of the people is one of fear and suspicion. The worshipper does not love his god, but fears him. The same mental act which is produced when the worshipper approaches his god, is also produced in children and wives when they approach their fathers and husbands. The same is produced in subjects when they approach those who are in authority. The father of a family, as well as the king or chief of the tribe, holds the same relation to his children or subjects as the god holds to the nation. It may be said that children fear rather than love their fathers, and wives submit with dread to their lords. The obedience required of them is an enforced one; it does not spring from love, but it is caused by fear. The native rule is like the rule of his gods, it is stern and severe. If there is any love, it is swallowed up in fear. It may be said, however, that this is not a peculiar characteristic of the Yoruba people and religion, but a general characteristic of Pagan Africa.

In the Yoruba sacrifice are included fruits of the earth, such as bananas, kola nuts, meal made of beans, oil (generally palm oil), animals and human beings. Kola nuts occupy an important place in worship. Through it the god makes known his will to men. The worshipper, after separating the two halves of the nut, throws them on the ground; if the inner parts turn upwards they signify that the god looks with favor upon the worshipper; if they turn downwards they indicate the god's disfavor. In all human sacrifices the blood is the most important. It is offered as a libation to the god and poured on the ground. While the worshipper may become impoverished by constant sacrifice, the sacrificer or medicine man is often enriched by it. Salvation sought through such a system is one of sacrifices and works.

The gods often reveal their minds to men by means of omens. If one, on the eve of an expedition, were to hit his left toe against an object, it presages evil; if the right toe, the result would be a success. Often the traveler is obliged to return home and wait for a favorable omen. If a snake is seen crossing a path, it means that some misfortune will happen to the beholder. Shooting stars are sure signs of the removal of friends from earth by death. The flight or cries of certain birds point to disaster.

The Pagan system of Yoruba worship, like all religions which are in a state of childhood, is not philosophical but poetical, a religion inspired by fear rather than love. There is no element found in it which is not present in similar religions. God is the fundamental conception; worship of Him includes prayer, which is an expression of the soul's yearnings, and sacrifice, which is made to appease God and escape danger. "Nor is it possible to conceive the existence of a race, properly human, without some germ of the sense of spiritual mystery which so rapidly widens out into an apprehension of that Infinite 'whose center is everywhere, and whose circumference is nowhere.' But such an apprehension involves the feeling of dependence, subordination, the craving after harmony with that larger power which is dimly discerned. And it is in this distinctively human apprehension which, while fairly discoverable in the humblest, remains in the highest humanity wholly unresolvable into any forms of the logical understanding, that we must seek the essential nature of religion.'"[*] We cannot deny to these people the possession of a religious or a moral sense. Both exist, though corrupted and distorted. At the root of their religion is God, yet it leads away from God, and finally loses Him, because it has from the start a wrong conception of His nature, and confounded Him with His works. The study of the philosophy of religion is bringing us nearer and nearer the truth that the conception of God is universal, and that it is only the "fool that saith in his heart there is no God." "In this experience of God, every soul of man has a part. He is not far from every one of us; in Him we live and move and have our being.

    * The Essential Nature of Religion, by Picton.

It is possible for every soul, however degraded, however ignorant and humble, to feel after Him and find Him (Acts xvii: 27-28).

The knowledge of God is common knowledge. However imperfectly and pervertedly men may hold it and express it, all have it, so that when the higher Christian truth comes to a soul, it does not come to one ignorant of God, but to one that, from its earliest days, has felt his presence and power."[*]

    * The evidence of Christian experience; Theistic philosophical presuppositions; Stearns.

CYRUS C. ADAMS
One of the Editors of *The Sun,* New York; Geographer and Africanist; Member
of the American Geographical Society; Late Delegate to the International
Geographical Congress, at London; Member and Contributor of the Brooklyn
Geographic Institute and the National Geographic Society at Washington, D. C.

Some Results of the African Movement

BY
CYRUS C. ADAMS
GEOGRAPHER, EDITOR *New York Sun*

The particular results of the African movement of which I shall speak to you have little to do with exploration, commerce or other material outcome of the work in Africa. Let us consider rather some of the ideas to be derived from the experience of the past generation of African workers. If we wish to study Africa, if we wish to work for Africa, at home or there, what ideas, what lessons drawn from experience, will help us to start right, and to make our energy most effective? I shall try to indicate some of these lessons. It is a wide subject and in this paper I can do no more than briefly to emphasize, without enlarging upon these ideas.

To do good work we must work intelligently and therefore must use as effectively as we can, the literary helps within our reach. We are confronted at once with the difficulty that the mass of literature is already too enormous to be examined except by specialists. Much of it is very valuable, much is commonplace, much is worthless. Then a great deal of the best material is not accessible to those who read English only. The best and latest works on Liberia, on the rich and populous west and central Soudan, the Cameroons and German East Africa have not yet been translated from the German. The fullest summary of the Congo basin and the remarkable work there, in all their aspects, is published in French. Considerable of the most valuable material is scattered through the publications of geographical societies and has not appeared in book form at all. There have recently been published or are now preparing some compendiums on Africa and some bibliographies. They will be very helpful but not wholly adequate for our special needs. I believe money, time and energy will be economized if those persons whom America sends out as missionaries, teachers or merchants are helped, first, to get right at the gist of the most reliable literature about the particular districts to which they are going; and second, to become thoroughly imbued, before they leave home, with some of the fundamental ideas, the outgrowth, sometimes, of bitter experience, that seem necessary to success. Here is an illustration or two of what I mean:

The Scottish mission at Blantyre in the Nyassa Highlands, was founded upon the idea that the missionaries might well combine with their religious and educative work, the functions of a civil government and even of commercial and industrial enterprise. It was simply an attempt to carry out the views of Livingstone, himself, who discovered this land; and the history of that endeavor is one of the most instructive chapters in the story of African missions. I can only say here, the experiment was a dismal failure, even scandal resulted, and in the blackest days, that splendid work was saved from utter collapse, apparently, by the deciding voice of one man in Edinburgh. Let governing power, commercial endeavor and religious and educative influence, work for good ends in parallel lines which, you know never run together, and the desired unity of effort is attained. Combine these various functions in one agency, and disaster seems inevitable among these barbarous tribes. This was a lesson that was not learned except by actual experiment.

Again, do you suppose that when the missionary societies began to send medical missionaries to Africa, they had any very clear idea as to what the greatest potency of these physicians and surgeons would prove to be? It is already found in some places, that these specialists are striking at the very root of an evil which, perhaps more than any other one influence, keeps the African native degraded. That is the superstition which has invested the fetich doctor with mysterious power over human life and happiness. No man can grow while he believes the fetitch doctor can exorcize the evil spirits that make him ill, or sell him charms that bring victory in battle. No man can progress so long as a greedy chief, eager to seize the little property his subject has gathered, may call in the fetich man to declare him a witch, and condemn him to death. The glimmer of an idea is dawning upon many of these people, that the real healers are these men who have come among them and that there is nothing supernatural about their skill. They are beginning to see the imposition that has kept them prostrate. Governments have observed this tendency of medical work and it is helping to stimulate them to supplement the influence of medical missionaries in more drastic fashion. In an immense area of inner Africa, to-day, it is a crime to practice fetichism. The law has lately been proclaimed throughout the great territory of the British South Africa, from the South African Republic to Lake Nyassa, that any fetich doctor will be severely punished if convicted of practicing his arts.

These are two among many facts and ideas, the results of experience, that should be collated from the best sources for the benefit of those who are preparing for missionary work, with a view to instructing them in the nature, conditions and methods of their future activity before they ever see Africa.

When we study Africa we must bear one thing in mind. That is that many books on Africa contain an undue admixture of crude personal impression which has passed, too often, for statement of fact. Two observers in the same field may give diametrically opposite views of it, the fact being, perhaps, that the more unfortunate pioneer, overcome by unaccustomed hardships, weary and homesick, sees everything as through smoked glass, very darkly. The late Montague Kerr, the first explorer to completely cross Mashona Land, wrote me once that he had seen nothing there giving promise that the region was worth occupying. He enlarged upon this statement in his book; and yet some thousands of white men are living there to-day, and two railroads are pushing towards the country. Now it takes time and study to learn to read critically about Africa, to learn to discriminate between what is best to retain and what to reject; and those who dip only here and there in desultory fashion into the immense mass of literature will get hardly the faintest idea of some mighty influences, of which I shall speak, that are working as quietly and as potently as leaven, preparing the native mind in wide districts to become fertile soil in which the seeds of a higher life may germinate and thrive.

I know of nothing, apart from the desire to Christianize these millions of men, that would so stimulate the practical interest of our philanthropists in the best African work as to make it possible for them, who cannot themselves give months and years to the study, to see clearly the trend of this African movement; and I know nothing that would be more useful in preparing young men for practical service than to guide them to those things in African literature that will most help and edify them.

Where are the two or three educated young men specially qualified for such work who will give the requisite study to this literature, in the English and other languages, that will fit them to compile, with critical care, a list of references to the books, monographs and maps that have special bearing upon the work we want to do? I do not mean a bibliography of Africa for that work would be colossal and, for our purposes, redundant and unwieldly. The bibliography of Congo alone, now preparing, will contain 4,000 titles. But we need to be directed to the volumes and pages in which the best information may be found about regions in which Americans are to labor; their geography, resources, climatology and hygiene; character of natives; their amenability to good or bad influences; methods approved for winning their confidence and affecting their lives; coöperation given by governments to religious and educative work; their provisions for safeguarding the people from pernicious influences and the work done by government and commerce to elevate them; in general, the results and teachings of experience thus far. We need concise digests of the most helpful things that are not accessible except in foreign languages; and attention should particularly be called to any writings that give a good idea of the scope of this whole African movement; of the colossal-forces that are moving for the mastery of that continent; and of the profound, the astonishing effect already apparent throughout large areas.

A concise monograph showing what these forces are and how they are beginning to affect African barbarism does not exist. When written, it should be a most effective instrument in stirring the hearts and impelling the cooperation of our philanthropists in the cause of African regeneration. These things will cost some money, but they will pay.

Students of Africa like such work as the Haussa Association is doing. It was organized in 1892 to prepare for missionary work in that fine part of the Sudan between the Niger and Lake Tchad. Unable yet to enter that region, the society's agents have gone to accessible places where they may meet Haussas, have studied their language, whose field is far wider than that of any other tongue in Central Africa, and have collected much information to serve them when the time is ripe for entering the land. I have talked with missionaries in New York, just embarking for Africa, who had never read anything of the region for which they were bound, and knew nothing even of the hygienic rules they should observe to preserve their health. Hereafter such ignorance should not be possible.

A gentleman in Europe, learned in African matters, has written a careful book in which he has attempted to figure out, in percentages, just what this and that part of Africa will be worth to civilization and commerce. I believe that this is labor lost. There is no oracle among us to tell what the future of Africa will be. Just as the discoveries of five years revolutionized our notions of the hydrography of the Congo basin, so time and again have we seer the verdict passed by explorers upon this or that region or people overthrown by later studies. We do not yet know enough about Africa or the potentialities latent in her 175,000,000 of people to give value to any hard and fast estimate as to their part and place in future history. Africa's future depends upon her resources still almost untouched, the abilities of her people still unfathomed, and the capacity of the human race to advance and to this capacity no prophet has a right to assign limits. I say this much because certain writers have assumed that their dictum about the ultimate destiny of Africa is worthy of attention. If anyone were to ask me what the world will do with the desert of Sahara, I should tell him that we do not know; but we know, at least, that an edge of that desert has been made to blossom by the irrigation works of the French. The story of the white man's enterprises in Africa, every year for the past eighteen years, teaches us that pessimistic conclusions are not warranted by any events, however inexplicable or disheartening they may seem. We might fill all the sessions of this congress with illustrations of this fact. When Stanley began to plant his stations on the Congo he could induce hardly a native to lift a pound of freight or to sell an hour of service. For years, labor was brought to the Congo from Zanzibar and the Guinea coast. Even Chinese were imported to work on the railroad. But to day, Congoland is not importing labor. Fifty thousand of the people who live there are working for wages. They man the stations and steamboats carry on their backs thousands of tons of freight, and their humble service both in peace and war, is helping to develop their country. It was with the guns in their hands that the Arab slave raiders were driven out of the Congo basin and the natives themselves are grading the bed, and laying the rails of the railroad, that is now advancing a quarter of a mile a day.

Eighteen years ago Colonel Chaille Long said in his book that Central Africa was a plague spot, that its people were miserable wretches, and he protested against sending any missionaries to Uganda in answer to Stanley's call, because they would meet only with misery and speedy death without any results to justify their martyrdom. To day 50,000 of these Uganda can read. Two hundred native churches are scattered over their country, and the largest church at Mengo, the capital, holds 3,000 people.

The man who dedicates himself to Africa will find in facts as they are, a sufficient tax upon his resources and energy. He should be taught, early in his training, not to borrow needless trouble from, nor to be unduly perplexed by the dictum, so lightly spoken of writers who imagine that their few months or years in Africa qualify them to sum up and pass final judgment.

When we make it easier for our people to study the whole African movement what are some of the ideas that are likely to get firm lodgement in their minds? I will tell you what I think some of them will be.

As far as we can see, Africa, or the most of it, is for the African. He has a land in which other races cannot swarm as they have over America. His is the only race that has lived, thrived and done a man's full work in every climate of the world. A few papers have recently been written in Europe to show, some that the native population of Africa is increasing, others that it is diminishing. I have seen no facts or arguments at all convincing in favor of the latter hypothesis. The most careful observers believe that in certain districts intestine wars or slave raids have diminished the population to a marked extent; that other areas which have suffered from evils less formidable are holding their own, and that Africa, as a whole, is growing in population. It is observed that certain regions have recuperated from evils that devastated them with remarkable rapidity. One of the best authorities on the statistics of the world's population (*Der Bevölkerung der Erde*), in its edition of 1891, assigns to Africa a population exceeding by 42,000,000 the total number of inhabitants in the three Americas, and the West Indies. We have no reason to believe that if the Caucasian race could invade Africa in myriads they would or could wipe out the native people, for the Negro is not made of the stuff that breaks and disappears, like the Pacific islander and the American Indian, upon the intrusion of other peoples.

Every European government in Africa is seeing more and more clearly that the native is the largest factor in determining the prosperity of Caucasian enterprises there; that the more the native is elevated the more money can be made; and so some of these governments are conspicuously bending their energies to improve the condition of the natives, and the world never saw before such colossal efforts to this end among barbarous peoples, nor such significant results in so short a time.

It is found that a very large part of these natives have offered little or no obstruction to the introduction of governments and other agencies of civilization. It is an impressive fact that, in the course of a few years, the agents of the International Association of the Congo, from which the Free State issued, made over 1,000 treaties with Negro chiefs in the Congo basin, by which they voluntarily ce ed their sovereign rights, accepted the government offered to them, and all this work was done without firing a shot.

We may be thankful for the selfishness that is the basis of some of the most powerful influences yet brought to bear upon the African native. It is no mere love of humanity that has impelled the European States to divide these regions among themselves. We can hardly realize here the intensity of the struggle for existence in many of the overcrowded regions of Europe. Their industries, their manufactories are enormously productive but the people will suffer for food unless they can export. It was the crying need for new markets. for new sources of raw material, that drove these States into Africa; and we should be glad for Africa's sake that they have gone there to make money.

We believe that it is immoral to waste or destroy useful things. Day by day, this moral truth is now being inculcated in the minds of many thousands of Africans by men who are not teachers of morality but whose purpose is to protect a source of wealth.

All over the Congo basin is a species of the rubber plant whose product is worth exporting though it still has to be carried on the backs of men around 235 miles of cataracts. The native method of getting the sap is to cut off the vine, thus destroying the plant. There are nearly 150 stations of the State and of the Belgian and Dutch trading companies scattered over the upper Congo and most of them are centers of the rubber trade. Everywhere the natives are told:

"Rubber is valuable to you, for we give you cloth and wire and beads for it. It is valuable to us or we would not buy it. But you have been killing the vine, destroying that which is good for you and us. Bula Matari has made a law forbidding anyone to kill the rubber vine and you must not do so any more. This is the way to get the juice. Tap the vine, the juice will flow out for you, the wound will heal, the vine will produce again. But if you kill any more vines the law will punish you."

And it does if they forget the prohibition. The result is that these thousands of rubber gatherers are beginning to protect the vine and are telling their children: "There is a plant that is good for men. You must never kill it." Surely this inculcation of one vital principle of morality by a government whose arm reaches far and which has the strength not only to teach but to insist and persist until the lesson is learned is an important fact in this African work.

We know that very serious injustice has been done to natives by agents of governments in Africa. Instances of this sort from the Congo are now being investigated at Brussels, and it is high time, for the gravest outrages have been committed there and elsewhere. But we must not think because young men in the depths of Africa, unworthy of their trust, have been guilty of cruel and scandalous acts, that the government is indifferent to native welfare and unmindful of justice. The laws for safeguarding the natives are all right. The observance of these laws has fallen short of that measure of protection, of forbearance and mercy that the world must demand now and hereafter. But we should know that this sort of crime against the native is an incident, inexcusable to be sure, but not a policy. The regulations to secure the just and considerate treatment of uncivilized peoples, probably, were never more wisely devised than those of the various powers in Africa, with one exception. The world wants justice and protection for these natives and none will insist upon it more strenuously than the people of the leading powers that are identified with the African work.

We protest against the evils of the drink traffic. They are bad enough. But do we not see, even now, some signs amelioration? The Royal Niger Company has just announced that it has doubled the import tax on spirits with the expectation that it will considerably reduce the trade. The British South Africa Company has just proclaimed its positive prohibition of the sale of spirits to natives throughout its immense domain. Such sales to natives are strictly forbidden in more than nine-tenths of the Congo basin. We take it for granted that missionary influence will be for good. The point I wish to make is that though various evils are marking the progress of the African work, they are, as I verily believe, but a drop in the bucket as compared with the fundamental and lasting good that governments and commerce are doing and will do.

What grander thought can be conceived of the African native than that he himself shall be made the agent of the regeneration of his land. That is the idea, expressed or implied, underlying the policy of the African governments. He is not to be a ward of the nations, placed on a rerseve like the American Indian; and see how skillfully some of the governments are managing him to bring about his willing compliance with their desire that he shall become the potent factor he must be in the development of Africa.

A small tax is now levied upon 60,000 native huts in Mashona Land. That is right. Paying taxes is one of the privileges of civilization. The natives who pay this hut tax, were living, until recently, in those places that were loftiest and most difficult to reach, in constant terror of the Matabeles who killed them, burned their villages and carried off their women and cattle. The only hope in the lives of these miserable people was that they would escape the Matabele raids. Now they are living as safely as our own farmers. The valleys are covered with their gardens and their herds are multiplying. It is right that they should pay for the blessings of the wise and humane government they now enjoy and that has made life worth living; and what a wonderful impetus in the way of development is this fact that they have good government and are helping to pay for it. Now the

Mashonas, like all Kaffir tribes, are rather thrifty. They hate to part with money or cattle; and Sir Cecil Rhodes's government is taking advantage of this trait to get them to work and train them in methods of work. The Mashona hut-owners are told:

"You may pay the hut tax in money or cattle; but if you wish to keep these, come to our officials and work a month. You will be well fed and at the end of the month you will owe the government nothing and you will then have eleven months to devote to your fields and your herds."

So thousands of these Mashonas are supplying their labor to the government in lieu of paying the tax. They are working on the railroad to the Indian Ocean, in the mines, in the townships, on the highways. They are well kept and well treated and it is found that many who came in to work a month remain six, and pocket their wages. It is also seen that their wants, though very simple yet, are increasing a little. They have discovered, for instance, that a blanket is a very comfortable thing on the cooler nights in their country. Now this revolution in native aims and conditions of life is occurring in the veriest wilderness of Africa where, ten years ago, no white man could venture except at imminent peril.

If you can give a barbarous people the protection of a good government and induce them to work, all things are not only possible but are coming. So we see throughout an enormous area from the South African Republic to the north end of Lake Nyassa, in a considerable part of German East Africa, in Uganda, and for thousands of miles along the Congo and its tributaries, the effort is constantly widening to give government, which means good order and protection, to these tribes and to require from them what it is right they should pay for the security of life and property they are beginning to enjoy for the first time in their lives.

The laws of the Congo State provide that crimes against native persons and property shall be severely punished; and though these laws have been violated by agents of the State, it is none the less true that as fast as the State has been able to extend its influence, inter-tribal wars and the practices of cannibalism and human sacrifices have been suppressed; and simultaneously the State is requiring from the villages thus protected a tax payable in rubber.

The question, "Will the native African work?" is no longer a conundrum. It seems only yesterday that the white agents in German East Africa were writing, that to procure the essential native labor it would be necessary, in effect, to reduce the people to slavery; that is, they were to be forced to work. There is not a government in Africa, to-day, that needs to import labor. The cry from all over South Africa, where an enormous amount of manual labor is required, is, "Do not send us laborers. The natives give us cheap and effective service."

You have heard of the fierce Matabeles, trained for war and not for work. Work was fit only for the women and slaves. They have, no longer, need for the assegai and shield. They could not go on the war-path if they would Their thoughts, turned from the pursuit of war, are now bent on getting ahead in the world. The men who, four years ago, could not own cattle because cattle were the prerogative of the king, now have their herds and farms. Who would have thought when the African Congress was held in Chicago, that it would have been written in this century: "Prospectors, in pairs or singly, wander all over Matabele Land and, far from being molested, they are hospitably received. The Matabeles are not a difficult people to deal with. They are pleased to see the white men in their country. They were cruel at the bidding of their king. As soon as the barbarous system that ground them down was destroyed, they became quite reconciled to the new order of things."

Eight hundred of these soldiers who fought in their impis three years ago, to drive the white men out of the gold fields, came unbidden, in August last, to Bulawayo and secured work in the brickyards and other industries of the place; and the barbarous African is not only beginning to work his way to a higher place, but also to fight his way there, if need be. It was chiefly the former cannibals of the middle Congo, who chased Stanley down the river crying: "Meat, meat," who were the agents in driving the Arab slavers out of a vast region which will, probably never again be scourged by the evil that kills eight people to enslave one.

The fact that in many ways, the native is putting his own shoulder to the wheel in this enormous work is clinching the conviction that has been growing for years, that all of tropical and sub-tropical Africa, the greater part of the continent, is for the Africans, just as India is for the East Indians, though a British possession.

The missionary and the trader are sometimes preceding this extension of government influence, sometimes following it. Now one, now another is the pioneer; and the more there are of them all, the better. Experience in some large districts seems to show clearly that if you can double the points of contact between the natives and the civilizing influences, governmental, religious, educative, industrial, commercial, you more than double the good results; for the multiplicity of reputable foreign enterprises and stations, as a rule, increases the security of the native and hastens the day when the fact begins to dawn upon him that the good things brought to him, in other words, civilization, mean a diminution of his sufferings and an augmentation of his well-being. The constant effort must be to impress this fact upon him and when he clearly sees it the victory will be two-thirds won.

I see not a particle of inducement for Afro-Americans to go to Africa to earn the wages of a day laborer. The work required in every field needs something more than strength of hands. Any foreigner who cannot devote to Africa special gifts or attainments in some direction, or the self-effacing zeal of the Christian missionary or teacher, had better keep away. He can make a more comfortable living at home and Africa does not need him.

But it would be surprising if Afro-Americans should not become prominent in one or another of the great departments of this movement. The field of missionary and educative work seems especially to invite them. Their capacity for the work, their strength to help Africa if they will only put it forth, needs no argument. I am glad the day has gone when every untruthful statement about Africa can be met only with a little argument and less knowledge. It is much easier and more convincing to be able to point to precedent and fact. If any one were to tell me that the millions of Afro-Americans, stronger every day as they are, cannot, if they have the impulse and the zeal, make for themselves a chapter in the history of Africa's development that shall be an enduring monument to their love of God and man, I should simply point to that little colony of freed slaves on the Grain Coast, struggling as they have been and still are. What work has Liberia done in politics, in agriculture, in morals, in religion that she need be ashamed to compare with the best results of European domination on Africa's coasts, and I do not except the British settlements of Sierra Leone and Lagos? Who would belittle the part that Liberia played in freeing West Africa from the curse of the slave trade; or what thinking man would dream of denying that the handful of freed slaves was a boon to Africa when he sees aborigines of Liberia fitted to take some part in her public affairs, prominently engaged in agriculture or commerce and spreading the tidings of the Christian faith among their people?

Strive to get your ideas of Africa and the African work from the sources that are, admittedly, most reliable.

Look upon all estimates of Africa's ultimate value to the world as purely tentative, for they may be proven, in the course of Africa's evolution, to be far from accurate.

Remember that we are still in the early stages of African work, that much that is done is experimental, and that all the ideas that promise improvement in policies or methods should be widely published and studied if found worthy.

In all your efforts, keep before you the thought that Africa is for the African; that the summing up of the work is to help him to help himself; that the destiny of his continent depends upon his development; and that in every stage of his progress his life and property should be shielded by laws as efficiently enforced as our own. I believe that no missionary center is true to duty that fails to make injustice and inhumanity known, and in such cases America should swell if she does not lead in a chorus of indignation and protest that cannot be ignored, and that shall teach governments and trading companies to look well after the fitness of the agents they send to Africa.

Remember that government and commerce are and should be the natural allies of missionary enterprise, each having its own ends in view, but all essential factors in the same great scheme. I do not believe that more eloquent tributes have ever been paid to the value of missionary work than those of men who have been prominent in the Congo government service. If the whole work thrives, there must be co-operation and mutual helpfulness; and the world should hear of any attempt by government agents or traders to impede or interfere with the development of missionary or educative endeavor. Neither public opinion nor the governments themselves will countenance such interference.

Do not encourage interference, at least for the present, with any native customs that are not unsurmountable stumbling blocks in the way of the work. Missionary societies may draw a useful lesson from the example of the British South Africa Company, which is telling all the natives under its rule that it will not interfere with their laws and customs save that there must be no more raiding, no more murder and no more witchcraft. Establish the essentials of progress first, for premature attention to non-essentials may retard the general advance.

Mr. Droogmans, a Belgian writer, has called attention to the fact that recent years have seen Austria, Norway, Sweden, and Switzerland, none of them having possessions in Africa, organizing societies, raising funds, earnestly and actively promoting philanthropic work in that continent. We have been lagging behind, not because we have less love for humanity, but because we have not been organized as they are abroad for effective appeal to the philanthropic spirit of our people in behalf of Africa. The World is full of that spirit now and we can hardly conceive of the change that fifty years have brought. We can scarcely realize that up to the middle of this century the principal article of African commerce was man. How ghastly now appear the Spanish statistics of their traffic recorded, not in numbers, but in weight of slaves. Ten thousand tons of Negroes exported in a year!

I should be glad to see among the practical results of this congress, a new department in some existing society, or better yet, a new organization here in the South, whose special aims should be:

A more effective organizatiou of the philanthropic impulse and spirit that pervades our own country, for the promotion of good works in Africa.

The preparation of literary helps and guides for the use of those who wish to study the whole subject or parts of it.

The collection of data, by correspondonce and exchange of news with philanthropic African and missionary societies, at home and abroad, relating to the treatment of native tribes by foreign agencies of every sort, so that the influences at work and the measure of justice and humanity accorded, may accurately be presented for the judgment of public opinion.

J. C. HARTZELL, D.D.

Corresponding Secretary of the Freedmen's Aid and Southern Education Society of the Methodist Episcopal Church; Formerly Editor of the *Southwestern Christian Advocate,* New Orleans; For twenty-five years connected with the work for the colored people

J. C. HARTZELL, D.D.
Corresponding Secretary of the Freedmen's Aid and Southern Education Society of the Methodist Episcopal Church; Formerly Editor of the *Southwestern Christian Advocate,* New Orleans; For twenty-five years connected with the work for the colored people

The Division of the Dark Continent

By
REV. J. C. HARTZELL, D.D.
CORRESPONDING SECRETARY FREEDMEN'S AID AND SOUTHERN
EDUCATION SOCIETY

Fifteen years ago, Victor Hugo said: *"In the nineteenth century the white has made a man of the black; in the twentieth century Europe will make a world out of Africa."*

The fulfillment of Victor Hugo's prophecy has begun. During the past few years, the world has witnessed results in the dividing of the African continent among the nations of Europe which have been unparalleled in the annals of history and which mark a very important episode in the progress of the world. These results indicate the rising tide of Christian fraternity among nations; and also demonstrate to the Christian student of history that God is preparing the way for a rapid and mighty uplift of the African continent, not only in material things, but also for her millions of black people, of whom the world knows so little, and concerning whom there are such conflicting theories and prophecies.

The preparation has been long, extending through many centuries, even reaching far back into pre-historic times, but the culmination has been sudden, remarkable and fraught with far-reaching consequences to that continent, its people, to Europe and to the world.

The continent of Africa lies in the eastern hemisphere, south of Europe with the Mediterranean Sea between, and the Red Sea separates it from Asia on the northeast, except the Isthmus of Suez, a narrow strip of land between that sea and the Mediterranean. As the Suez canal crosses this neck of land, Africa, in fact, is a vast island. On the north is the Mediterranean, on whose banks have arisen and passed away empires and civilizations. On the west is the Atlantic from the Straits of Gibraltar to the Cape of Good Hope. On the east and south are the Suez canal, the Red Sea and the Indian Ocean. In comparison with Africa, America and Australia are new discoveries. Our oldest traditions and most ancient history are African. The Phoenecians had settled in Syria and Egyptian civilization had begun its wonderful growth long before Abraham left his father's field, and while Europe was yet occupied by wandering tribes of barbarians. Only in recent times are the sources of Egyptian civilization being solved. Its history includes thousands of years before Christ.

The territory of the dark continent includes 11,500,000 square miles, and lies in about 70° of latitude and about the same of longitude. It is three times larger than all Europe, and about two-thirds the size of both North and South America, and three times as large as the United States. From Cape Bon to Tunis, on the north, to Cape Agulhas near the Cape of Good Hope, on the south, it is five thousand miles; and from Cape Verde on the west, to Cape Gardafui on the Indian Ocean, in the east, it is 4,500 miles.

It seems incredible that this continent, so vast in extent and in resources, just south of Europe, and on the highway from Europe to India, more easy of access from Europe than America, and much of its northern border lying on the highway of empire, as it traveled from Asia westward, should have so long been neglected and left in doubt and uncertainty.

This fact is emphasized when we remember what has been accomplished in comparatively few years in America and Australia. Only four hundred years ago Columbus accidentally run on the shores of this western world, with its sixteen millions of square miles of territory. There were probably four millions of aborigines in North and South America, and of these, perhaps half a million were in North America. These aborgines were the remnants of civilizations of whose origin we have no data. What marvelous changes have come in four brief centuries! Those remnants of civilization have disappeared and those copper colored barbarians are exterminated or without influence, and one hundred and thirty millions of people of European origin or descent have spread over this vast territory. In the United States alone are fifty-five millions of white people, and in Canada, just to the north, are nearly four millions more. And what prodigious advances in art, science, literature, agriculture, manufacturing and in moral activities! And again, what wonderful results in the extension of American influence in all the world, in business, diplomacy, education and missionary enterprises.

Australia gives another remarkable contrast. Only a hundred years ago the first convict settlement was made in New South Wales. Half a million of the lowest type of humanity were scattered over this domain, which is about as large as the United States or Europe. It is only about fifty years since the real transformation began. The result is wonderful. That half million of savage people have given place to three million whites, mostly of British origin and the annual trade amounts to $600,000,000.

On the other hand, Africa, with a population estimated at from one hundred and fifty to two hundred millions, one-ninth of the world's population, with ancient and at times powerful settlements on its northern borders, with both its coast lines known to the most powerful and populous nations, has remained until recent times, practically unknown. Its people, century after century, have continued to babble their one hundred and fifty languages and to live and die in the midst of their vast natural domain unreached by the thought or inspiration of the great world without.

And what adds pathos to this remarkable picture, is the fact that all other races united in a determination not to enslave each other, but to combine in the enslavement of the African. There are about thirty millions of Africa's sons and daughters in North and South America, the inheritance chiefly of slavery, and the descendants of freedmen. It is estimated that up to 1860 during three hundred and sixty years, fifteen millions of Africa's sons and daughters have been carried to America and Europe as slaves. It is also estimated that for every slave delivered into bondage the life of another African was sacrificed, so that thirty millions of these barbarous people have been murdered or sold into slavery, as the result of the accursed traffic in which, until within a few years, every Christian nation on earth had a part!

Bishop William Taylor tells that in one of his missionary tours along one of the many highways for centuties made bloody and horrible by the dying victims of the slave-trade,he lay at night on the ground trying to sleep. The moon shone brightly, and as the scenes of murder and cruelty which had been enacted on the spot where he lay came to mind, voices seemed to come out of the ground and cry to him: "O! man of God, why have you been so long coming?" So to-day may we not think of the aching heart of Africa crying out to the civilized world: "Oh! brothers, why have you been so long coming?"

When and by whom was the dividing of the Dark Continent begun? Whether Egyptian civilization, which began thousands of years before Christ, was indigenous or came from Asia, we do not know. Owing to Egypt's prehistoric origin, we cannot consider her people in the question before us.

The first foreign people to establish a colony and acquire territory on the northern coast of Africa were the Phoenicians, eleven hundred years before Christ. The Phoenicians were a wonderful people, occupying a little strip of land two hundred miles long and ten miles wide on the east end of the Mediterranean. Tyre and Sidon were their great cities They gave the world the alphabet and the science of numbers, and to Europe its first impulse toward civilization. They were great colonizers. They were darker skinned than the other Syrians, and were the sons of Ham.

The Greeks, sixty-three years before Christ, made the first European settlement in Africa. Cyreniaca, as the region was called, came to be a place of commerce, travel and pleasure-seeking for the active, cultured Greeks.

Later on, all northern Africa fell under the Roman sway.

How much was known of the Dark Continent early in the Christian era, is indicated by a map made by Ptolemy, the famous Alexandrian astronomer who flourished one hundred and forty years after Christ. Six hundred years before, Herodotus had given a summary of what the world knew of Africa. During that time the whole world had grown larger. Still the knowledge of the Dark Continent was confined to the shores of the Mediterranean and Red Seas, and down a few hundred miles on the east and west coasts. The continent itself was untouched.

The Sahara Desert was a tremendous barrier to movements southward. Egypt, in the height of her greatness, was more concerned about Asia than Africa. The camel had not yet come into general use as a means of travel and burden-bearing. Nearly all Europe and Asia were open to choice, and besides the native tribes resisted the encroachments of their neighbors. It is reported that the Phoenicians, six hundred and ten years before Christ, circumnavigated the continent, going down the Red Sea, round the Cape of Good Hope, up the west coast, and entered the Mediterranean by the Pillars of Hercules.

It is interesting here to note that there are those who claim that the discovered ruins of ancient cities, forts, mines, etc., and the testimony of the earliest travelers, demonstrate that in different parts of the Dark Continent there were in ancient times large centers of civilized people who, overwhelmed by the surrounding barbarous nations, or yielding to the inevitable tendencies of human nature, lapsed into decay. It is now, for example, considered fairly certain that the land of Ophir, where the ships of Solomon and his friend, Hiram of Tyre, went once in three years to bring back gold and precious stones and other merchandise, was in the vicinity of Zambesi, far down on the eastern coast of Africa. The recent opening of the gold-producing countries south of Zambesi-- Mashonoland and Manica--and the evidences of ancient mines found there, have served to confirm many in the opinion that the Ophir of the Bible was not in Arabia but in Africa. It now looks as if Africa would lead the nations of the world in the production of gold. (Last year the yield was $40,000,000, mined almost entirely by Negro laborers).

I have found one thing to the credit of Nero, the Roman tyrant. Sixty years after Christ, he sent an expedition to explore the source of the Nile. This is the first attempt we have on record of an enterprise which, eighteen hundred years later, our own Stanley completed.

Following the Roman conquest, the next great effort in dividing the Dark Continent was the invasion of Mohammedanism. For hundreds of years after the Roman conquest and the division of the empire, there was continued fighting along the Mediterranean, interfering with all exploration and new settlements. One episode, however, is worthy of mention. Four hundred and eighty years after Christ, eighty thousand Vandals (men, women and children), crossed from Spain to North Africa. For a hundred years these Teuton people held their own, but finally disappeared from history and blended with other peoples. The time had not come for people of our blood to have a hand in the division of the Dark Continent.

The Islamic or Arab conquest began 640 years after Christ, and in seventy years Europe was swept out of the Dark Continent and all North Africa was practically Mohammedanized. Wave after wave of Arab immigrants poured in. Cities were built, and great progress made in agriculture, commerce and art. For 750 years this process went on, so that at the close of the fourteenth century Mohammedanism had crossed the Sahara, had a good footing in Soudan, in the Niger region, as well as in Abyssinia and down the East Coast to Sofala, where the Portuguese in the sixteenth century found rich Arab cities. Caravan routes, with the use of camels, were established across the desert. Regular reports and annual pilgrimages to Mecca from different parts promoted knowledge of countries and people. Learning was advanced. At present the Mohammedan University at Cairo is one of the world's great seats of learning. When asked by a traveler what was taught there, the reply was: "We teach God."

Here, then, we have the first serious division of the Dark Continent. It was from Asia and Mohammedan, and not from Europe. Similarity of climate had much to do with bringing this to pass. Islamism brought with it political organization, some civilization, commercial activity and the establishment of slavery as an institution.

Europe next comes to the front in the work of exploration and division of Africa in the person of Prince Henry the Navigator, of Portugal. Columbus was born twenty years before, and Luther twenty years after the death of this remarkable man.

A water route to India, round the Cape of Good Hope, was one of the dreams of that day. Portugal seems to have been providentially prepared for her great work at this time in Africa. In view of her achievements on the Dark Continent, the Pope conferred upon her king the title of "Lord of India." which is attached to the crown to our time. In seventy years Prince Henry and his successors traced the contour of the west, south and east coasts of Africa, initiated the modern European colonization of the continent and began that division which is only now being completed. In 1520, the beginning of the sixteenth century, Portugal was mistress of all the coast of Africa except the Mediterranean and Red seas; forts were built, treaties made with the native tribes, Catholic stations established, and attempts made to convert the natives. But the power of this plucky little kingdom was destined to wane in Africa as well as at home.

Portugal inaugurated the slave trade. Antonio Gonsalvo brought home some gold dust and ten slaves in 1443. These were probably the first slaves taken from Western Africa by Europeans. They were presented to Pope Martin V., and be conferred on Portugal the right of possession of all countries discovered between Cape Bojado and the Indies. Portugal also had the first of many chartered companies to trade in African gold and slaves.

While Portugal was practically mistress of Africa during much of the sixteenth century, England, Spain, and France were absorbed in the acquisition of territory in the New Western World. Cortez had conquered Mexico (1520), Magellan had passed the straits bearing his name, the Spaniards had introduced slaves into the West Indies (1508), Cartier had entered the St. Lawrence (1535), and France began settling Canada (1542), and the year previous DeSoto had been on the Mississippi.

The world was entering upon a new era. The thirst for gold grew rapidly as the stories of exploration and conquest multiplied. The time for European rivals in Africa had come. The slave trade had already grown to be the chief African traffic. Indians had proved a failure as slaves in America. A few Negro slaves admitted into the West Indies had proved such a success that the traffic had grown enormously. In 1516 Charles V. granted a patent to a Flemish trader to import four thousand slaves annually to the West Indies. The Pope opened a slave market in Lisbon. As early as 1537 it is said ten to twelve thousand slaves were taken there annually, and sent to the West Indies. In 1562 Sir John Hawkins, in spite of the protest of the Queen and many philanthropists, inaugurated the slave trade for England, which later on was chartered by royal authority.

For one hundred and fifty years, from 1550 to the close of the seventeenth century, one by one, the leading nations of Europe began to get footholds on the African coasts, especially on the west. (England, 1553; France, Holland, 1595; Denmark, and last, Germany, 1681). There came to be sharp rivalries. Later on were conferences and diplomatic congresses, during which Portugal was gradually pushed out, and foundations laid for the permanent division of the continent.

The slave trade was the great industry contended for and carried on. In 1748 there were 97,000 slaves carried to America by all nations, and up to that time the total number was probably a million. During the eighteenth century six millions were carried to America, besides the horrible traffic which was kept up to the coasts of the Mediterranean, to Egypt and to Asia, which had been carried on from time immemorial. It is estimated that the profits of the slave trade in the seventeenth and eighteenth centuries from the Dark Continent were equal to that on gold and all other products.

The eighteenth century was practically a century of stagnation so far as the division of the Dark Continent was concerned. European wars had much to do with this. The great nations were busy with their own interests and the protection and extension of their colonial possessions elsewhere. So far as Africa was concerned, the civilized world united in the awful crimes of devastation and slaughter incident to the slave trade. Toward the close of the century this unspeakable crime against humanity resulted in 200,000 slaves a year being exported, one-half to America and the West Indies and the other half to the East Indies, Egypt and the Mediterranean cities. But during this century the voice of

God had begun to speak in thunder tones through such men as Wesley and Wilberforce, in England and elsewhere, and the tide of sentiment against the traffic at the close of the century was powerful and effective. Denmark was the first to forbid the traffic in 1792. The reformation went on, and in 1815 the powers signed a declaration at Vienna, declaring the trade repugnant to humanity and its abolition highly desirable.

The year 1815 marked a new era in the history of the world, an era destined to have much to do with the Dark Continent. The long Napoleonic wars were over, and the dream of France for supremacy beyond the seas was dissipated at Waterloo. As to Africa, but little change had been made in European possession except in Egypt, where England's diplomacy and money had gained a paramount influence, which continues to grow more and more absolute until the present time. An Egyptian debt of $400,000,000, owned mostly in England, indicates the inevitable, as soon as Turkish power can be ignored, and the jealousy of other European nations appeased. The new era was destined to see a long period of peaceful development throughout the world. In America, our own republic led the way. Undreamed-of results in world-wide prosperity, in invention, learning and moral activities were the result.

Europe at this time had only a few stations and factories on the coasts, and but little occupation beyond the seaboard. Interior Africa was an unknown blank. There was no real thought of the continent as a whole, as in the case of America or Australia. Germany, in the modern sense, did not exist. France was only awakening to a new desire for colonial expansion. England was busy with the development of Canada, Australia, India and the East, and cared for Africa only as a way station to her Asiatic empire. The nations which had possessions made but little effort to strengthen or extend them. The total commercial value of African trade in 1815, including slaves, was only $150,000,000. The exports were but $65,000,000, and half of this from Egypt and the countries of the Mediterranean.

For sixty years Africa was to have practical peace, so far as the outside world was concerned. All this, as we see it now, was Providential. It gave opportunity for a period of preparation in Africa herself, and in the thought and conditions of the outside world.

This period of preparation resulted in great changes both without and within the Dark Continent. In the outside world there was an entire change of sentiment as to the relations a parent country should sustain to her colonies. The question at issue was Imperialism on the one hand and Federation on the other. Imperialism taught that colonies were private properties of the crowns, to be administered for their benefit with but little thought of the colonists themselves. The Federation idea, which came at last to be accepted as the true Imperialistic policy, was that colonists were to be regarded as parts of the whole nation, with rights and privileges and claims for protection and help, the same as the subjects who dwelt under the more immediate shadow of the throne. England had been taught a good lesson in the loss of her American colonies. This growth of right sentiment toward colonists was accelerated also by the increasing independence of thought among the colonists themselves, and also by the need of new fields for occupancy by the crowded populations at the home centers.

Another matter of world-wide interest and importance affecting Africa in this preparatory period was the gradual suppression of the African slave-trade. So far as that trade with Europe and America was concerned, its destruction was practically reached in 1850. Our own country ended it forty years before. The discussions in public assemblies and in literature, the contests over legislation and in diplomatic circles, all helped to educate the world's conscience concerning the black races, and to develop Christian sentiment and interest toward their continental home.

After the suppression of the slave-trade in the West, the horrors of the Arab-Asiatic traffic in human souls were brought to light by Livingstone and others. This served to combine philanthropists and statesmen for its destruction, and centered the world's thought anew upon Central Africa. The emancipation of the millions of Africans in our own country during this period had a powerful effect upon the world's thought and conscience concerning black humanity.

Thus, Providence was preparing the outside world for its final responsibility toward the Dark Continent. The only European nation to gain any new foothold in Africa during that sixty years of preparation was France. She conquered Algeria, and laid the foundation for the future French empire in North west Africa. It has been an expensive purchase to her, costing $750,000,000, and many hundreds of thousands of lives. But the results have been great, and Algeria, soon to be connected by railway across the Sahara desert with Senegal, on the West Coast, 2,500 miles to the South, is destined to be a great country.

In 1820 the Republic of Liberia was founded under the auspices of the American Colonization Society of the United States. England cared for her interests in the south and elsewhere. Egypt pushed a little farther down the Nile. The Suez canal was built. France was seeking a foothold in Madagascar.

While this transformation of sentiment and policy were going on among European nations, Africa herself was being prepared. This preparation was the result chiefly of exploration.

The world needed to know what the Dark Continent really was in extent, in physical resources and possibilities, the location of her mountains and plateaus, and her lakes and rivers, the nature-of-her climate, and the character of diverse and vast populations.

How marvelously the answer to these and similar questions went on through those sixty years of preparation. Every European center had its organization of learned men, whose sole purpose was to study Africa. Scores of powerful search-lights were turned on the Dark Continent. Egyptology rose to the rank of a science. Questions of geography, ethnology, history, language and religion as related to Africa, commanded fortunes in money, and the best brain of many of Europe's leading statesmen and scientists. It was an era of exploration and discovery by a long line of heroic men, and a few equally heroic women, such as has never been equalled in numbers or heroism in the exploration of any other continent.

I cannot attempt to even catalogue their names, much less their deeds. They were God's forerunners opening the way for the nineteenth century to make a new world out of Africa.

We must, however, pause long enough to mention two names--England's Livingstone, and America's Stanley. The former died alone upon his knees in the heart of the continent for which he gave his life; and his dust, after being carried many hundreds of miles to the seacoast by his faithful black attendants, now sleeps in Westminster Abbey, among England's greatest dead.

Stanley lives to aid in the work of nation-building in the land he helped discover. His wonderful journey across the continent, and the discovery of the great Congo waterway, may be said to close the period of preparation and to inaugurate the national scramble which was soon to begin.

From this time on African exploration and occupation came to be a kind of holy crusade. Germany had become interested in the wonderful continent whose rim only was mapped out in the school-days of many now living. Stanley's hunt for Livingstone, and Livingstone's tragic death, had awakened tremendous enthusiasm throughout the civilized world. Missionary enterprises multiplied, and the day for Africa's opportunity hastened.

The greatest single event preparatory to the final division of the Dark Continent was the founding of the Congo Free State. This was done under the Christian and heroic Leopold of Belgium. He had no children of his own, and it is said he adopted Africa as his child. Stanley was still in the heart of the Dark Continent when, September, 1876, Leopold called a select conference of distinguished geographers and philanthropists to consider the question of an international movement in the interests of African civilization. We need not go through the various steps by which this new State was established. Stanley was Leopold's faithful lieutenant, and gave five years to its organization. The result was the establishment of a Negro Empire, which begins with the mouth of the Congo and extended eastward a thousand miles into the heart of the continent, and reached a thousand miles north and south. Its flag is a field of blue on which shines a single golden star. The United States was the first to recognize that flag as the ensign of a friendly power. This new nation, born in a day, includes 770,000 square miles of territory, and about 15,000,000 of people. Its territory is larger than New England, New York, Pennsylvania, Ohio, Indiana, Michigan, Illinois, Minnesota, Missouri, Kansas, Colorado and Utah. Its central government is in Belgium and twelve governors-general, over as many districts, represent the home authorities.

Glorious little Belgium! Or rather, glorious Leopold, in whose Christian and philanthropic soul this marvelous work was begun!

While the development of the Congo Free State was going on, other nations were looking out for larger possessions on the continent. More or less conflict in opinion and policy resulted. This made necessary the celebrated "Berlin Conference," held in 1884. The first, and perhaps the most important result of this conference was to completely recognize the permanency of the Congo Free State. This new African empire was the pivotal center of friendly international co-operation. A representative was present from the United States.

The congress opened the Congo, the Niger and the Zambesi, and other rivers to the free trade of the world. It also settled definitely the law of occupation as to territory, and made it necessary for any nation intending to acquire new territory on the continent to notify all the powers represented in the conference.

We have now reached the culmination of the Providential events leading to the division of the Dark Continent.

It would be interesting to follow England and France and Germany and Italy and Portugal and the other nations, in their spirit and methods in holding the possessions which they had and in securing more wherever possible. "Influence," as applied to the extension of a nation's power over vast territories, and the German suggestion "Hinterland," or the land beyond, came to be accepted as international doctrines, and the lines of agreement between great sections of territory, extending many hundreds of miles, were fixed.

But we need not enter into these details. It will suffice to group the permanent results of this Continental scramble, as shown by the latest attainable data. France has the largest slice; namely, three millions of square miles. Her chief African empire is in the Northwest, and extends from Algeria down to Sierra Leone, more than two thousand miles. It includes the largest portion of the Sahara region, the region of the Upper Niger and the valley of the Senegal river. She also has Madagascar and its dependencies.

England comes next with her more than 2,500,000 square miles, and a late Royal proclamation has added more. British Africa is in three great sections, and are known as British Guinea on the West, British South Africa, and British East Africa. British South Africa extends from Cape Colony, fifteen hundred miles northward, through the center of the continent, touching the Congo Free State. British East Africa begins at Zanzibar, extends northeast to Abyssinia, westward to Congo, and northward to a yet undefined line toward Egypt. That undefined line probably means that when Egypt becomes a British province, the intermediate territory, now in revolt under the Mahdi, will also become British, making a continuous stretch to the Lower Nile, a distance of twenty-five hundred miles.

Portugal has nearly 900,000 square miles, divided about equally on the southeast and western coasts.

Germany has about 825,000 square miles in three parts; one on the west near the equator, one on the southwest coast, and one on the east coast, bounded by the sea on the east, British East Africa on the north, British Central Africa on the south, and the Congo Free State on the west.

Rejuvenated Italy has about 600,000 square miles along the Red Sea, the Gulf of Aden, and the east coast, including Abyssinia.

Spain has about 215,000 square miles on the West coast, made up largely of the Sahara region.

In the center, recognized and protected by all, surrounded by the possessions of England, Germany, Portugal, and France, is the great Congo Free State, which, like the golden star on its flag of blue, shines as a star of hope in the midst of the Dark Continent.

The Turkish section at present includes Egypt and Tripoli, 800,000 square miles, but the grip of that Asiatic power grows less and less upon African soil.

This leaves unappropriated only about 1,000,000 square miles. The lakes of Africa include about 68,000 square miles.

We have thus briefly outlined the dividing of the Dark Continent. How quickly it all came to pass when the world and the continent itself, in God's own time, were ready. Three thousand years ago the Phoenecians began to nibble at the great continent on its extreme northern edge. Since then Asia and Europe have been mostly discovered and settled, and America and Australia have been discovered and become seats of vast empires of power and usefulness. And yet, only ten years ago, of the 11,500,000 square miles which make up Africa, not more than 2,500,000 were occupied by European nations and the Boer Republic in the far south. Only the rim of the continent had been touched. To-day nearly the whole has been gobbled up, and all Europe combines to pour in upon the Dark Continent the light and life of Christian civilization. Who can comprehend the results sure to come? Under the protection and leadership of Protestant England and Germany, Republican France and rising Italy, the power of Mohammedanism will be broken, and the Crescent in North Africa will wane before the uplifted Cross; the last vestige of traffic in human souls will be swept away; her rivers and lakes will become highways of commerce; railways will be built along her valleys and across her many plains; instead of slave-gangs and slave-traders' highways of crime and agony, will be the school-house and church and pathways of peace and prosperity; and fetish heathenism among her millions will gradually give way to the worship of the true God.

But we must not expect results too soon. Great preliminary questions are yet to be settled. The climax now reached in the division of the continent, by which the best thought and civilization of Europe are pledged and enlisted *means supreme opportunity* for Africa. A general European or Asiatic war would cost Africa a generation of progress. Exploration must be completed; the economic value of the continent must be further tested by actual settlement. Africa has few ocean harbors, and no really great system of lakes like our own, and her large rivers reach the sea with difficulty, and at times over falls, instead of being continental highways to and from the ocean, like the Mississippi, the Columbia or the Amazon. Will systems of railways supply these deficiencies? Africa is essentially a tropical country. The equator passes through the center, and only portions of the north and south ends are in the temperate zones. No great nations have yet been developed between the Tropics of Cancer and Capricorn. Will Africa be an exception? If so, will it be by colonization, or by development of the black races already on the ground. Time will solve these and many other questions. *To-day, I repeat, is the hour of Africa's supreme opportunity.*

A single concluding remark. The African is a belated race. God sees to it in due time that every section of His family of races has a chance. The sons of Shem had their. They rejected their Lord, and are eliminated from the governing factors of the world.

The sons of Japheth now rule, and will continue to rule if true to their Lord; denying Him, their power will also pass away. It seems now that the sons of Ham are to have their chance. How soon, or to what extent they are to rule, we know not. We may rest assured, however, that the long ages of heathenism, which have enveloped hundreds of millions of God's children in black, are about ended, and this belated African race will have its opportunity.

> "Joy to thy savage realms, O Africa!
> A sign is on thee that the great I AM
> Shall work new wonders in the land of Ham;
> And while He tarries for the glorious day
> To bring again His people, there shall be

A remnant left from Cushan to the sea,
And though the Ethiop cannot change his skin,
Nor bleach the outward stain, he yet shall roll
The darkness off that overshades the soul,
And wash away the deeper dyes of sin.
Princes, submissive to the Gospel sway,
Shall come from Egypt; and the Morian's land
In holy transport stretch to God its hand;
Joy to thy savage realms, O Africa!"

THE PARTITION OF AFRICA

The following table has been compiled by Mr. E. G. Ravenstein, F.R.G.S. The population figures are necessarily in most cases only the roughest estimates:

BRITISH AFRICA:	Area Sq. Miles	Population	Inhabitants to Sq. Mile
Gambria	2,700	50,000	19
Sierra Leone	15,000	275,000	18
Gold Coast	46,600	1,905,000	41
Lagos and Yoruba	21,100	3,000,000	142
Niger Territories and Oil Rivers	269,500	17,500,000	65
British Guinea	354,900	22,730,000	64

Page 58

	Area Sq. Miles	Population	Inhabitants to Sq. Mile
CAPE COLOLY (with Pondo Land and Walvisch Bay)	225,940	1,728,000	8
Basutoland	10,300	219,000	21
Natal	20,460	544,000	22
Zulu and Tonga Lands	9,790	173,000	18
British Bechuanaland	71,430	50,000	0.7
Bechuanaland and Protectorate	99,500	80,000	0.8
Matabili, Mashona, and Nyasa Lands, etc.	524,000	1,600,000	3
British South Africa	961,420	4,394,000	4.6

	Area Sq. Miles	Population	Inhabitants to Sq. Mile
ZANZIBAR (Protectorate, with	1,040	200,000	192

Northern Ports)			
Ibea, to 6° N. latitude	468,000	6,500,000	14
Rest to Egyptian frontier	745,000	6,000,000	8
Northern Somali Coast	40,000	200,000	5
Sokotra	1,380	10,000	7
British East Africa	1,255,420	12,910,000	10

BRITISH AFRICA -- Continent:	Area Sq. Miles	Population	Inhabitants to Sq. Mile
Mauritius and Dependencies	1,030	393,000	381
St. Helena, Ascension, and Tristan da Cunha	130	6,500	50
Total British Africa	2,572,900	40,433,500	16

FRENCH AFRICA:	Area Sq. Miles	Population	Inhabitants to Sq. Mile
Tunis	44,800	1,500,000	33
Algeria	257,600	3,900,000	15
Sahara	1,550,000	1,100,000	0.7
Senegambia (old professions)	15,000	180,000	12
Gold and Benin Coasts	50,000	600,000	12
Sudan and Guinea (remainder)	525,000	10,000,000	19
French Congo (and Gaboon)	320,000	6,000,000	19
Tajura Bay (Obok and Sibati)	7,700	70,000	9
Madagascar and dependencies	228,000	3,520,000	15
Comoros	760	64,000	84
Reunion	770	165,000	214
Total French Africa	3,000,630	27,099,000	9

PORTUGUESE AFRICA:	Area Sq. Miles	Population	Inhabitants to Sq. Mile

Portuguese Guinea	11,600	150,000	13
Angola	517,200	3,500,000	7
Mozambique	310,000	1,500,000	5
Madeira	320	134,000	420
Cape Verde Islands	1,490	111,000	74
St. Thome and Principe	460	21,000	45
Total Portuguese Africa	841,070	5,416,000	6

Page 59

SPANISH AFRICA:	Area Sq. Miles	Population	Inhabitants to Sq. Mile
Tetuan, etc. (Morocco)	30	16,000	530
Sahara (Rio de Ore, etc.)	210,000	100,000	0.5
Canaries	2,940	288,000	98
Gulf of Guinea	800	33,000	41
Total Spanish Africa	213,770	437,000	2

GERMAN AFRICA:	Area Sq. Miles	Population	Inhabitants to Sq. Mile
Togoland (Slave Coast)	16,000	1,150,000	72
Cameroons (Kamerun)	130,000	2,600,000	20
Southwest Africa	322,450	117,000	0.2
East Africa (with Mafia)	353,500	2,000,000	6
Total German Africa	821,950	5,867,000	7

ITALIAN AFRICA:	Area Sq. Miles	Population	Inhabitants to Sq. Mile
Eritrea	52,000	300,000	6
Abyssinia	195,000	4,500,000	23
Somal Galla, etc	355,300	1,500,000	4
Total Italian Africa	602,000	6,300,000	10

SUMMARY:	Area Sq. Miles	Population	Inhabitants to Sq. Mile
British Africa	2,572,900	40,433,500	16
French Africa	3,000,630	27,099,000	9
Portuguese Africa	841,070	5,416,000	6
Spanish Africa	213,770	437,000	2
German Africa	821,950	5,867,000	7
Italian Africa	602,000	6,300,000	10
Congo State (Belgian)	764,000	15,600,000	18
Boer Republics (Swazi Land)	168,120	948,000	6
Liberia	37,000	1,000,000	27
Turkish (Egypt and Tripoli)	836,000	7,980,000	10
Unappropriated	1,486,710	23,919,500	16
Lakes Chad, Victoria, Tanganyika, Nyassa, etc	67,850		
Total Africa	11,512,000	135,000,000	12

Unappropriated Africa includes Morocco (219,000 square miles, 8,000,000 inhabitants), Bornu with Kanem (80,000 square miles, 5,100,000 inhabitants), Wadai (172,000 square miles, 2,000,000 inhabitants), Bagirmi (71,000 square miles, 1,500,000 inhabitants), etc.

FREDERIC PERRY NOBLE
Secretary of the World's Congress on Africa at the Columbian Exposition; Author of "An African Devil-Mission;" "Chautauqua as a New Factor in the American Life;" "Natural Religion Prophetic of Revelation;" "The Missionary Occupation of Africa"

FREDERIC PERRY NOBLE
Secretary of the World's Congress on Africa at the Columbian Exposition;
Author of "An African Devil-Mission;" "Chautauqua as a New Factor in the
American Life:" "Natural Religion Prophetic of Revelation;" "The Missionary
Occupation of Africa"

THE OUTLOOK FOR AFRICAN MISSIONS IN THE TWENTIETH CENTURY:
Epitome of an Essay at the Atlanta Congress on Africa

BY
FREDERIC PERRY NOBLE

SECRETARY
OF
The World-Congress on Africa at the Columbian Exposition
CHICAGO, AUGUST, 1893

AND

AUTHOR OF
An African Devil-Mission; or, The African Slave-Trade of To-Day;
Another Devil-Mission; or, Christendom's African Rum-Traffic;
Captain Great-Heart and the Holy War; or, The Story of the Salvation Army;
Chautauqua as a New Factor in American Life;
Natural Religion Prophetic of Revelation;
AND
THE MISSIONARY-OCCUPATION OF AFRICA: A STORY OF CIVILIZATION

(In Preparation)
[The book now preparing and the present essay have each been separately entered according to Act of Congress in the year 1895 by Frederic Perry Noble in the office of the Librarian of Congress. Washington, D. C. All rights of reproduction, translation and use are without exception reserved by the author].

Copyright, 1895, by Frederic Perry Noble

After darkness, light! May Atlanta's congress advance Africa's annexation to Christ's kingdom.

PART I.
ANALYSIS OF THE ESSAY.

Statement of the Divisions of the Subject: Political partition; Religious partition; Non-Statistical results; Reinforcement for missions; Conclusion.

Division A: Political Partition

- The positions of Belgium, France, Germany, Italy, Portugal and Spain
- The position of Britain
- The meaning and outcome of the European position in its bearing on slavery,
- Muhammadanism and missions

Division B: Religious Partition

- The Christian protagonists: Abyssinian, Copt, Greek, Protestant and Roman
- Christian churches and communicants in connection with Anglican (and Episcopal), Baptist, Congregational, Lutheran, Methodist, Moravian, Presbyterian,
  Roman and undenominational missions
- Summary of statistics for Protestant and Roman missions

Division C: Non-Statistical Results

- Non-denominational societies and other auxiliaries
- Gains and rising ratios of gain
- Negro Christianity in the Americas
- Its influence on African evangelization thro Baptists, Methodists and other Protestants

Division D: Reinforcements for Missions

- Christian women
- South African Christianity

- Native agency
- New methods or new applications of old ones: evangelism, including education; self-support; industry; medical missions

Conclusion: What shall Christianize Africa?

- Fellowship between Catholics and Protestants; the methods and principles of Krapf and Mackay; the purification of Christendom by Christianity; wealth; prayer; *GOD.*

PART II.

SUMMARY OF THE ESSAY

Introductory Statement

Four large facts bear upon the outlook for African missions in the twentieth century. Africa bye-and-large is in the grip of Christendom. Secular agencies as a whole will work to the advantage of religious forces. European powers protect missionaries and sometimes promote missions. The results of Christian missions in Africa now, at the close of the century beginning 1795, surpass what Carey the Baptist, Coke the Methodist, Johnson the Anglican and Moffat the Congregationalist could have dreamed. The Christian womanhood of the United Kingdom and the United States; the British and Dutch Christians of Cape Colony and Natal; and the Negro churches of Africa and the Americas are doubling the force.

Division A: Political Partition

Belgium, Britain, France, Germany, Italy, Portugal and Spain are making Africa an appanage of Europe. The millions of Negroes inhabiting the Antilles, South America and these southern states endow the western world with African interests. Five of the first-mentioned powers rank as Catholic nations, three as Protestant peoples. The Roman states comprise Belgium, France, Italy, Portugal and Spain. The Protestant powers include Britain, Germany and the United States; but Finland, Norway, Sweden and Switzerland also contribute to the Protestant conquest of Africa. Britain has swarmed into the cardinal coigns of African vantage. She is at the cape and the Zambezi; at the head and mouth of the Nile and the Suez canal; along the Atlantic and the Niger; and on the Indian ocean and the Red sea. The best portions of Africa for men of Saxon stock are in British hands.

The back-bone of the slave-trade is broken. Europe is actually achieving somewhat toward the suppressal of slaving.

The partition of Africa is striking the sword from the grasp of Islam. Since 1890 Muhammadanism south of the equator has received such blows that it cannot there lift the heel against Christianity. Between the equator and the tenth degree north, east of Adamawa, Islam is more than ever a waning force. What it may, perhaps, have attained, is merely a military success. Beyond the tenth degree Abyssinia, England in Egypt and France in Berber and Mediterranean Africa prevent the Muslim theocracy from regaining power. The Senusiya and the Saharan and Sudanese Islamites need not be feared. The solidarity and strength of the Muhammadan states of Central Sudan have in the last five years sustained severe shocks. The number of African Muslims has been grossly exaggerated. Instead of numbering one hundred or eighty or sixty millions, they, according to the highest authorities on Africa and especially as to Islam in Africa, number but forty million.

For the first time in fifteen hundred years Christian missions are to have a fair chance and an open field. Most of the obstacles have now been passed. The crescent sinks. Protestantism moves toward federation. Rome revives. Europe takes Africa seriously in hand. Great Britain and the United States, the two Protestant and Teutonic powers that wield the moral headship of humanity, are the powers of most influence in the spiritual regeneration of Africa and those most richly endowed for the betterment of her peoples.

Division B: Religious Partition

In the conflict with Islam and paganism Protestantism and Rome are the spiritual protagonists. The Abyssinian, Egyptian and Greek churches effect practically nothing for the evangelization of Africa. The Greeks (Orthodox) number less than fifty thousand; the Kopts may amount to six hundred thousand; and perhaps the Ethiopic church is three million strong. The Roman communion claims a population in every class numbering one million, two hundred thousand. The Protestants comprise at least one million, five hundred thousand souls. Probably the grand total for Christianity in Africa and the adjacent islands, including the native converts won by missions proper, amounts to five millions, seven hundred and fifty thousand. Against these may be set three hundred thousand Hindus and Sikhs, only four hundred and thirty thousand Jews, forty million Muhammadans (possibly even less), and over one hundred million pagans. But the Abyssinian, Koptic and Russo-Greek church-men in Africa need missionaries. In South Africa Dutch Presbyterianism as a whole is too often a mere form of doctrine. In the Spanish, Portuguese and French possessions, according to Catholic authorities, the Christian character of the colonists connected with the Roman church leaves very much to be desired.

[Mr. Noble does not deem it advisable or judicious as yet to publish any statistics as to the native churches and native communicants connected at the present day with Anglican, Baptist, Catholic, Congregational, Lutheran, Methodist, Non-Denominational, Presbyterian, or Unity of Brethren missions. He is engaging in correspondence with each and every mission-society throughout the world that works among African peoples, in the hope that they will enable him to supplement his tentative estimate with the freshest and most authoritative data as to the religious census of African missions.]

So far as the statements of the agencies for missions on the continent and the islands permit an approximation toward the number of native communicants, Rome would seem to have two hundred and fifty thousand of these in Africa and the African isles of the sea; and Protestantism as many if not more. Excluding adherents, who presumably number additional hundreds of thousands, the total of native communicants won since 1795 by strictly missionary work in Africa and Madagascar together would appear to be represented to-day by at least five hundred thousand native members of the Christian church in its Latin and Teutonic branches.

Division C: Non-Statistical Results

Interdenominational, non-denominational or undenominational agencies for African missions are at once an effect and a cause of these activities. Nearly one-third of the non-denominational organizations devote themselves to evangelism pure and simple. The remainder consist of medical mission-societies; of bodies partly philanthropic, partly religious; and of publication-societies whose colporters are missionaries. As representative or typical auxiliaries to societies for evangelization may be mentioned religious tract societies; Bible societies; associations for free distribution of the Scriptures; international unions of missionaries; associations for planting Sunday-schools abroad; alliances of theological seminaries to promote missions; world-wide leagues of young people in every branch of Christ's church; Christian associations of young men and of young women; and the volunteering of students for service as missionaries. Rising tides of intelligent interest and men and means are coming from these unused reservoirs.

[Mr. Noble here omits other statistical data as not yet ripe.]

The Christianizing of the American Negro is another result. Europeans often reproach American Christians with attempting little and accomplishing less for the African. They forget--or ignore--the black Christian of the Antilles, South America and the United States. Merely in the last-named country the Protestant communions alone had two million, six hundred and seventy-three thousand, nine hundred and seventy-seven Negro members in 1890. This is ten times as many black communicants as the native church-members connected with Protestant missions in Africa. Moreover, this astounding and stupendous result is the outcome, (except so far as the existence of about five hundred and twenty-five thousand Negro Protestants in 1861 is concerned), of but thirty-three years of effort. Missions among the freedmen of the United States and their children (in one-third of the time that European societies have been active in Africa) have accomplished more than ten times as much.

The Negro of the United States and the West Indies has already rewarded his Christianizer. The Anglican, Baptist, Basle, Congregational, Episcopal, Methodist and Presbyterian missions in Africa have enjoyed the services of Negroes from America. Six Negro Baptist, five Negro Methodist, bodies engage in missions among African peoples. The Anglican Negro church of Sierra Leone is the child, grown to independence, of the Church Missionary Society. The British Wesleyans have made their mission in Cape Colony a separate conference. Liberia's Negro Baptists, Methodists and Presbyterians have grown into independence. These five organizations of African Negro Christians represent thousands of communicants.

Division D: Reinforcement for Missions

Christian womanhood, American and European, Catholic and Protestant, exerts itself for Africa, the Antillean Negro and the freedman of the United States. Now that the Muslim or pagan populations of northern and tropical Africa open themselves to woman more and more, she will render yet greater service. The Kaiserswerth deaconess, the Protestant woman-missionary and the Roman nun or sister have an enlarging part in the evangelization of Africans during the twentieth century.

Colonial Christianity in South Africa constitutes another reinforcement. The Anglican, Congregational, Presbyterian and Wesleyan clergy are no less alert to meet the need of the colored natives than of other men. So are some ministers of the Dutch church in Cape Colony, notably Andrew Murray, and a few individual

Boers of Orange State and Transvaal. The religious [?] population of *Cape Colony* now numbers over seven hundred thousand, and supports at least sixteen local agencies for missions among African heathen. The Reformed church reports forty native helpers and about four thousand native communicants among its two hundred and six thousand, seven hundred and seventy-seven members. The Episcopal communion claims eighty thousand communicants in *British South Africa,* the Wesleyan church one hundred and eleven thousand members. What might not Cape Colony do for Christian missions between the years 1,900 and 2,000?

Native agency furnishes another occasion for hopefulness. The native missionary societies of Negro Anglicans in Sierra Leone and Lagos, of the Malagasy Congregationalists and of the Egyptian Presbyterians have already afforded instances of Christian aggressiveness on the part of the Negro Protestant in Africa. If we would save tropical Africa, we must save the Negro of the Antilles, South America and the United States.

Tho testimony on the whole so far bears against the Negro as a missionary-- the fault is not in the race. Time and culture are removing the vices, the infirmities, the difficulties manifested by imperfectly cultured and unripe individuals.

New applications of old methods form a fourth ground for hope. Evangelization must remain the chief agency for inspiring the African with life. Did not Mackay of U-Ganda, the most all-around, the most finely equipped personality that has yet devoted himself to Africa, write: "Whatever U-Ganda needs, there is at least 'one thing needful'; and any thing we do, if it does not aim at imparting a knowledge of that, and bear right down on it too, will be of comparatively little value"? This, be it remembered, is the testimony of an ideal industrial missionary, who, however, was also much more than a mere industrial missionary[*]

* Mr. Stanley regards Mackay as "the best missionary since Livingstone."

. Yet the evangelist must continue to be more and more aided, as he has ever been assisted, by the artisan. Industrial and medical missions will fill larger spheres, but industrial institutions will have to guard against secularism swamping spirituality. Societies that, in order to raise revenue for missions, engage in agriculture and commerce, need to guard against the same liability of injury to religious interests from mundane matters.

The self-sustaining missionary, when compelled to resort to farming or trade or hunting or other worldly means of keeping alive, is prevented from fulfilling the real duties of a Christian worker for the Muhammadan or pagan. Apart from the climatic and hygienic difficulties, the fact that such missionaries are regarded as mere self-seekers renders it unlikely that self-support as a method of mission-work will supersede the mission with a salaried staff of men and women sustained by a strong society.

As yet it seems hardly feasible to attempt to gauge the sphere and to forecast the future of medical missions proper in Africa. Until we obtain data bearing on the entire continent and on all the adjacent islands, it would be wiser to suspend judgment as to the place of medical missions in African evangelization as a whole.

Conclusion: How Evangelize Africa?

Americans and Europeans may learn from the African. Muhammadan missions afford suggestive hints. The Negro genius can enrich us. White men must set aside all supercilious sense of superiority.

Protestants, if they wish to enjoy the fullest return from woman's work, will gain more from unmarried women organized than from unmarried women unorganized.

Rome, if she is to make lasting impression on the tropical African, must adopt the course urged by her representatives in African missions. She must employ Protestant methods.

Christian missions, as Krapf indicated, must set up series upon series of supporting stations along each of the main axes of Africa; and then, as Mackay urged, must universally utilize the principles and procedure of the normal school, planting this at scores on scores of strategic centers. America and Arabia, as well as Africa itself, should be made recruiting fields for Christianity to secure colored missionaries who shall do for the Arab and Berber and Malagasy and Negro what none but a native can do.

Christendom needs purifying at the hand of Christianity. Europe and her African colonist, especially (according to Mackay the Scotch Presbyterian) the British inhabitants of Cape Colony, would do well to end their liquor traffic and trade in lethal weapons with the native, the holding of serfs by Christians and the red-handed treatment of aborigines. The United States must do justice to the Negro, or else meet a wrath of God the just that shall be a worse wo than that of 1861-65. When Christians prove strong enough in America and Europe to remove these stones of offence from the paths of African missionaries, Christian missions among African peoples can forge forward with a hundredfold greater speed and sureness.

The conversion, consecration, crucifixion and surrender of Christian wealth to service would work miracles in the evangelization of Africa and her children.

The Negro Christian, especially the Negro Baptist and Methodist, needs to wake to his peculiar duty and privilege in regard to Africa and the Negro. If merely the black Baptists and Methodists of the United States, now numbering, say, three millions, would concentrate on missions among Africans and would make a business of training Negro missionaries, this single agency could, humanly speaking, win tropical Africa for our Lord and Master within a century.

The crowning ground for hopefulness as to the outlook for African missions in the twentieth century is that Christian missions are God's work. The existence of so many native Christians in Africa, of such vast numbers of Negro Christians in the Americas, proves His presence and leadership. It looks now as if the African missions of Protestant churches could enter the twentieth century with twenty-five hundred American and European missionaries on the dark, long-lost continent and its isles; fifteen thousand native mission-workers; and among the communicants a Gideon's band of twenty-five thousand men and women chosen and consecrate. How many more Rome will throw into the conflict for a continent cannot be stated, but her ideas for the conquest of Africa are sublime. The day when Africa shall yield dominion to Him who is King of kings and Lord of lords may not be imagined, but if we do our part, generation after generation, or, if need be, through centuries on centuries, we may leave results to God.

> Say not: "The struggle nought availeth,
> The labor and the wounds are vain,

The enemy faints not nor faileth,
And as things have been, they remain."

If hopes were dupes, fears may be liars;
It may be, in yon smoke concealed,
Your comrades chase e'en now the fliers,
And but for you possess the field.

For while the tired waves, vainly breaking,
Seem here no painful inch to gain,
Far back, thro creek and inlet making,
Comes silent, flooding in, the main.

And not by eastern windows only,
When daylight comes, comes in the light;
In front the sun climbs slow, how slowly,
But west ward -- look! the land is bright.

    532 Washington Boulevard, Chicago, Illinois, U. S. A. November, 1895 and January, 1896

JOHN H. SMYTH, LL.D.
Editor of *The Reformer,* Richmond, Va. for Nine Years
Minister to Liberia

The African in Africa and the African in America

BY
THE HON. J. H. SMYTH, LL.D.
EX-MINISTER TO LIBERIA

The fact will be readily admitted by those most familiar with the sentiment of a large and not unimportant portion of our American citizenship, who, by the fortunes and misfortunes of war, viewed from the standpoint of one or the other combatants of the sanguinary struggle of 1861-62-63-64, were made equal before the law with all other citizens, that as a class they are averse to the discussion of Africa, when their relationship with that ancient and mysterious land and its races is made the subject of discourse or reflection. The remoteness of Africa from America may be a reason for such feeling; the current opinion in the minds of the Caucasians, whence the American Negroes' opinions are derived, that the African is by nature an inferior man, may be a reason. The illiteracy, poverty, and degradation of the Negro, pure and simple, as known in Christian lands, may be a reason in connection with the partially true and partially false impression that the Negroes, or Africans, are pagan and heathen as a whole, and as a sequence hopelessly degraded beings. These may be some of the reasons that make the subject of Africa discordant and unmusical to our ears. It is amid such embarrassments that the lecturer, the orator, the missionary must present Africa to the Negro in Christian America.

In view of recent newspaper articles about migration of Negroes to Liberia, so much has been recently said by men of African descent of prominence, and by men of like prominence of uncertain descent, and by men of other races than the Negro, of Liberia and Africa generally, that I deem it a duty as an American citizen and a Negro, in vindication of the men and women of like descent with myself, citizens of the United States, to state some facts explanatory of and in rebuttal of much that has been said, ignorantly, unwisely and unsympathetically, to the detriment of the effort being made at self-government in Liberia, West Africa. The people who constitute the inhabitants and citizenship of Liberia (the largest portion of the latter class are American Negroes from the Southern part of the United States) are possessed of and imbued with the sentiment and the civilization peculiar to this section of our country. That these immigrant Negroes who migrated to West Africa, or began migration as far back as 1820, and who continue to go thither, have a better field there, with less embarrassing environment, to prove their capacity for self-government, for leadership in Statecraft than their brethren in the northern, western and southern portions of the United States, will scarcely be seriously denied or questioned. This conceded, it seems to me that wisdom, self-respect, race loyalty, and American patriotism would show themselves richer to withhold judgment as to the success of the experiment being made in Africa for self-government until such time as this immigrant people and their descendants have lived in Liberia, Sierra Leone, the Gold Coast, the Camaroons and other parts of West Africa long enough to assimilate the sentiment of liberty and rule, the general heritage and possession of the native African, than it has shown itself in echoing the expression of opinion of white men, whatever their learning or literary capacity, who estimate the progress of the Negro by the standard of their own race with its superior opportunities, advantages and facilities.

Until we have demonstrated ability for organization, for government, and have shown effective cohesiveness and leadership here in the United States, it may be a little immodest to hastily and unadvisedly make up the record adverse to our immediate kith and kin, who less than sixty years ago made the first step on lines of independent form of government of themselves, and have successfully maintained themselves against the greed of Spain, the aggrandizement of France, and the envy and cupidity of the merchant class of England without active assistance or defense of our formidable North African squadron; without an army and without more than one gunboat, the property of the Republic.

Liberia is the only democratic republican form of government on the continent of Africa of which we have any knowledge. The civilization of the people constituting the majority of the citizenship of Liberia is American. It embraces that phase of our American system which has made the autonomy of the south distinct from that of all other parts of our common country. This is the resultant of the outgrowth of the laws and customs of the severalty as well as the jointness of that system of government which exists in the South. In so far as the civilization of the United States on analysis is differentiated as northern, southern, eastern, and western, and in the south as Virginian, Carolinian, Georgian, it may be said, that the people composing the nation have transferred such American phases of government to this part of Africa.

The pioneers of this colony, the descendants of them, and the immigrants that have gone from here at varying periods of time within sixty years, like those of us who have remained, have been the unhappy victims of the influences of an alien, racial oppression; are fragments of races and tribes, and lack much in capacity for maintaining a stable form of government without the aid which comes from the moral support of the United States. But notwithstanding the embarrassments and difficulties of this youthful nation, the elements of success are being gradually, surely and deeply laid in industrial and agricultural concerns. The masses of the people are directing their effort to agriculture, the development of the soil, and are leaving the matter of coast-commerce or barter to the few.

No epitome or summary of Liberia would be worthy of the name which failed to take note of the renaissance of education under the scholarly Blyden and Freeman, both of whom have been presidents of Liberia College. When the former scholar came to the presidency of the college, then was commenced the work of the adaptation of the training of the youth for the definitive and distinct purpose of advancing the nation on the line of race. This institution has sent forth strong Negro men, who are unperverted in their instincts, strong in their race loyalty, and unhampered by a civilization upon which the individuality of the race is not stamped. Such a civilization, unmodified, is unsuited to the African in Africa, or out of Africa and although it may develop him religiously, in manly, self-reliant feeling, it will make him a weakling and will be destructive of true manhood, self-respect and race integrity. In illustration of the method of training the mind of the Negro youth of Liberia, the following from the inaugural of the late president of the college, Dr. Edward Wilmot Blyden, on assuming the presidency, will make clear Liberian higher training. After alluding to the leading epochs in the history of civilization, the theocratic, the Greek age, the medieval age, the modern age and its subdivisions, the age since the French Revolution, the distinguished president said of the curriculum of the college: "We shall permit in our curriculum the unrestricted study of the first four epochs, but especially the second, third, and fourth epochs, from which the present civilization of Western Europe is mainly derived. There has been no period of history more full of suggestive energy, both physical and intellectual, than these epochs. Modern Europe boasts of its period of intellectual activity, but none can equal, for life and freshness, the Greek and Roman prime. No modern writers will ever influence the destiny of the race to the same extent that the Greeks and the Romans have done. We can afford then to exclude them as subjects of study, at least in the earlier college years, the events of the fifth and sixth epochs, and the works which in large numbers have been written during these epochs. I know that during these periods some of the greatest works of human genius have been composed. I know that Shakespeare and Milton, Gibbon and Macaulay, Hallam and Lecky, Froude, Stubbs, and Green, belong to these periods. It is not in my power, even if I had the will, to disparage the works of these masters; but what I wish to say is, that these are not works on which the mind of the youthful African should be trained.

"It was during the sixth period that the transatlantic slave trade arose, and these theories--theological, social, and political--were invented for the degradation and proscription of the Negro. This epoch continues to this day, and has an abundant literature and a prolific authorship. It has produced that whole tribe of declamatory Negrophobists, whose views, in spite of their emptiness and impertinence, are having their effect upon the ephemeral literature of the day, a literature which is shaping the life of the Negro in Christian lands. His whole theory of life, quite contrary to what his nature intends, is being influenced, consciously and unconsciously, by the general conceptions of his race entertained by the manufacturers of this literature, a great portion of which, made for to-day, will not survive the next generation.

I admit that in this period there have been able defenses of the race written, but they have all been in the patronizing or apologetic tone, in spirit of that good-natured man who assured the world that

'Fleecy locks and dark complexion
Cannot forfeit nature's claim.'

"Poor Phillis Wheatly, a native of Africa, educated in America, in her attempts at poetry, is made to say, in what her biographer calls 'spirited lines,' 'Remember, Christian Negroes, black as Cain, may be refined, and join the angelic train.' The arguments of Wilberforce, the eloquence of Wendell Phillips, the pathos of Uncle Tom's Cabin, are all in the same strain, that Negroes have souls to save as white men have, and that the strength of nature's claim is not impaired by their complexion and hair.

"We surely cannot indulge with the same feelings of exultation that the Englishman or American experiences in the proud boast that we speak the language that Shakespeare spoke. The faith and morals which Milton held, for that "language" in some of its finest utterances patronizes and apologizes for us, and that "faith" has been hitherto powerless to save us from proscription and insult. It is true that culture is one, and the effects of true culture are the same;

but the native capacities of mankind differ, and their work and destiny differ, so that the road by which one man may attain to the highest efficiency is not that which would conduce to the success of another. The special road that has led to the success and elevation of the Anglo-Saxon is not that which would lead to the success and elevation of the Negro, though we shall resort to the same means of general culture which enabled the Anglo-Saxon to find out for himself the way in which he ought to go."

But to return. It was not the privilege of ancient foreign civilization to know Africa except superficially, and with equal truth it may be asserted that the world of foreign races to Africa is ignorant of Africa now, and always has been as to her races, although millions of her sons and daughters, and their million descendants, have been placed in most intimate and unfortunate relation with many great and remarkable alien races.

This absence of knowledge concerning a continent so related as Africa has been to the past and present of European and American nations, may be accounted for in the selfishness of man's nature, the disposition to concern one's self, to the exclusion and the neglect of others, with racial characteristics which create an interest in those of a race for that race alone, which produces pride of race, a possession of every race, unless destroyed by oppression, which produces indifference to other races than one's own, save in so far as others may be made to conserve the interest of one's own race.

The continent of Africa is to-day the most interesting of the eastern hemisphere to the scientist, the political economist, the philanthropist and the religious propagandist, and the plunderers of weak and defenseless humanity. It will not be possible for me to speak of the races of the whole continent. My purpose is to speak of Africa in America and Africa in Africa, confining myself to a portion of the races of West and Central Africa, for the purpose of arousing an active spirit of inquiry as to a continent and a people, to which we are bound by the blood that courses our veins and by whatever of self-respect we possess.

We are taught by holy writ that God set bounds to the habitations of men. One race he established upon the continent of Africa, another upon the continent of Asia, another upon the continent of Europe, and a heterogeneity of races upon the continent of America, and fragmentary peoples inhabit the isles of the sea. In this various apportionment of races, wisdom and beneficence are shown. If we fail to see the former, we cannot doubt the latter, since "He does all things well."

In the light of these facts I fail to see a providence in bringing the Negro here, in making of him, at best, a moral and mental imitation of an original such as he can never be. Every step made by the Negro and his progeny, brought here a man and trained a slave, has continued him slave, though the institution as such has perished. The inherited taint of the institution has removed him further and further from the land of his fathers, from his tribal and racial traditions (valued heritages of a people), and has tended to make latent in him, if it has not wholly destroyed his best racial peculiarities and characteristics. In making us Anglo-Saxons by environment, we have lost not only in soul, but exteriorly, as objectified in the various types among us, nomenclature colored people. However distasteful to the Caucasian the statement of the fact may be, the Negro who has grown to manhood under their alien Christian civilization, alien to the Negro and [in many respects] to Christ, is in his virtues and vices more Caucasian than African.

These considerations are serious to the Negro who feels any pride in being connected with races which aggregate, as known, more than 200,000,000 souls, who have an inalienable right to a continent as rich in its flora and fauna and mineral deposits (to say the least) as any other the sun warms with its heat and upon which the rains descend to make fruitful. Serious, indeed, must these considerations be to the Negro of the Americas and the Antilles, the descendants of those races whose moral elevation and mental ripeness in the morning of time manifested themselves in the conception and execution of those wonders of the ages, the pyramids, the sphinxes, and that musical colossus, Black Memnon, so fashioned that for two hundred years, on the rising of the god of day, as its rays shone upon it, it became musical with the concord of sweet sounds. Serious must these considerations be to the descendants of those races who erected these most beautiful temples and obelisks which have existed for centuries, the superscriptions within and upon which are yet to be interpreted by the descendants of Negro architects and builders; the ruins of which, in their moral sublimity, stand as sentinels of time all along the delta and banks of the Nile, and are seen at Alexandria, Philæ, Elephantiné, Thebes and Karnac, representing their builders feeling after God in their desire for immortality.

These works of art and utility survive, in ruins, the perished civilizations of Asia, the cradle of the human race, and will survive the civilizations of Europe and this last, vigorous, Herculean civilization of America, which is but an evolution of Europe. These ruins have been the surprise and admiration of all other civilizations. These ruins have seen other civilizations in their dawn, their noontide, and will, notwithstanding the vandalism of the Caucasian, continue beyond his day. Those perished peoples of Africa furnished Europe with letters, sciences, and arts, although we, their lineal heirs, by the selfishness, greed, and ingratitude of the Caucasian, have been denied, until within the century, the title of human beings, and within three decades have-only been regarded as equals before the law in a land of liberty and law. Two hundred and fifty years have removed us to a far greater distance from Africa than the geographical measurement that separates America from Africa, and to-day that continent is perhaps of less interest to the educated and refined Negro of America than to his thrifty, industrious, and adventurous white fellow-citizen.

There is error in a system of religion, a mistake in a system of education that so alienates brother from brother and sister from sister. Especially is this so when they trace their lineage from the same race stock.

It is lamentable that two hundred and fifty years have removed us to a far greater distance from Africa than the geographical measurement which separates America from Africa, and to-day that continent is perhaps of less interest to the educated and refined Negro of America than to his thrifty, industrious, and adventurous white fellow-citizen.

Says an eminent English divine: "Neither Greek nor Roman culture had power to spread beyond themselves, and we have the testimony of the Emperor Julian to this. He considered the barbarous western nations incapable of culture. The fact was that Rome did not try to civilize in the right way. Instead of drawing forth the native energies of these nations, while it left them free to develop their own national peculiarities in their own way, it imposed on them from without the Roman education. It tried to turn them into Romans. Where this effort was unsuccessful, the men remained barbarous; where it was successful, the nation lost its distinctive elements in the Roman elements, at least until after some centuries the overwhelming influence of Rome had perished. Meantime they were not Britons nor Gauls, but spurious Romans. The natural growth of the people was arrested. Men living out of their native element became stunted and spiritless."

The peculiar character of a nation is not lost in Christianity, but, so far as it is good, develops and intensifies itself. People should be allowed to grow naturally into their distinctive type and place in the world.

The wrong done us here in America, the wrong done us in Turkey in Asia, and Turkey in Europe, and Constantinople, is being recognized at the center of Anglo-Saxon civilization, as is honestly indicated by utterances such as these: "It is too late to ask, 'Are we our brother's keeper?' Three centuries ago the plea might have seemed specious, but since then Europe has made itself guilty towards Africa of the blackest series of crimes that stain the foul record of civilized history. The actual appalling state of things in Africa is the result of the policy of Europe towards the African races. European contact has brought in its train not merely the sacrifice, amid unspeakable horrors, of the lives and liberties of twenty million Negroes for the American market alone, but political disintegration, social anarchy, moral and physical debasement, the decay of the simple arts and industries which had been developed during centuries of undisturbed and uneventful existence. Christian Europe, it is true, no longer openly tolerates the slave trade, but Christian Europe furnishes the arms by means of which the slave trade is carried on. The European explorer paves the way for the Arab man-hunter; in his track follow not the blessings of civilization, but conflagration, rapine, and murder, and European trade, while extinguishing native handicrafts, places within the African's grasp the power of self-destruction by spirits and of mutual destruction by firearms.

"We are now consciously confronted by all these evils and responsibilities. They have been slowly forced upon our recognition as one traveler after another opened a chink into the darkness of the heart of Africa. That a debt of reparation is due from the white man to the black can no longer be denied. It *must* be paid somehow; it *may* be paid for weal and not for woe. A duty left undone is a Nemesis, pursuing to destruction; a duty to be done is simply a problem to be solved. Which shall it be for us? The public voice has already spoken. The blunder and the crime of the abandonment of Khartum will not be repeated. Henceforth, at least ostensibly, the salvation of Africa is the policy of Europe.

"There remains, then, only the question as to the best means of carrying it into execution. And here, too, ignorance is giving place to better knowledge. Our conduct is, as it were, shaping itself, and for once commercial and national advantages are found combined with the highest interest of humanity."

I am aware that it will be insisted by some who have failed to give this matter the consideration which it merits, that we are a part of the greatest composite nationality, and therefore, any influence that would make the Negro less American and more African than he is, would be injurious to the best interest of our American nation. I would gladly impress upon persons entertaining such thoughts, that race allegiance is compatible with patriotism, with love of the land that gave us birth. This has been abundantly shown to be true with reference to the Jews. Whatever doubts may be entertained upon this point on account of their wide religious divergence from other religionists, must undergo a change in the presence of the admonition given in a missive sent to Israel by the prophet Jeremiah, and which has been faithfully conformed to by Israel and the descendants of Israel: "Serve the King of Babylon, and live. Build ye houses and dwell in them; and plant gardens and eat the fruits of them. And seek the welfare of the city whither I have caused you to be carried away captives, and pray unto the Lord for it; for in the peace thereof shall ye have peace."

Though we are a part of this great national whole, we are a distinct and separate part, an alien part racially, and destined to be so by the immutable law of race pride, which is possessed by our white fellow-citizens, if not by us. The sentiment, the something stronger than sentiment which makes an English American proud of his connection with Britain, a French American proud of his connection with La Belle France, and a German American fondly attached to the memories of the fatherland, and all European races of their Aryan descent, has something that partakes of the moral sublime. Truly "language and religion do not make a race."

The characteristics, peculiarities, idiosyncrasies and habits have been determined by what has been displayed and noted of Negroes under influences foreign to them and beyond their control. This has been the cause of inaccurate knowledge of the races of Africa on the part of the whites, and inaccurate knowledge on the part of the Negroes themselves.

The elements of character of American whites are to be learned in the light of their free, unhampered ancestry and brethren in Europe.

* Partitioning of Africa between European Nations and Races.--Edinburg Review, Oct., 1889.

The civilized Negro here has but recently emerged from slavery and been recognized a freeman; and though guaranteed in the possession of political rights, is still hampered by his inability to understand himself, by the conviction that on account of the political unity of the races here, his end must be reached by pursuit of the same line followed by the controlling races.

The condition of the race past and present here makes the American Negro African, without the peculiarities of his race; an African only as to the hue of his skin and his blood. The black man here is Americanized, and as a sequence, sectionalized.

Now the difference between Africa in America, and Africa in Africa being recognized, let us look to Africa in Africa. The races of Africa have not been a subject of Caucasian study.

The Egyptian, Carthaginian, and Moorish people are imperfectly known, and the interior, eastern, western races, are still more imperfectly understood, and for very prudential reasons,--the uncompromising conditions of climate toward European peoples, and the almost insuperable difficulties of ingress to the country. Says Amelia B. Edwards, in her cleverly written book, "A Thousand Miles up the Nile," of African races: "As with these fragments of the old tongue, so with the races, subdued again and again by invading hordes; intermixed for centuries together with Phoenician, Persian, Greek, Roman, and Arab blood, it fuses these heterogeneous elements in one common mould, reverts persistently to the early type, and remains African to the last. So strange is the tyranny of natural forces. The sun and soil of Africa demand one special breed of men, and will tolerate no other. Foreign residents cannot rear children in the country. In the Isthmus of Suez, which is considered the healthiest part of Egypt, an alien population of twenty thousand persons failed in the course of ten years to rear one infant born upon the soil. Children of an alien father and an Egyptian mother will die off in the same way in early infancy, unless brought up in simple native fashion. And it is affirmed of the descendants of mixed marriages, that after the third generation the foreign blood seems to be eliminated, while the traits of the race are restored in their original purity."

Another reason, race pride, so natural to all races, will always be a good and sufficient reason to deter the Saxon from recognizing excellences in a race foreign and alien to his race. Now, if we would know the Negro in his African home, we are to seek that knowledge of his true character through him.

The testimony of Africans, distinguished for their knowledge of their countrymen, for their learning and character, should be looked to, and consulted as authorities in these matters. The Arku and Ebo races are not to be known through the flippant and inconsiderate statements of some ignorant European who finds to his surprise and annoyance that he cannot successfully take advantage of them in a business transaction, and as a consequence declares the former people a deceptive, ignorant class, and the latter an insolent, lazy set. You are to read the history of these races in the light of what the learned Dr. Africanus Horton has written in his "Africa and the Africans," and what his lordship Bishop Crowther experienced in his successful labor of love among his own and other races.

A comprehensive knowledge of the Christian, Mohammedan, and heathen Africans of Central and West Africa must be read in the light of the full and exhaustive information to be found in the writings of Edward W. Blyden, D.D., LL.D., late president of Liberia's college. Christianity in the third and fourth centuries among the Africans must be studied, in the Africans' fathers, and in Lloyd's North African Church and in Abyssinian traditions.

The missionary work in West Africa in the fifteenth century may be read in the voluminous Spanish and Portuguese and Italian state papers and travels. A few most valuable ones as to the Congo races are to be found in an English translation made during the reigns of Henry VIII. and Elizabeth. Bishops Crowther and Colenso may be read on African character with profit. There are two classics, African, which should be read: A. H. L. Heeren, African Researches, and a portion of Herodotus.

For quite fair treatment of African character, French and German explorations are interesting, and in English, Mungo Park, Livingstone, and Gordon Pasha.

Having directed attention to the means and some of the sources to be relied on for facts concerning native African character, I now point to some illustrations of error and wrong in dealing with the African in Africa.

It is not to our century alone that we are to look for active but mistaken effort to christianize Africa. There has existed no African mission, which, in the same period of time, attained to such proportions as the Portuguese mission in the Congo region during the fifteenth century. A cathedral and churches adorned, beautified, and glorified that portion of West Africa, and a Congo gentleman, after pursuing the necessary course of study in Spain prescribed for the priesthood, was made a bishop, and returned to his country to carry on the work of christianizing his people through the religion of Catholic Rome. All this work passed away. The ships which brought priests as outward passengers took the human product of the race back as homeward cargo. The theory and practice of the European being in opposition, the one to the other, the work perished. The fetich of the cross in the hands of the Portuguese, did not deter them from knavery and theft and murder, and the Congoes concluded that their fetiches were less harmful than the alien Portuguese.

Africans cannot be influenced by aliens, who, however Christian, seek to subvert their manhood. With the African at home, service to God and service to his fetich will not be yielded if manhood be the sacrifice.

He may be forced to accept a dogma or a religion, but will not receive either under such circumstances. Alien races can aid the progress of Christianity and civilization among Africans, but cannot control it with hope of ultimate success in Africa. Mr. Venn would have probably ranked, as the chief work of his official life, his careful and prolonged labors for the organization of native churches. All his measures converged to this point, the formation wherever the Gospel was proclaimed, of a native church, which should gradually be enfranchised from all supervision by a foreign body, and should become, in his phraseology, "self-supporting, self-governing, self-extending." He carefully discriminated between missionary: work carried on by foreigners and Christianity acclimated and so become indigenous in a national church. The one was the means, the other the end; the one the scaffolding, the other the building it leaves behind when the scaffolding is removed; the one subject to constant changes and modifications, as fresh circumstances develop themselves, the other growing up to the measure of the stature of the perfect man, only changing by gradually putting away childish things and reliance on external help and control.

In the British colony of Sierra Leone opportunity is afforded to study native character, as at no other place with which I am acquainted. The representatives of not less than a hundred tribes may be seen here and of not a few races. Here one may see the stately and grave Mandingo, the diplomatic Soosoo, the frail but handsome Foulah, and the paragon of men, the magnificent Jollof, "his complexion free from any taint of Abyssinian blue or Nubian bronze, intensely, lustrously, magnificently black."

Of the foregoing races there has been no acceptance of anything of foreign civilization. These races represent a very high and unique type of Mohammedanism and Arabic training. They have adopted the religion of the Prophet and made it to conform to themselves. They have written their own

111

commentaries on the sacred book. They are not controlled by the Arab, the Persian, or the Turk as to their conception of the Koran. Their women share in common with the men in the instructions of the masters. But there are two distinct races here, and some of each of them in Liberia, the Ebo and Arku races, among whom is displayed the highest type of English civilization, with their free, unhampered peculiarities and idiosyncrasies. These two races control and direct commercial interest in Sierra Leone, on the Gold coast and at Lagos, and have brought peace to war and order from confusion in the independent Negro nations of Abbeokuta.

Among these races, in religion are the Crowthers; in medical and surgical science, the Davises and Hortons; in jurisprudence, the Lewises and McCarthys; in pure scholarship, the Blydens, Coles, and Quakers; in the mercantile profession, the Boyles, Williams, Grants, and Sawyers. The time was when these two races were opposed to each other, but happily much of the tribal hatred has been destroyed by contact and education. These people are distinct in their bent of character. The Arku race is marked by a suavity of manner, a disposition to please, which borders on obsequiousness, and are industrious. They live upon a very little that they may save very much. They are never found to be improvident. The women make most affectionate wives, and have no peers in the world in their disposition to prove themselves helpmeets. It is said that the refusal by a husband to allow an Arku wife to help him, not infrequently causes marital difficulties. She prefers to trade than to remain indoors attending to her domestic affairs and babies. In complexion this race represents the average dark complexion of the American Negro.

The Ebo is a proud, daring race. They are always industrious, are found of display, and in their hospitality are ostentatious. It may be asserted that there exists no evidence to show these people ever to have been pagan, in their home on the Niger or elsewhere. As a race they have never received either Christianity or Mohammedanism, but claim to believe sincerely in God. Those in the British colony have assimilated Christianity and some have attained to the highest culture and refinement. The first Negro graduate of Oxford was an Ebo. The most distinguished physician--Negro physician--living up to 1884 was Dr. Horton, an Ebo. The knowledge of reading and writing and ciphering, in short, rudimentary training in this colony, has been very thorough. To Wilberforce and Venn be lasting honor and praise for their effective work in the British colonies of West Africa.

The entire coasts of this continent are surrounded by and permeated with a deadly malaria which makes Africa feared. In the future there will be cause for, and there will be much rejoicing that an Almighty wisdom has made the coasts generally alluvial, and has given a few broad and possibly navigable high ways to the interior, the banks of which are charnel houses to aliens.

The aboriginal tribes and races subject to Liberia, excepting the American Liberians, are estimated at three-fourths of a million souls. The principal races here are Mandingos, Kru and Graybo and Bassa people, cognate races; Veys, Golas and Pesseys. My contact has been with these races in the civilized settlements, and in their own towns and villages. It would be a task to describe them with the accuracy their tribal and racial differences merit.

The Mandingos are a Mohammedan, proselytizing race, strictly sober, industrious, intellectual and sincere, serious men. Their women are handsome and models of chastity. The English explorer, Winwood Reed, in his Savage Africa pays them this compliment reluctantly. Marriages rarely occur between women of this race and Christians or pagans. The Kru race, evidently a central African people, occupy that portion of country lying between Grand Bassa and Cape Palmas, and are to be seen on every ship from Sierra. Leone to Congo river. To West African commerce he is an indispensable factor, since European sailors cannot work the cargo of a ship south of nor in the port of Freetown. This race is divided into two classes, mariners and agriculturists, the latter being typical landsmen in ignorance of the sea. The sailor class, like their class among the Caucasians, are simple-hearted, improvident, and are devotedly attached to their families. Wherever found, these men may be recognized, the identification being an India ink mark extending from the root of the nose to the hair, and an arrow-shaped mark from the ear tending toward the center of the cheek. They have much cunning in their nature, are not wanting in courage, are marked for endurance and industry as laborers, but so far as training in books has been carried on among them, they have shown themselves possessed of ordinary intellectual ability.

To the Kru race the two Americas are chiefly indebted for the catching and embarking of Africans upon slave ships. It is currently reported and generally believed these people have never themselves been enslaved. The Spaniards, Portuguese, English, and American pirates, in the interest of the nefarious slave traffic, gave them immunity from capture and slavery for the invaluable service they rendered their bad cause. Strange as it may seem, they are said never to have

113

held slaves, nor do they to-day hold slaves, and will not keep one as a slave in their household. A slave may be adopted in a Kru family, may intermarry with the race as a freeman, but not as a slave. Physically, they are a very superior race of men and women. The Greyboes resemble in appearance the Krues, with the exception of a lighter complexion, being a dark reddish brown, and are dissimilar in being more intellectual than the Krues. They have the scriptures, and other books of their history and traditions, written in Roman characters in their own tongue. The guttural sound of the Dutch language is peculiar to both the Kru and Greybo languages. Intellectually, the Greyboes are a very remarkable people. The most eminent surgeon Liberia ever had was of this race; so also the first Hebrew scholar. They are a warrior race, powerful in stature, very brave, and marked for their courage, as the Americo-Liberian's experience attests. They have their own representatives in the Legislature. The Bassas are inferior to the Greyboes, and in some respects not the equals of the Krues. Notwithstanding this fact, they have produced soldiers of no mean order, and assimilate the Christian civilization about them as readily as the Americo-Liberian acquires their language.

In this matter I am reminded of the very great importance of the native languages as a valuable auxiliary in the spread and extension of civilization among African races. To use the terse language of his lordship, Bishop Crowther, "men think accurately in their own tongue."

The Golas as a race are courageous and intrepid, and kindly in their relation with the Americo-Liberian, preferring peace with them to war. The Pesseys, once a martial race, have by internal dissension and wars with other races, to an alarming extent lost their independence and many of that once noble race have been made captives to other peoples and slaves. As slaves they are highly valued, being indefatigable laborers, and therefore admired bondsmen by their masters. Their language has the softness and liquid sweetness of Italian, being in striking contrast to the harshness of the Kru and Greybo tongue.

Now I approach the consideration briefly of a people little known to the explorer of Central or Western Africa, though unquestionably a Central African people, but destined to be, should they prove as numerous as supposed, one of the first races of the continent, the Veys. Complexionally, this race is black and brown, the women of which are distinguished for facial beauty, and the symmetry of physical proportion, while the men are not wanting in elegance and strength of physique. They have grace in carriage, and in language there is a sweetness and harmony in utterance that reminds one of what music is. They have wonderful address, great tact, and the women possess the airs, graces and fineness which are attributed to the women of France.

The Veys do not display industry in manual labor to the extent of other races. They prefer those callings and employments which require the smallest amount of physical exertion. Notwithstanding this fact, there are blacksmiths, cloth weavers and skillful workmen in silver and gold, but the majority of them are mercantile in their tastes and pursuits, and are, therefore, traders.

This race is highly intellectual. As a semi-civilized people they claim the first importance among the West African and Negritian races. The acquired philological capability of the Veys is not traceable to any ulterior influences, but is from within. Domestic slavery exists among them, and their laws are not unlike those of ancient Rome and old Saxon enactments and customs. The children follow the condition of the mother. If the mother be a bond-woman, the issue is a slave. Marriage between slaves and free persons are prohibited, and where the prohibition is disregarded, the offender, the slave, is punished with death. Manumission is very rare among the slaves, and neither obedience or industry in peace nor heroism in war mitigates the condition of the slave. Once a slave, always a slave. The system in its operation is of a patriarchal character. A parallel; By reference to Stubb's Constitutional History of England, vol. I., page 44, we read of the ancient Saxons. Rudolph, the author of the Translation, Sancte Alexandri, writing about A. D. 1863, describes the Saxons of the early Frank Empire thus:--*--*--*--* "Of distinctions of race and nobility they are most tenaciously careful; they scarce ever (and here the writer quotes the Germania) allow themselves to be infected by any marriages with other or inferior races, and try to keep their nationality apart, sincere and unlike any other. Hence, the universal prevalence of one physical type. The race consists of four ranks of men, the noble, the free, the freedmen, and the servi. And it is by law established that no order shall, in contracting marriages, remove the landmarks of its own class; but noble must marry noble, freeman, freewoman; freedman, freedwoman; serf, handmaid. If any take a wife of different or higher rank than his own, he has to expiate the act with his life."

I should perhaps leave an impression which would be misleading as to Liberia and Africa unless I be more explicit. If you have observed, in any utterance of mine, anything about Africa which seems to possess in itself, or as to the races of that continent, a roseate hue, be pleased to remember that I have faintly, and with unartistic hand, shown you a part of this garden of the Lord and limned its inhabitants with the pencil and brush of an amateur; and I appeal to Mungo Park, the sainted Livingstone, Barth, Schweinfurth, Nachtigal, and I may risk Stanley in the rear of this galaxy of friends of Africa, for more accurate data and for larger and fuller experiences. But I may astound you when I say that Africa fears not the invasion of her shores by Europe and the rightful acquisition of her territory, and that no Negro who knows Africa regards the European's advent there as a menace to the progress and advancement of her races, except when they bring with them rum and firearms. I am pronouncedly, and have been since I first stepped upon the soil of my fatherland in 1878, an African colonizationist, but I am so in a strictly qualified sense, as is shown in the official statement made to my and your government--made from the United States Consulate-General, Monrovia, under the date of February 21, 1883.

It may not be inopportune or out of place to say, in the interest of the prospective immigrant and in the interest of Liberia, that it is perhaps unwise for persons to emigrate here simply for the purpose of being free and enjoying complete civil liberty and social equality. The State is young, and, though poor in developed resources, is vigorous in purpose and effort, and needy only of additional influences of civilization which are possessed by those who, at their homes, have displayed the ability of independent labor and proprietorship. That is to say, that the man needed as an immigrant here is one who, in his home, displays industry and fixedness of purpose sufficient to cause him to stick at work of some kind until he has earned and saved enough to purchase a comfortable home, is competent to control it and does control it, or a man who has entered upon a business and has self-denial enough to continue in it to the end of respectably supporting himself and family, or who has made himself a boss of some supporting trade--a man who is not directly dependent upon being a common servant, and who is not an ignorant laborer incapable of turning up something by his innate good sense and the God-given push within him.

Liberia possesses no large class of citizens who need or are able to employ a servant class from a foreign country. Intelligent laborers are needed, not ignorant ones. The constitution of this Republic guarantees to each immigrant so much cultivable land. The purpose of such grant is obvious; the improvement of it, the means of supporting one's self from the soil, is the consideration for the gift, thereby winning from the forest and jungle valued lands capable of indefinite production, and winning from ignorance the native races by the pursuit of the arts of peace. Such results can be obtained alone through intelligent, persistent industry.

All agricultural labor, all coast labor, loading and unloading vessels, and fishing, all house service, are carried on, in general, by aborigines. Farm labor is worth from $2.50 to $4.00 per month, exclusive of housing and feeding. This is paid principally in goods, or one-half goods and the other half money. Where this labor is well fed, and treated well, it is honest and reliable -- where these conditions are met there is no lack of it. The labor performed by the citizen class is farm proprietorship, trader, merchant, mechanic, professional, and governmental. There is a minority of farm laborers of the civilized Liberian class.

A clear understanding of the conditions of labor here is important to that class of foreign Negroes who contemplate settlement here. The possession of a few hundred dollars, skill in labor, and executive ability, constitute a capital that cannot but secure a most comfortable living here with a probability of wealth.

Unless the Negro out of Africa goes to Africa seeking a home because he has none; goes of his own volition, with as correct a knowledge of Africa as may be obtained from the writings of trustworthy African travelers and explorers and missionaries, reinforced by race loyalty, and with greater confidence in himself and his race than in any alien self and alien race; goes from a sense of duty imposed by his Christian enlightenment, and not unprovided with ability and previous experience to organize and control labor, with as ample means as he would go with from the Atlantic coast of the United States to the Pacific slope for the purpose of engaging in business, he is wholly and entirely unsuited for Africa, and would impede by his presence not only the progress of Liberia (if he went thither), but any part of Africa by his unprofitable presence, and ought to be denied the right to expatriate himself.

If by anything that I have said you have been impressed with the fact that you are descendants of African races and as a consequence that you are a separate and distinct people from Caucasian races, and that the highest excellence to which an individual can attain must be to work according to the bent of his genius, and the other to work in harmony with God's design in his creation, on his race line; if I have impressed you at all with the wisdom or propriety of confiding in the highest Negro authorities and the best alien writings, for reliable data respecting our race in the fatherland, and thereby awakened in you an interest and sincere desire for the well being of Africa and her races, for our people, and for accurate information concerning that most ancient, and most mysterious of lands; then I feel conscious of having made a contribution of information not wholly valueless to my countrymen that may tend to modify and dissipate general ignorance of us and of our antecedents and their country; and I have done something toward awakening your dormant self-respect, and given you some conception of the dignity which attaches to Negro manhood, and created in you a preference for your race before all other races; and this sentiment, if produced, will place you *en rapport* with the Negroes in Africa, who have no conception of any land greater, more beautiful than their own; any men braver and manlier than themselves, any women better, lovlier, and handsomer than African women. Then you will retire from this place with a feeling of stimulus rather than of satiety, of unrest rather than of repose; then shall I retire from my effort to interest you in Africa in Africa, and Africa in America with satisfied pride in having performed something of duty as a Negro-- clear in his conviction of the high destiny in reserve for Africa and its races, and of your duty to be loyal to the race, since true allegiance will make us sharers in that glory which the sacred writing declares shall come, when Ethiopa shall stretch forth her hand unto God.

The Policy of the American Colonization Society

BY
THOMAS G. ADDISON, D.D.
DELEGATE OF THE AMERICAN COLONIZATION SOCIETY

The Rev. Thomas G. Addison, D.D., attended the Congress as a representative of the American Colonization Society, and, although not on the program for a paper, made a short address in which he said in substance that the society which he represented was frequently misunderstood and misrepresented as desiring to get all the Negroes out of this country. Nothing could be farther from the truth. For the welfare of the little Republic of Liberia, which it founded, the Society desired to see only a limited number of emigrants going there from this country at present, and these should be of the very best class in character, general intelligence, industry and thrift. There were more than a hundred thousand applications from Negroes in the United States for assistance in emigrating to Liberia now on file in the office of the Society, and new applications were received daily.

The Society had adopted the following outline of its policy:

1. "Colonists aided hereafter to be selected with special reference to the needs of Liberia, and to be located with more care and to better advantage to themselves.

2. Funds held in trust for education to be applied in ways to aid and stimulate the Liberian Government to more energetic action in establishing and fostering an efficient system of public schools rather than in merely supporting independent schools.

3. The society to make special effort to collect and diffuse more full and reliable information about Liberia and Africa, and, as a bureau of information, to make itself practically useful both to Liberia and the Negroes in the United States desiring to emigrate there.

4. The Society to promote in every possible way the establishment of more direct, frequent, and quicker communication between the United States and Liberia.

5. The chief end of the work of the Society to be in the line of enabling and stimulating Liberia to depend less and less upon others and more and more upon herself."

It would be seen at once that it proposed with its present limited means to leave emigration to Liberia largely to pay its own way hereafter, and to make use of its means in furnishing fuller and better information about the country, improving its schools, its agriculture and other industries, and attempting to bring about more direct, quicker and less expensive means of communication between the United States and Liberia.

The thousands of letters received by this Society annually from Negroes in the United States show conclusively that a very large number of these people feel that they are and must continue to be at great disadvantage in a country dominated by the white race, that they are engaged in a hopeless conflict, and they desire, more especially for the sake of their children, to escape from this hostile environment.

The main purpose of the Society is to assist in building up a Negro Republic in Africa, a civilized, progressive, Christian nation, for the sake of itself, for the sake of the benign influence it may have on the Two Hundred Million, (200,000,000), of the native people of that great continent, and in the general interest of the race.

Whatever may be the final outcome it is safe to assert that the results thus far are creditable to the Liberians. Liberia is still in its infancy, that country is not yet a United States, and Monrovia is not yet a London, or New York. For forty-nine years it has, however, without any foreign governmental protection or assistance, maintained an independent government and in an orderly manner by the votes of its electors changed its legislative and executive administrations at the regular periods prescribed by its constitution. In all that time it has had no violent revolutions and on no occasion has substituted force for law.

Many of its citizens have displayed intelligent industry and enterprise, have acquired and cultivated large and productive coffee farms, bringing them a handsome income annually, built themselves commodious brick residences, and furnished them with all the comforts and even luuxries of a well arranged English or American home. They have given their children a good education and contributed liberally for the support of schools, churches and other public institutions. No better citizens can be found in any country. What these men have done may be done again by any immigrant of like character, intelligence and industry.

The government of Liberia gives to each immigrant 25 acres of good public land, and at almost a nominal price he can purchase as much more as he desires. As this land produces two crops of vegetables each year, it is an easy matter to raise enough to support a family. A coffee grove can be planted at once, which if properly cultivated will begin to bear in from three to five years, and in from five to ten years can be made to bring its owner an income in gold of at least $1,000.

All that is wanted is a Negro of good character, intelligence and pluck, and all this can be realized in a land where he will enjoy without let or hindrance the fullest civil and social equality.

The American Colonization Society desires to see only such men as have been alluded to emigrating to Liberia, men that can help build a state and not men who will be only an additional burden.

Hitherto emigrants have settled largely in the tide water region, where on account of malaria and other causes, the conditions are not so favorable to health and enterprise. The Society now proposes to assist in forming settlements in the higher and more healthful region above the first rapids in the St. Paul river, in the vicinity of Mt. Coffee, and from this departure it looks forward to great benefits to Liberia, better health, greater industry, improved agriculture, the building of good roads, and the introduction of new and valuable domestic animals.

On Health Conditions and Hygiene in Central Africa

BY

ROBERT W. FELKIN, M.D., F.R.G.S., F.R.S.E.
LECTURER ON DISEASES OF THE TROPICS AND CLIMATOLOGY,
EDINBURG MEDICAL SCHOOL

Mr. President and Gentlemen:

It is with diffidence that I accept the very complimentary invitation I received on the 18th of November to contribute a paper on Health Conditions and Hygiene in Central Africa to your Congress. Had it not been that I am greatly interested in the civilization of Africa, I must have refused the invitation, as the time at my disposal is totally inadequate to do justice to my theme. You must kindly excuse all shortcomings, but I will not waste time by making further excuses, which I feel under the circumstances to be unnecessary.

There are various reasons why it is difficult to do missionary or civilizing work in Africa. Although the climate is the chief barrier, it is not the only one. What then are the others? To my mind they may be summed up briefly as follows: Difficulty of transport, ignorance on the part of missionary societies at home and of the agents sent out, and again, the faulty selection of those agents. Let me then say that all persons should be examined before they are accepted for work in Africa. The individual should be of slightly bilious or, better still, bilio-nervous temperament or else of a sanguine temperament, but that is not quite so good. Persons having a lymphatic temperament should be rejected. No one who has a syphilitic, rheumatic, scorbutic, or malarious history should go to the tropics, nor should persons who have heart disease or a nervous family history be permitted to go. Eyes and ears should be sound. No one should go under twenty-five years of age. Women with any tendency todiseases peculiar to their sex should not be allowed to go. Phthisical persons should be rejected. Many of the deaths which take place would be avoided if the foregoing points were kept in mind.

The next point is that the persons selected should have some instruction as to the climate of Africa, the kind of life they will have to lead, the people they will mix with and the precautions which they must take if they are to be of any use in Africa whatever. To my mind it is both foolish and wicked to send out young, ignorant, unhealthy persons to try to work for the Master in Africa. If they live to return home after a few month's work, they are in most cases invalids for life, a burden to themselves and to the church which sent them forth. Africa is thick with the graves of men and women who might have done good work at home. Providence will not take "special" care of the weak or the foolish, let their intentions be never so good.

With regard to training before a person goes out, a full medical training with special instruction in tropical diseases would be good, but, apart from this, "first aid" should be taught, also how a house is to be built, how drainage is to be dealt with, etc. A little knowledge of carpentering and smith work, as well as boot repairing, is also of use. The people sent out should be "handy" ones, not bookworms. These remarks apply to white and colored people alike, and it must not be forgotten that Negroes from America cannot expect to be able to settle in Africa without some hardship and difficulty.

The outfit should be ample, first-rate goods must be sent, but lavish expenditure is not needed.

Another point is the difficulty in transport. The coast line is the most fatal region in Africa, and till we have railways we cannot expect very great things. For the last fourteen years I have, in season and out of season, been calling out for railways. Now several are being built, and it will soon be possible for missionaries to be taken rapidly across the zone of death which girdles Africa, to the comparatively healthy land, which forms the great central plateau. In any case, however, those going to Africa should begin to take three grains of quinine daily for a week before landing and go on doing so for six or eight weeks thereafter, but to this I will refer again, only noting that the drug should not be taken with either tea or coffee, as is so often done, with the effect of bringing discredit on a useful, indeed the only prophylactic drug we possess.

I must pass over details of personal outfit, merely saying that especial attention should be paid to solar helmet, woolen shirts, thick stockings and good boots. Cholera belt should always be worn, a good hammock is useful, and a mosquito netting indispensable.

The arrival on the coast of Africa should be timed to be at the coolest time of the year. This time varies in different regions.

With regard to transport, at present men must carry the loads; each load should weigh 40 to 45 lbs., never more. Oblong cases are best and the goods in them should be well assorted, so that a large number of cases need not be opened *en route.* One of the great drawbacks to all expeditions has been in the size of the cases sent out by outfitters. They are always too heavy and much time is wasted and many lives lost owing to the delay in repacking goods before starting for the coast. I never heard of an expedition which did not suffer in this way.

In order to be successful, the expedition should leave the coast as soon as ever possible and porters should be ordered beforehand so as to be ready to start directly it arrives. It may be needful to camp for a day or two away from the coast to get the expedition shipshape, but each delay is dangerous.

All young or inexperienced men make the initial and grave mistake of starting with too long marches. They want to "get on", to beat the record, or perform some such foolishness. The result is that their porters break down and that they themselves get over-fatigued. My strong advice is to make haste slowly. A five or ten miles' march a day at first is ample; a little longer after a week on the road if it is necessary. A halt should be made for rest on Sundays, if in a good camp, but not if the camp is badly situated. The porters should be well treated, firmly but kindly. It is regrettable that it should be necessary to mention this point, but it *is* needful. The leader of the expedition should always march in front, so that he may be on the spot if any difficulty occurs. The second in charge should march in the rear to look after stragglers.

The only rules I can give for the march are: have coffee, or cocoa and biscuits before starting; do not start till after sunrise (after the grass is dry is best); do not march under the noon-day sun, and, with the object of avoiding chill, put on a light wrap when halting. At the end of the march, before cooling down, take a bath (not too cold) and have a good rub down with a rough towel. If possible, get the march over by 11:00 A.M.; if that is impossible, march, say, from 7 A.M. to 10:30 A.M. and again from three to five or six P.M. Do not drink much on the march; it is a mere question of habit. Cold tea is the best drink. It should be taken in small quantities, but it should be made properly in order that it may quench the thirst. Take a metal teapot, holding a quart; put in it two teaspoonfuls of tea, then heat the dry pot to a temperature about that of boiling water. Then fill the pot with actually boiling water and decant the infusion at once and cool it in a basin. If the water be allowed to stand on the leaves, the fluid is not so good for quenching the thirst. Never touch alcohol in any form on the march. If it is taken at all, it should not be taken until evening, and even then it is better omitted from the dietary.

It is most important to select a good site for a camp. Take the highest ground available, avoiding as far as may be, the vicinity of swamps, river banks, gullies or valleys, and even in a plain try to camp on a mound, for malaria clings to the ground and 15 or 20 feet make all the difference to the salubrity of the site.

On arriving at the camp, mark off the place for the laterines well to the leeward, have a trench dug round the tent, especially if the halt is to be for more than one day; have a good fire before the tent door. Personally I prefer a grass hut to any tent, but if a tent is used, it should be one with a double roof and the best I know is Edgington's green tent for tropical Africa. The best size is 9 by 7 by 7; it weighs 90 lbs. In any case the tent must protect from sun, rain and wind and should be well ventilated. Whilst the tent is being pitched, the water supply should be seen to. Set a watch over this supply, if needful, to prevent the porters bathing in it, as they so often do before a supply for cooking is obtained. All the water should be filtered (Pasteur's filter should be used) and boiled before use. Food should be well cooked on the march; it is s mistake to eat badly prepared food and native food does not at first suit the new comer.

Marches try the temper very much, owing to the frequent discomfort and *contretemps.* Men should be "slow to anger," and make it a rule to employ the soft answer which turneth away wrath. It is advisable, on the march at any rate, for each person to have his own cook, and have his meals by himself. This may be thought curious advice, but if my authority is not forcible enough, I can quote a far higher, which will at once be acknowledged, namely, that of General Gordon. He told me that it was his strong advice to every African traveler, and that it would tend to avoid most of the quarrels which are the curse of African travel. One man wants meat, another does not; one man likes his food cooked in one way, one in another. Why fight about it? Let each cater for himself. It is a fact that a boon companion in a temperate climate may be a very fiend in Africa; therefore avoid all occasions for strife; bear and forbear. I might give many other details on camp life, but these few must suffice.

I now turn to the important point of fixing on a permanent settlement, and notice some point which will tend to render it as salubrious as possible. It is a mistake to hurry in the choice of a settlement, and as a rule the permanent settlement should not be made until after a year's residence in a district, for it often happens that a very short distance off a better site may be found than the one which at first sight seems best. A rough and ready method of finding out if a district is malarious is to apply the "spleen test." If the majority of the natives have enlarged spleens, go elsewhere if possible. If few of them suffer the place should be fairly healthy.

The settlement should be at as high an altitude as possible, on a slope with well-wooded land to the windward and with a stream at the bottom of the slope, but not too near. Find out from the natives the prevailing local winds, so as to get your settlement sheltered from them if you can. The cultivated land should be placed to the lee of the compound. Do not cut down a single tree unless absolutely necessary, before a survey of the place has been made. It should be remembered that disturbing the land developed malaria, therefore camp away whilst the site is being prepared and the compound being built.

The following notes on the choice of a permanent settlement may be of use:

With regard to elevation of the site, instead of selecting a spot close to a river or in a valley, or even upon low-lying land, a considerable altitude should be secured, if possible. Hill stations are always the best, but a spot even from 50 to 200 feet above the surrounding country will always be beneficial. It is well also, if practicable, to secure a position which will readily furnish natural drainage. Ravines and their entrances are almost always unhealthy from their being often traversed by chilling winds, of which there is an up current by day and a down current by night. But the worst form of ravine is a long, narrow valley which becomes contracted near the outlet. Places situated at the base of a hill should always be shunned. In the tropics it is usually found that at the base of hills the vegetation is rank and luxurious, suggesting that the locality is consequently healthy. But no greater mistake could be made, for this luxurious vegetation is the result of an excessive amount of moisture; the rain collects upon the hill tops, flows down their sides and thus keeps the land near their bases in a constantly moist condition. This condition, however, may be modified where a deep ravine exists near the base of the hill. This may carry off the drainage, and the land beyond the ravine may be quite healthy.

Depressions in plains are worse than those on the hills, since drainage is always liable to occur in the latter, and thus even a gravel basin lying in a plain may be constantly damp on account of drainage into it. Then, again, the proximity of marshes must be carefully avoided; all places near to a marsh at a less altitude than 1,500 feet are to be avoided. It must also be remembered that malaria originating in a marsh may be carried horizontally as well as vertically, and at least a mile distant from a marsh must, if possible, be found. It is true that malaria is probably not diffused on a calm day to a greater distance horizontally than vertically, but winds and air currents blowing over a marsh may convey it to a distance of even two or three miles. As a rule, a mile of water renders a place safe. If, again, a belt of dense forest trees should intervene between a marsh and a proposed settlement, they may act as a screen or filter and render the spot healthy unless they are removed or burnt down accidentally.

The brushwood and vegetation around the station must be cleared away, for they not only check the free movement of the air, but thereby create a stagnant stratum of still air highly charged with decaying vegetable matter. It is, however, well to encourage the growth of short grass around the station; it cools the ground by protecting it from the sun and by increasing evaporation. It may be mentioned here that the removal of dense brushwood is even dangerous to the natives, and should only be permitted during the hottest part of the day. With reference to the soil itself, the most important point to consider is dryness, and, where the choice is open, gravel is best for a foundation, unless it be situated so low that the subsoil water is very near the surface and so renders it damp. Gravelly hills furnish the best of all sites, and the springs at their feet are usually pure. If a high, bare or nearly bare site can be found, it is to be preferred. Diluvial deposits brought down by floods are never desirable; here are often alternations of sandy loam and clayey strata, with vegetable matter disseminated through it. The alluvium often contains iron and alumina with siliceous particles and probably underneath stiff clay or clayey brick earth will be found. This stratum is often only two or three feet beneath the surface. Europeans will never be able to maintain health on such a soil, since malaria is very rife there and the water very impure. All clays and marls are unhealthy, for only the most complete and deep subsoil drainage can make them suitable for dwelling on. Clayey soils require to be doubly drained.

Chalk and limestone, however, form healthy soil if unmixed with clay, but in this case again it is not uncommon to find clay underlying them, and this, receiving the drainage percolating through from above, renders them malarious. Rocks may be regarded as healthy, with the exception of decomposing ferruginous granite. Sandstone is healthy, but the water found in its vicinity is frequently impure. Siliceous sands may be good when extending to a great depth and free from organic matter. They are naturally dry and healthy, and the water near is usually good. But other sands, argillaceous, calcareous and the like, especially when mixed with organic matter, or lying above a layer of clay or laterite, are damp and consequently unwholesome.

Having settled upon the ground it has now to be prepared for building. It must be properly leveled, with a slope of about one inch in six feet to insure surface drainage. Subsoil drains should then be sunk from five to eight feet deep in the ground, and placed about twelve feet apart. The surface drainage should be provided for by shallow, *open* drains. The foundations of the house should be excavated as little as possible in order to avoid more than is necessary disturbance of the soil. The house should be built on piles five feet above the level of the ground, and the surface under the house and round it where rain may fall from the roof should be paved or cemented, with a good gutter all round. Into all the details of building I cannot enter. They depend on building material obtainable, money available, etc., but the following hints may be given: Build the house with the gable towards the prevailing wind; let it be of two stories if possible. Have a good verandah all round it ten or twelve feet wide, and on the southern or western sides jalousies should be placed covering from two to four feet at the upper part of the verandah. The rooms in the house should be large enough to give each person 100 superficial feet or 3,000 cubic feet of space. The roof should be double, with an air-space between the two roofs. The windows should be made so that the upper part may open inwards and downward so as to direct the air upwards.

A good bath-house should be provided near the house, also a latrine, both being connected with the house by a *covered* way. The greatest care should be taken in seeing that the compound is kept clean, and that the garbage is daily removed. Earth closets are the best to use in the tropics, about twelve pounds of dry earth is required per head per diem. For the servants the trench system is the best; shallow trenches, twelve or eighteen inches deep, should be used; earth should be thrown over the excretas, and as soon as an acre or so of trenches are full the whole may be ploughed up and sown with vegetables. After three crops have been grown the ground may be used again.

The water supply needs great care, about thirty gallons per head per diem will be required. An artesian tube well will be advisable; forty feet of 1½ inch steel piping, in 5-foot sections, and a pump will cost about £4. I cannot enter into details, but it draws the water from the bottom and cuts off the direct entrance of water from higher levels. Whatever water reaches it must filter through a considerable depth of earth.

Water for drinking and cooking purposes must be filtered and boiled, *not* boiled and then filtered. If there is much mud in the water treat it with alum before filtering. As boiled water is not palatable, aerate it before drinking. This can be done by placing it in a porous jar and letting it drip down into a vessel placed below it.

Having now given some idea as to how to reach and how to found a fairly healthy home, it remains for me to give a few hints on personal hygiene.

A man or woman going to Africa as a missionary or civilizer owes it to society as well as to himself to use all precautions to retain health. I do not for a moment mean that he is to be namby pamby, or think that the slightest malaria is to be fatal, indeed fear causes more deaths than are pleasant to contemplate, but "sanctified common sense" must be used.

A man in the tropics must be temperate in all things; in food, in drink, in work and in play. He should have a hobby not connected with his special work. Boating, geology, anthropology; anything you like. Something to take his mind off the worries of every day life.

He should cultivate an even temper, should not be given to gossip, should not be "thin skinned," eccentric or a man of one idea.

Probably the following notes will give hints which may with advantage be followed: The hair should be kept short, the body perfectly clean, nor should the feet be forgotten. Dr. Murray advises the following tooth powder to be used night and morning: Sulphate of quinine, 3 drachms; oil of eucalyptus, 2 drachms; rose oil, 10 drops; Armenian bole, 1 ounce; camphorated chalk, 5 ounces. Triturate well, and keep in stoppered bottles, each containing one ounce. Carbolic or eucalyptus soap should be used.

Exercise is needed; it should be vigorous, so as to cause free perspiration, either a good walk for two hours, a hilly walk if possible, or tennis or riding or dumb-bell exercise. The exercise should be taken in the cool of the day and a bath and rubdown thereafter. All chill should be avoided, and note that just after sunset there may be a sudden fall in the temperature, therefore if out at that time a light wrap should be available. Again, about 4 A. M. it is apt to be very cold (relatively), and an extra blanket may be needed, or the fire in the hut or room stirred up. I got into the habit of waking about 3:30 A. M., and thus avoided many a chill. Speaking of fires, it is well to note that a fire is always useful if the weather permits; it keeps the room dry, it prevents malaria to some extent, it drives away mosquitoes; in the open, if built so as to give off a dense smoke, it keeps one dry, the smoke forming, as it were, a canopy above.

Always sleep in a mosquito net, whether there be mosquitoes or no. The net acts as a filter to the air breathed. It should be fine, and steeped in sulphate of ammonia, one part by weight to five parts of boiled water. This makes it uninflammable (Dr. Murray). A pint is required for one foot of net. Steep it for three hours, then dry and iron.

Never sleep on the ground; a few feet make all the difference. If compelled to sleep on the ground, which is hardly ever needful if a hammock is taken, have a waterproof ground-sheet, and to keep off snakes, scorpions, etc., place a coil of camel's hair rope round the bed.

Avoid fogs and night air; indeed keep indoors from sunset till sunrise if possible; never go out with an empty stomach. If bound to be out at night in a very malarious district, a respirator on which is placed a few drops of eucalyptus oil may be used with benefit.

Avoid chill after violent exercise or a wetting, change the clothes as soon as may be; put on an overcoat if an immediate change is not possible. Draughts should be avoided.

It is safe to say that quinine, the hydrochlorate by preference, is the only drug which is of use as a prophylactic against malaria, but it must be used with common sense. Unmeasured doses should never be taken, three or four grains a day is enough, taken with soup, never with tea or coffee, which beverages should not be taken for two hours after the quinine. I do not even think it a good plan to take these small doses of the drug for too long, as it is apt to affect the brain and nervous system, and also should fever occur, as is most likely, far larger doses of the drug will be required to cut it short than would otherwise be the case.

If in a healthy station, the regular use of quinine is unnecessary. Take it if on the march, if the rainy season comes on and when the rains cease, or if unwonted exertion has been undergone, or if sleeplessness occur.

Care must be taken to avoid the sun; the slanting rays of the morning and evening sun are to be feared. A good solar helmet should be used; an umbrella with a white cover is not to be despised. The small of the back too needs protection, and the flannel shirts should be made with a double thickness down the spine, or a good Kummer band should be worn. The neck should be free, no high collars being worn.

Dysentery may be avoided by care in respect of food and drinking water, and by avoiding depression and over-exertion.

I greatly regret that press of work prevents me from elaborating this brief paper as I would wish, and as the important subject demands.

MRS. M. FRENCH-SHELDON, F. R. G. S.
Lecturer on Africa
Organizer and Leader of an Independent Expedition for the Exploration of the
region of Kilima-Njaro in East Africa; Author of "From Sultan to Sultan"

Practical Issues of an African Experience

BY
MRS. M. FRENCH-SHELDON, F. R. G. S.,
AFRICAN EXPLORER; AUTHOR OF "FROM SULTAN TO SULTAN"

Lord Chesterfield has said: "I join behavior with learning, because it is almost a necessity, and they should go together for their mutual advantage." I venture to go further and say: *"Deportment is akin to religion."* Hence it becomes all those who aspire to propound the tenets of Christianity to deferentially behave as Christians--not to preach and teach one thing and live and enact another, while seeking to conduct the so-called benighted natives of Africa, or any other country, into the light of civilization and Christianity. Animated by the belief that all of God's creatures, in whatsoever clime, of different color, notwithstanding their environments or ignorance, if approached in the proper manner with justice, peace, and patient humanity, and the desire to, would find an echo in the natives' nature and arouse the better qualities and the good--which is the God--latent in the very lowest of God's creatures.

I hear considerable talk about the African question. I know not what the real import of this question is, as set forth by speakers I have not heard, but, mark you, if it means anything concerning the Afro-American and the native African being one and the same nation, amenable to the same treatment and consideration, and in any way as suggestive that the Afro-American's real home-land is in Africa, I must publicly disavow any belief in the doctrine, and will touch upon my reasons later on.

The greatest impiety and preposterous assumption on the part of human kind is the calling into question the rights of life or salvation of any of God's creatures. This belief was so grounded in my mind, which is predisposed by its Quaker heredity to peaceful solutions of questions, I determined, "if circumstances would lead me, to find where truth was hid." After pondering over the outrages and cruelties perpetrated by aliens in their invasive progress throughout Africa--after hearkening to the horrible tales of the natives' heinous deeds, their hopeless degradation, their utter devoidness of uplifting sentiments or tender emotions, I solemnly resolved to visit Africa on an independent, unsponsored expedition, unhampered by sectarianism, or state interest or commercial greed, or white companions or lieutenants, and visit tribes, as far as possible, where the white man's influence, the Arab traders' man-hunting were measurably unknown, and even where missionary influence might not yet have reached. In fact, study the raw native, the untutored, unrevised aborigine, with his vices, his ignorance, his intellectual poverty, and his possibilities in their primitive state.

After a dedication of years, gleaning from every source available what had been done, and determining what should *not* be done, getting glimpses into the superstitions, habits, and life and language of as many different tribes as possible, and submitting to training in order to be able to stand the necessary physical stress and hardships from exposure, unavoidable while marching through plains, forests, and over almost inaccessible mountain passes, swimming streams, and strove to nerve and discipline myself to a spirit of self-abnegation and fortitude which made it possible to face with some degree of complacency the very great chances of death, then I determined to make the experiment, cost what it would, in behalf of humanity, and succeeded far beyond my most fervent expectations, without bloodshed.

Suffice it, the world has become sufficiently familiarized with what it is please to call "the unique undertaking of a woman," and it would be entirely unnecessary to recapitulate all that.

Adopting the native *Inshalluh,* equivalent to our Christian *God writing,* the venture was made without bloodshed, and I have concluded that the extreme measures employed by some would-be colonizers, most explorers and treaty-makers are unnecessarily atrocious, and without the pale of either civilization or humanity. If, instead of carrying emblems of war and hostility into alien lands, they had carried *the emblem of God-which is love*--the results might have been immeasurable towards the religious progress, weal and higher development of millions of misguided, misjudged and oppressed creatures.

Foolish admirers and hero-worshippers are wont to say that this work, undertaken and accomplished, was because it was *destined.* To those persons I would say, that "she who did these things" *was not* born to do them, but took her "license in her work." I am wont to opine with the noble Henry Ward Beecher, "The elects are whosoever wills, the non-elects are whosoever wonts"--and Solomon said, "He that hath love in his breast hath spurs in his side,"--and so, I found it a great truth when put into execution. Allow me to reiterate, that it makes no difference *who goes* to Africa, or elsewhere as to the sequences of his or her work, it depends upon *how* they go,--*how* they behave; this reverts back to that universal link between deportment and religion.

Through independent action the conclusions which I will present without further preamble for your consideration, have been deductions made on the spot, and to which I am more fully convinced by present retrospection and prevailing tendencies. Before summarizing, allow me to make a brief departure on the question of the Afro-Americans. Unfortunately fanatical zealots have represented the Afro-Americans' rights of nativity in Africa, forgetting that after several generations that most of the negroes in America have become thoroughly Americanized; they are born Southerners and have no longer any proclivities for the life of the natives in Africa; and more than all that, they are now freemen in America, and the fact is that unless they have such qualities and such wealth as to give them certain powers and rights as leaders, or chiefs, if they returned, to most parts of Africa, they would find themselves thrust back into the conditions of servitude and slavery, harder to bear after their education and emancipation than was experienced during the old régime in the South. In affirmation of this point, of almost universal slavery amongst the natives even at this late day, it gives me great pleasure to refer as an authority to the celebrated Heli Chatelain, and other men of similar knowledge and experience.

Another point: What is being done so effectually in America, especially below Mason and Dixon's line, in manual, industrial, and agricultural training, which constitutes such an important part in almost all of the educational institutions inaugurated during the last thirty years for the Afro-American, is the *very necessity of Africa to-day,* upon which its future prosperity and the wholesome enlightenment pivots.

The basis of a future development of not only Africa, but the Africans, must be through agricultural and domestic and industrial means, rather than through purely denominational religious and educational methods of the ethical type. Any serious-thinking individual will be willing to admit that it is utterly preposterous and perfectly incongruous to the maintenance of his own self-esteem; that the fine distinctions and dogmas of various creeds can be made simple and interpretable to the primitive intellects of people who have no comparative knowledge, no education excepting such as the exigencies of their lives and their peculiar environments render, living for the most part pastoral lives, except as they follow the vocation of hunters and warriors, devoid of all refining surroundings, living in huts so meanly constructed that they are scarcely fit to be considered by us as decent shelters for animals, into which they must enter, while reducing themselves to the attitude of quadrupeds and creep in on their hands and knees; without light excepting that which emanates from their fires, huddled with their animals, men, women, and children, promiscuously--their bodies daubed with grease and clay to which soap and water are strangers,--can understand what it has taken enlightened races centuries to divide off in special and distinctive creeds for the acceptance of different minds. No! No! It is impossible.

The trouble has been that the foundations have not been properly laid; an infinite amount of philanthropic money, the sacrifice of lives, loss of time, has occurred through the fallacious methods of beginning at the steeple-top instead of building a foundation, letting the superstructure be a gradual evolution in a wholesome, natural, and steadfast manner. Sound through and through.

The love of prestige, glory and reputation prevailed universally in every tribe I visited. This made the open sesame for me to their most intimate lives and characteristics; for I maintained this prestige without ever deviating from its forms and ceremonies; and it is well that they have it, for it is through this one quality that civilization and christianization will be most readily accepted by them. A singular fact, that all the chiefs or sultans whom I encountered on the eastern coast, recognized the *dignity and might* of labor, inasmuch as in all the onward movements in this Western continent towards the progression and enlightenment of the world, some of the most affluent, most refined, most cultured of the upper class of men and women have devoted, tirelessly, their time, money, and energies to the acknowledged betterment of the populace, and this without price. Their assiduous, praiseworthy efforts have inducted a fresh, virile, energizing force, uplifting labor to the eminence of personal dignity, until it is regarded a shame for any mortal to exist indolently despite their position or personal tendencies otherwise.

It was the chiefs or sultans who were the expert craftsmen; they were the Fundas, or blacksmiths of the tribes, and they were proud of the production of a finely tempered, well-modeled spear, or knife, or delicately made metal-chains, as might any gunsmith or jeweler in civilized countries have been of similar work; and so proud and jealous were they of their particular class of work that they put what was equivalent to a sterling mark on all work made in their individual tribe, and after making a certain number of specimen patterns, some of the important, apt youth in the tribe, frequently the sons or nephews of the sultan, would be trusted to execute all other spears needed, exactly adhering to the sultan's pattern, and submit the finished work to the expert eye of the sultan to attest their quality and finish before this sterling mark could be placed upon them. Admitting that they do this work simply for self exaltation, or even for acquisition of riches, it is an admirable quality to deal with. After all, if we would admit it, our love of power, and love to excel, and love of adulation or admiration is what animates us to do the most valiant deeds and spurs us to the greatest perfection. It is the foundation stone upon which heroes stand, it is the root of progress, and if judiciously used, in the further instruction of the natives in Africa, it can be turned to immeasurable service in the gradual enlightenment of not only individuals, but of whole tribes; first, because of the power it gives the native, he will seek to learn certain useful things introduced by teachers, finding that each new acquirement gives him greater power; hence, with no nobler motive than the acquirement of knowledge simply for the sake of power, he strives to excel; presently, in due time, he finds that the knowledge is gained from the so-called enlightened teacher, and as a natural consequence, he seeks enlightenment to the fullest, mainly in the first instance, for his material betterment; but during this passing of ignorance to knowledge his mind quickens, becomes alert and susceptible, and his condition becomes truly amenable to the very best influences in life and education that may be offered him. This can be wisely followed up and turned to the best account in a spiritual, moral way.

This is practical--it is possible--it must be the way to first reach these people. Hence is it that I stand as one proclaiming the Gospel of Soap and Candles, Hammer and Saw, and Loom as the primary method of instruction for all so-called savage nations, and all mediocre people. For example, candles like those which I taught them to make [Mrs. Sheldon here showed a candle] brought light, brightness, and morality into their huts. Look you, how significant can it be used by those who have no thought but the religion of the people and the christianization of them. May the teacher who follows the Gospel of the Candle not use this as a symbol, and say in such terms as their natives can appreciate and comprehend, "as this light has brought you so much comfort in your material existence, this teaching which gives you light of the almighty God will bring you light and comfort for all your sufferings and sorrows, and be a guide for your future life?"

And this Gospel of Soap [Mrs. Sheldon showed a piece of soap made for the natives], may it not also be used with the same significance--"as this makes your body clean, and leaves a delicate perfume which delights your nostrils, this spiritual love which we will teach you of, will cleanse your soul as this cleanses your body."

Then, again, as for the Gospel of the Saw and Hammer, is it not rational to give to people the means to make decent homes, so they can understand why it is the Christians build and beautify a house in which they worship God?

Time has irrefutably demonstrated that all missionary and civilized work in Africa must be done through manual and domestic training and industrial schools, preparatory to whatever may follow in the way of higher education or christianization. My personal experience proves that you can develop exactly the qualities that you believe to exist in ignorant people, and after all is said, if one lives in harmony with their precepts and can openly submit to the native's extraordinary gift in detecting shams, he has done nobly. For after all is said, the greatest bane or sin of the native African is his primitive ignorance. Their language is circumscribed because they have no things in their lives to call for thought or give expression to, yet adroitly invent an appropriate for every new thing seen for the first time. The country is so vast--inhabitants numberless--yet for need of proper methods of transportation they have been shut off from the civilized influence of other countries, and with all the drawbacks that railroads may have, such as the introduction of avaricious traders, liquor, the vices of civilization, in greater proportion will be their civilizing influences, for it will be a deathblow to slavery; introducing commodities into Africa, which will make cultivation of their land easier and the reduction of their products into commercial values, and instead of using slaves as beasts of burden by transporting everything on their heads, the railroad will be available; and customs of other peoples will become known to them. As the natives are taught to read, they will become conversant with the outside world and what is going on, and many of them will be fired with a desire to visit other lands, and in these ways and commingling with others they will without intention imbibe knowledge of better life and condition, which they will return amongst their people and disseminate. Lateness in the development and enlightenment of Africa is by no means to be regretted, for it is in Africa as it will be in the development of the South, that all the experiments made heretofore in every avenue of life--the newest and most progressive methods of a mechanical, commercial or educational nature can be adopted without the expense of all that it has cost to bring them to perfection by more prosperous people. Take, for example, the city of Johannesburg in South Central Africa, which could only boast a few years ago of six thousand inhabitants, cut off far away from seaboard ports, taking weeks and weeks to reach the coast; whereas, to-day it is a thrifty, imposing city of over seventy thousand inhabitants, boasting of opera house, churches, beautiful residences, electric cars and electric lights, manufactories and a center of civilization, intellectual society and wealthy enterprises--where, to every white man who is working in the mines or on the railroad, according to Hon. Cecil Rhodes' statement some little time ago, there are a thousand natives. One cannot casually measure the influence that this one city will have upon the development of the surrounding country. Then, too, the railroad projected from Cairo to the Congo and to Cape Town will cut a bright ray of possibilities from the North to West, East and South Africa.

In view of this rapid introduction of commodities, comforts, luxuries and necessities by means of transportation which will bring about a better condition, not only for the natives, but for the white pioneers to live with some degree of immunity against former hardships, does it not behoove all those interested from divers reasons, with various aims in view, in a common sense, practical, and material way to make suitable preparation in sending out pioneers or teachers or preachers, or entering into commercial arrangements for the furtherance of their own or the African interest?

Is it to be affirmed, without contradiction by those sordidly interested, or the extremist, who claims the black man was born for bondage, that the future African will placidly remain a subjugated, coerced citizen of alien government? Such a stand must provoke a contrary thought to the matter-of-fact, cool-headed, neutral onlooker, who is not even animated by humanity as he deliberates over cause and effect.

May it not safely be prophesied that once enlightened, once realizing the immensity of their country, its limitless wealth, its grand commercial and other possibilities, these uncounted millions of people will struggle and fight to overthrow the governments they yielded so much to in their helpless days of blind, untutored ignorance?

In the unexplored regions, billeted out geographically by vague ink-boundary lines, marking alien proctorship of the various alien governments, may there not be tribes powerful in numbers, quick to recognize, possibly, with surprising latent intelligence their birthright to Africa, and with that knowledge, may they not strive to overthrow the English, German, Portuguese, Belgian, Dutch, French "Sphere of Influence" set up under false pretenses in their midst?

Africans, despite their ignorance, are human. They will fight as have other nations the world over, for country, for territorial boundaries--for their natural rights, for their beliefs, for their homes, for their women and children; and as do civilized nations this very day, to establish possessorship over weaker countries when an opponent avows a similar intention--they, too, will fight when self-interest is at stake, when even minor governmental or petty individual differences arise, if they pattern after the boastful nations of Christendom at this very time.

Unwittingly the whole world, self-duped, has been paying an involuntary tribute to the peaceful, submissive attributes of the beleaguered, hood winked African, to have so confidently presupposed that he will never feel his power as a nation and turn fiercely to throw off the shackles of subjugation, which pledge his allegiance to expatriation, and repossess himself of his birthright. Mark you, he will, unless terrorized into submission by unequalled methods of warfare. Then his patriotism must remain a paradox.

The Africans' greatest crime, after all, alas, has been their ignorance, their primitive ignorance, their simple arcadianism in morals and manners, wherein animalisms have had unguided sway. This must vanish before the resistless power of the world's constant progress, as the snow melts before the sun. The future of Africa, to the thoughtful, unprejudiced investigator, who knows something of Africa from having been in Africa, is startling! Its marvelous natural resources--its gold--its diamonds--its agricultural opportunities--its industries--its commerce--yet in their infancy, have already bestirred the alert, far-seeing, prosperous nations with great covetousness. Alien is elbowing alien to-day, in his endeavor to stake off Africa; each for his own country or personal aggrandizement. The contagion will soon take hold of the natives. However, the future conflict, when it comes, will be terrific between the white invader and the swart-skinned African--for the latter will surely awaken to the fact of the material value of all he has unknowingly abrogated and submitted to when acquiescing to treaties made under the guise of civilization and the assumption of benefiting his race. Light is radiating the Dark Continent. It is time the white man called a halt and reformed his methods.

In conclusion, as it has been attested by the most celebrated statesmen, the deepest thinkers, the closest students of political and domestic economy, allow me also to venture the remark that the greatest fulcrum of civilization is a legitimate commerce; and, to those who would preach, and teach, pray you, remember that there is something to impart as to the betterment of the life here on earth before you can successfully be a guide to or present any comprehensive view of the life hereafter, or clearly interpret the ethics of moral suasion to the Africans.

As the Africans say when they put the seed of a mango into the ground, when they are on a journey, "I plant it that my brother who comes ten years hence may have fruit to eat," so let us plant these little seeds of truth that those who come ten years hence may have the fruition of our forethought.

Abolish cant, and shams, seek to live according to the highest precepts; be humanly divine, merciful and noble when setting forth a code for others. Such humanity, such honest, exalted purpose, will impart a zest to all followers, and give all approached the one conviction that the element of *love* and *compassion* cannot be silenced:

> "In peopled cities, as in waste untrod,
> Its tones are mighty--'tis the voice of God."

It's true religion and the foundation of civilization.

African Slavery; Its Status and the Anti-Slavery Movement in Europe

BY
HELI CHATELAIN
AFICAN TRAVELER AND PHILOLOGIST; AUTHOR OF "FOLK-TALES OF ANGOLA"

It is my purpose to give in this paper a concise statement of the conclusions at which I have arrived, after fifteen years of theoretical and practical study, concerning; (1) Slavery and the slave traffic in Africa; (2) the efforts made by Europe for the extinction of these evils; (3) the duty of America in this mater.

Disposing of so little time for the treatment of this vast and complicated subject, I am obliged to leave out all discussions of controversive points, all quotations from travelers, philanthropists, and statesmen; all pictures of native African slave life, descriptions of the harrowing scenes presented by slave raids and slave caravans; all thrilling adventures and heroic feats of the recent anti-slavery wars in Central Africa, all, that is, that appeals to the emotional part of man, and be content with giving an outline of the subject in its three-fold aspect.

From time immemorial slavery has existed in Africa. The oldest records of the human race, the inscriptions of the Nile Valley, show us that negro slaves from the Sudan were then, as to-day, one of the principal articles of Egyptian trade.

Neither the institution of slavery nor the slave-trade were introduced into Africa or forced upon the natives by Arabic Moslems or European Christians. At all times, so far as human knowledge goes, slavery has been a constituent element in the social order of Negro Africa. It is said of two or three African Negro tribes that they object to selling their own tribesmen, and oppose slave-dealing in a general way. But these exceptions only confirm the rule that slavery is the universal practice of native Africa. There the trade in human beings is considered just as honest as trade in any other merchandise.

All those who want to work for the extinction of slavery in Africa should know from the start, that for one Arab or European slave-holder, slave-raider, or slave-dealer, there are hundreds of African slave-holders, slave-dealers, and slave-raiders. Therefore, in their efforts to conquer that monster they will have to face thousands of interested native opponents. This will be made clearer by a consideration of

THE SOURCES OF SLAVERY.

(1) Chief among these sources, because affecting every individual from his birth to his death, is the right of parents *to sell their children.* Every child that is born is the property, the chattel, of its maternal uncle ; in a few tribes of its father. The uncle or the father has the right to dispose of his property as he pleases. If he kills his human property, his neighbors, his clan, and his chief may show their reprobation of such a crime, but nobody can prosecute him, claim damages, or demand his punishment. If he sells his nephews or his children, sometimes separating child from mother, nobody seems to even think that he is doing wrong. The victim itself is no more recalcitrant than a young girl in our lands when she is sent for the first time to a boarding-school.

I have known many slaves who had thus been sold by their uncles, but never have I met one who protested against it. One reason why the victims so readily acquiesce in this iniquity is that they themselves expect to exercise, when grown up, this same privilege of selling their nephews or their own offspring. In the native mind anyone attempting to eradicate slavery is an anarchist, who saps the very foundation of parental authority, of private property, of social and political order.

The abuse of this parental right has assumed such proportions among the Lubolo tribe, in Angola, that these people seem to consider the breeding of children the easiest way of earning their livelihood. The high prices paid by the Portuguese planters have no doubt much to do with this monstrous phenomenon. If a man can save himself one or two years' care and labor simply by relieving himself of the support of one of his numerous nephews by selling him, why should he not embrace the opportunity?

(2) The least productive source of slavery is the right of a free adult *to sell himself.* Of course a man only sells himself when he has no cattle, house, or nephew to sell in his stead. This sometimes happens to gamblers, who, after having lost all their material and human possessions, stake their own liberty with a hope of recovering their losses. Runaway slaves, or liberated slaves, too, rather than be pounced upon and kidnapped, often prefer to sell themselves to masters of their own choice. In times of famine hundreds are compelled to exchange their liberty for the food which will keep soul and body together. In war, cowards would rather live as slaves than die as freemen.

(3) A third source is the sale of *insolvent debtors.* This only takes place when the debtor has exhausted all the resources of his material, animal, and human property.

(4) A fourth source is the sale of criminals by *legal action.* This does not differ in principle from the sale of debtors.

As there are no prisons in native Africa, punishment is either capital or pecuniary; the guilty party is sentenced either to death, or to the payment of a fine. In default of payment he is sold, and the plaintiff receives the price, or rather what is left after the deduction of the judge's fee. The principal crimes which feed the slave trade are witchcraft and adultery. The regular penalty for witchcraft is death; this may, however, by the cupidity of the chief or head-men, be commuted into banishment in slavery.

To send home a liberated slave who was sold by legal sentence for witchcraft is to expose him to certain death, or re-selling.

In the case of adultery, the regular punishment is a heavy fine for the male party, and death for the female party. Here, again, the cupidity of the offended husband often commutes death penalty into slavery and banishment.

(6) A sixth source is *kidnapping.* This is much more frequent than is generally supposed.

As a heathen African thinks it is a smart thing to tell a lie, or steal without being detected and punished, so his own conscience and his friends will not rebuke him if he kidnaps a person without getting himself into trouble. If, however, the kidnapper feels proud of his smartness, the victim is fully alive to the injustice committed.

While all the slaves I have known, who had been sold in consequence of a legal sentence, or by their parents, showed no resentment against the authors of their enslavement, those slaves who had been kidnapped generally related their misfortune with tears in their eyes, and entertained a secret, though forlorn, hope of regaining their liberty and returning to their homes.

I shall never forget the case of a fine, young Mushilange, from the center of the Kongo State, who had been kidnapped in a shameful manner. He was my fellow passenger with 200 other slaves, on the finest ship in the Portuguese Navigation Company, about five years ago, between Loanda and San Thome. His name was Musulu. Having come with a caravan of countrymen to trade at Kasanji, on the Kuango river, he was there taken ill. His companions left him in charge of a well-known native trader, with means to keep him until recovery. But, instead of sending him back to his country, the Kasanji trader sold him for about thirty dollars to a Portuguese trader of Malange, who, in his turn, sold him to a planter at San Thome for about seventy dollars.

All my efforts, while on shore at San Thome, and later by correspondence with a lawyer friend on my return to America, all my efforts to redeem Musulu, even at a high price, proved vain. Although my lawyer friend was, perhaps, the most influential man on the island, he declared that he was powerless against the coalition of all the planters and functionaries whose business interests are bound up with this nefarious traffic. If the slave had been redeemed, and brought by me to Europe or America he might have become an object lesson on slavery, rousing public opinion against the hateful system.

(7) A seventh source is *capture in war*. Captives are sometimes held at ransom. If there is no hope of their being redeemed at a reasonable price by friends, they are sold to traders for what they can fetch, and if the supply exceeds the demand they are butchered. Young or middle-aged women are seldom slaughtered. They are welcome additions to the harems of the victors, and can easily support themselves by field labor.

In purely native Africa slaves are so cheap and the demand for labor is so limited, that waging war for the main purpose of slave-raiding is of rare occurrence, except among cannibal tribes, when they are crazed by the craving for human flesh.

Most of the slave raiding wars are caused, not immediately but through one, two or three intermediary links, by the demand of semi-civilized Mohammedan Hamites or Negroes in the Sudan, of well-to-do Egyptians, Moroccans, and Arabs, of oil kings in the Niger basin, of white planters wherever sugar-cane, coffee and cocoa are grown on a large scale; and last, not least, by the demand of the European governments and expeditions for native soldiers or carriers.

The introduction of guns and powder into a new region is almost invariably the signal for a raid on some weaker tribe. The price of the slaves sold at the coast enables the victors to equip themselves for another greater raid. Thus the famous Mushidi of Katanga or Garenganze, being supplied with fire-arms and powder from both the east coast and the west coast, could, he a simple trader, found a vast empire on the ruins of unprotected and unarmed native towns and tribes.

Thus also the Makioko, though vassals of the great Lunda nation, managed to raid and finally all but annihilate their own suzerain nation, thanks to the powder and guns they obtained from Benguella. In exchange for these guns and ammunitions, the Makioko flooded the plantations and fields of Angola and St. Thomé with Lunda slaves.

This proves that the approach of secular civilization far from weakening, at first stimulates the horrors of the traffic.

Knowing now in what different ways Africans are enslaved, let us consider

THE LOT OF THE AFRICAN SLAVES.

Here we distinguish between slaves of heathen Africans, slaves of Mohammedan Arabs or Negroes, slaves of European or civilized native planters.

(1) In *primitive African society,* as we have already seen, almost every free person is or has been what *we* would call the slave of his or her uncle. The wants of the people being so very limited, there are no large plantations nor factories. The king, the headmen, the poor freemen and the slaves live on the same food, dwell in similar huts, wear the same sort of garment or show the same absence of clothing. All the slave has to do for his master is to fetch his water or his fuel; to assist him in planting his fields when the rains begin to fall, and to help him in harvesting when the season for it has come. All, or nearly all, that the slave earns beyond what he does for his master is his private property. With this he can improve his condition, buy himself wives, and other slaves. In Old Calaber slave-holding by slaves is so common that you often can hear of slaves belonging to slaves of slaves. As any person of royal blood may by a reverse of fortune become a slave, so any slave may by industry and thrift redeem himself, take his seat among the tribal headmen, and aspire to the kingship.

Among cannibal tribes, however, the prospect of figuring as a delicacy at a banquet of the tribe must considerably mar the patriarchal features of this phase of slavery.

(2) In the *Mohammedan* field, the slave who survives the horrors of the raid and of the caravan journey to the coast, and who safely reaches his destination in the house or in the fields of a Mohammedan master, may deem himself happy when he recalls the frightful scenes he has witnessed, but his lot is far from enviable. Although it is an exaggeration to say that the Koran teaches and encourages slavery and slave trade, it is bad enough that it allows these evils; even in recommending mild treatment Mohammed was not in advance of the moralists of his age. On the whole, slavery among Mohammedans is severer than among untutored Africans in the same measure as the Mohammedan culture surpasses that of the heathen, yet it seems to be less cruel than European slavery.

The Oriental may be a sharp and active trader, but he never equals the European as an exploiter of human labor in plantation or factory work. Nor does he, no more than the Portuguese and French, hurt the tenderest feelings of human dignity by drawing that fatal color-line in which the Anglo-Saxon seems to take such unjustifiable pride.

Slaves are hunted by Moslems (Arabs, half-breeds or Mohammedan Negroes) for the three following purposes: (1) To supply labor for their fields and plantations in the Soudan, in Zanzibar and the adjoining coast-belt; (2) to supply negresses for the harems of Turkey, especially Arabia, Egypt, Tripoli, and Morocco; (3) to obtain carriers for the trading caravans taking European goods to the interior and bringing down in exchange the tusks of ivory and the balls of rubber so much coveted by Europeans and Americans.

(3) The worst form of slave labor is that endured on plantations owned by *Europeans,* or civilized natives. The assertion that Europeans hold slaves, as also the statement made above, that the approach of civilization causes a revival of the traffic, may cause surprise, and requires some explanation.

Whenever Europeans undertake a work requiring a large force of men for a long period, they soon find out that free men and women either do not care to work, because they do not need to, or if they be willing to work, they want some pay, and as soon as they have the goods they proposed to earn they return to their homes and have a good time enjoying the proceeds of their labor. At the first rainfall, when all available hands are called for, to sow and plant the fields, it is well nigh impossible to retain a native whose home is not beyond reach. The result is momentary stagnation in the white man's work; in some cases its ruin. Hence hatred of the white man against the Negro, whom he calls an incurable idler and fit to be only a slave. Hence, also, the excuse for securing slave labor. Under the pretense of redeeming slaves-- which, in native parlance, continues to be simply buying and selling men--agents, either native or white, are promised so much a head for every slave they bring. The farther the slave comes from the better, as there is less fear of his running away.

These agents scour one region after another, trying to induce chiefs to procure the number of men and women needed. The chiefs are provided with guns and powder, and either they themselves or their correspondents in the interior make raids on weaker tribes and sell the captives to the middle-men, who bring them to the white man's agent, who redeems them. These poor creatures are redeemed from the status of patriarchal native slavery into the status of European plantation slavery. No more free time, no accumulation of private property, no hope of redeeming one's self by thrift, no home life, no possibility of flight. From morning till night unremitting toil in the broiling sun, under the lash of the driver, either without pay and with insufficient food, or with insufficient pay wherewith to buy the needed food. No other prospect than that of being slowly worked to death.

It would take me hours to relate the harrowing scenes of cruelty which have come to my notice without my seeking them--scenes exceeding all that my imagination could conceive; and yet the perpetrators of these crimes were Portuguese, English, German, yea, American gentlemen, or civilized and baptized natives.

Nor are the planters alone guilty of slave trade! It is a well-known fact that the expeditions of celebrated explorers were largely composed of slaves, whom their masters had to replace by causing new raids. The native soldiery of European governments is largely composed of so-called redeemed slaves, for the redeeming of whom the government pay special agents so much per head without investigating the manner in which the recruits have been secured.

Railroad companies, too, have indirectly encouraged the traffic. For about one year the Kongo State kept a recruiting officer in Angola trying to outbid the native and Portuguese dealers in human flesh. All the papers in Angola denounced the fact month after month, but those papers are not read outside of Angola. The contract system which in the Portuguese colonies has superseded slavery pure and simple is openly acknowledged by planters, newspapers, and statesmen in Parliament to be nothing but the old slavery legalized under a new name.

The trade in palm-oil, which upholds the British and German navigation companies on the West Coast, is largely founded on slave labor, and would come to a standstill if slavery were suddenly and effectually abolished.

From what precedes it will readily be understood that *native* slavery cannot be abolished by mere legislation. There must be a radical change in the native conception of property, of punishment, of marriage, of kinship, accompanied by a transformation of the social and political order. Arab slavery can be abolished only by subduing Moslem powers, and by converting Mohammedans to Christianity. As to *European slavery,* there is no other remedy than energetic and wise anti-slavery societies, represented on the spot by their own agents, who shall see to it that the wise provisions of national and international laws are not frustrated by the cupidity of planters and residents, or by the neglect of bribe-taking officials.

In concluding this chapter on the status of African slavery we are strongly reminded of a great truth scientifically revealed by the patient work of ethnology. I mean the psychical unity of the human race, the fact that in a given stage of development, irrespective of race, language, climate, and time, mankind shows a wonderful uniformity in conceptions, customs and institutions.

As the mythology of the African Negro differs but little from that of the Greeks and Romans, so the status of African slavery at the present time is almost identic with that of slavery among the Greeks in Homer's and Herodotus' time, and differs in no main point from the slavery of Greece and Roman Italy in the golden age of these two countries.

It may astonish some who know Greeks and Romans only from school-books, that among the ancient Greeks the parents could sell their children; that capture in war, slave-raiding, kidnapping, sale of insolvent debtors and self-sale were also the sources that supplied the system; that the great heroes whom our people are taught to admire were monstrous slave-dealers; that Julius Caesar, for instance, sold on one single occasion in Gaul, 63,000 captives; that in the most glorious times of Athens and Rome the slave population bore to the free the ratio of three to one; that in Sparta the proportion was seven to one; that the Helots were systematically slaughtered by the free citizens to keep down their numbers and their spirits; and that in the Roman empire man-hunting was reduced to a system]in order to supply the deficiency caused by the excessive mortality of the slave population.

ANTI-SLAVERY MOVEMENT IN EUROPE.

On Livingstone's tomb-slab in Westminster Abbey are engraved these, among the last words which he wrote: "All I can add, in my solitude, is : May Heaven's rich blessing come down on every one--American, English, or Turk-- who will help to heal this open sore of the world," the slave-trade.

During his thirty years' pilgrimage through the African bush, Livingstone had again and again appealed to the heart of Christendom for the healing of this open and bleeding sore. About the same time as he, Baker, Speke, Burton, Cameron, Nachtigal and Stanley had revealed the existence of the system and the traffic in all sections of the continent; but over the excitement created by their geographical discoveries, the sufferings of the slaves were lost sight of.

Public attention was about that time absorbed by the civil war in America, then in Europe by the Italian and Prussian struggles, culminating in the Franco-Prussian war.

In the Brussels conference convened in 1876 by the king of the Belgians the abolition of the internal slave-traffic of Africa began to appear in the background, the front-rank being still occupied by scientific and practical exploration.

In 1885 the principal task of the Berlin Conference was to avert European war by preparing the peaceful partition of Africa and laying the foundation of the Kongo State. Yet the act of the Conference declared in article IX that all slave-trade by land as well as by sea, and all transactions connected therewith, were contrary to the principles of human law as recognized by the civilized powers.

As the first Brussels Conference had been chiefly scientific, so the Berlin Conference was mainly political.

It was reserved for the second Brussels Conference in 1889 to be frankly humanitarian and to become the Anti-slavery Conference *par excellence.* In this gathering all the civilized powers, including Turkey, Persia, and the United States, emphatically declared slave-dealing and slave-holding to be crimes; they bound themselves to immediately take measures for the suppression of the traffic within their boundaries, and to prepare the gradual emancipation of all slaves. No doubt the motives of the single governments were interested and rather hypocritical, but the Act they promulgated is, as it stands, the Charter of the African's personal liberty; its provisions are wise and only need to be carried out honestly in order to bring about the final extinction of the traffic and of slavery in all its forms.

It is to be hoped that the clauses inserted with regard to the rum-trade, that other gigantic monster, may be the germ of a new humanitarian Conference which will effectually protect the natives of Africa against the wholesale poisoning to which they are subjected by European and American commerce.

The anti-slavery conference of the powers was in part the result of an anti-slavery movement inaugurated by Cardinal Lavigerie.

At the head of an African pilgrimage, the Cardinal appeared in the summer of 1888 before Pope Leo XIII and eloquently pleaded the cause of the victims of the Arab slave-traders.

The Pope, who had just published his bull "In plurimis," on the emancipation of slaves in Brazil, was well prepared to appreciate the appeal. He commissioned the Cardinal to agitate Europe on this question, and to organize a regular crusade against the Mohammedan slavers. He also supplied him with the necessary funds.

Wherever the Cardinal went, in France, Belgium and England, his addresses drew enthusiastic crowds; $300,000 were subscribed in a short time; thousands of men volunteered to join the Cardinal's new order in the war against the cruel Arabs, and new anti-slavery societies sprang up in France, Belgium, Germany, Switzerland, Austria, Holland and Sweden.

At first the movement professed to be purely humanitarian, but soon it became apparent that the direction of the movement was entirely controlled by the Pope through Cardinal Lavigerie and his assistant Monsignor Brincat; and that the campaign in Africa would be carried on in the interest of the Roman Catholic Church.

This discovery cooled the zeal of many Protestents, who withdrew from the first organizations and started rival Evangelical associations. This Protestant movement was encouraged by the Evangelical Alliance in 1888, at Berlin, and with greater force at the Ecumenical Conference of Florence in 1891. It must be confessed with shame that the Protestants have nowhere waked up to the importance of the questions at issue; and they have not, because they are ignorant of the facts. The Evangelical anti-slavery societies of Germany and Switzerland are doing, or preparing to do, a noble work, but their efforts are dwarfed into insignificance by the systematic, enthusiastic, universal and persistent movement directed by the Pope and supported by the whole Catholic Church. In a single day $100,000 were collected by the Catholic Church for her anti-slavery societies.

In great Britain Commander Cameron tried in vain to organize anti-slavery work. His failure was due, perhaps, to his own personality, and to the military methods he advocated, but also to the existence of the old British and Foreign Anti-slavery Society; that is, in reality, to mistakes of Cameron and to misapprehensions of the public. But few people are aware that the excellent British Anti-slavery Society limits its activity to influencing legislation and governments, and that practical work for the relief of slaves lies outside its programme.

It was at the request of this society that the British government asked the King of the Belgians to convene the great anti-slavery conference in Brussels, and the anti-slavery society took no small share in the deliberations.

Excepting occasional echoes of the European press, this great humanitarian cause has not yet been presented to the American public, and it would, therefore, be premature to blame this country for having done nothing for the healing of Africa's bleeding sore.

If the good name of Protestantism, as a promoter of liberty and happiness is to be preserved, the people of the United States and Great Britain must gird their loins for wise, energetic and successful effort on behalf of suffering slaves in Africa.

In the five years which the powers have had for the execution of the articles of the Brussels Act, much has been done in some lines, but much remains to be done in all lines.

The power of the slave-raiding Arabs in German East Africa and in the Kongo State has been attacked in its strongholds and completely broken. The two governments concerned have shown so much the more zeal as those Arabs were their political and commercial rivals, and the plundering of their stations and caravans proved to be a profitable business. Many hundreds or thousands of slaves have been liberated. Some were turned over to Catholic or Protestant mission stations, but these being unprepared to receive large numbers, the governments could not resist the temptation of compelling these liberated slaves to enlist in their colonial troops or to do unpaid or underpaid government labor on roads, etc., thus reducing them again to some of the worst forms of personal slavery.

In the Nyassa region England has shown vigor in putting down slave-raiding, but in Zanzibar and in West Africa she has winked at the trade as soon as her political interests appeared to be safe.

The provisions of the Brussels Act regarding the rum trade have proved altogether inadequate, while the prohibition to import arms appears more and more to be frustrated by clandestine importation, resulting in the massacre of unarmed populations by scoundrels who managed to obtain fire-arms from smuggling traders or unfaithful government officials.

All the money which the governments of Europe can secure from their parliaments for African work is inadequate for their ambitious schemes of expansion and annexation. Therefore the humanitarian work of civilizing and christianizing the liberated slaves devolves mainly on the charitable societies founded for this special purpose.

The Brussels Act provides that all slaves applying for certificates of freedom shall at once receive them, and that anybody attempting to deprive them of the same shall be punished as a slave-dealer. But owing to the fact that this article is not known among the slaves for whom it was made, I have never heard of one instance where its application was claimed.

The Catholic anti-slavery societies have helped the Kongo State in putting down the Arab slaves by military expeditions; they have built forts and taken weak tribes under their protection, gathering thousands of refugees into new villages and towns; Catholic male and female orders have been entrusted with the education of the large colonies of young freedmen and freedwomen, which the Kongo State is establishing at various points.

The evangelical anti-slavery societies of Germany and Switzerland are still raising money in order to establish refuges and industrial stations for liberated slaves. The German societies have no intention to extend their operations beyond the limits of German colonies. The Swiss society will establish its station in British territory back of the Gold coast.

Compared to the vastness of the field, the aggregate work of all existing agencies is only like a drop in a bucket.

Ethiopia is stretching out her hands unto America, the great, the rich, the mighty, the generous. Shall America be less liberal, less humanitarian, less Christian than little Switzerland, than Catholic Austria, than frigid Holland and Scandinavia? All these countries have no colonies or political interests in Africa, yet as soon as the appeal from Africa reached their ears, rich and poor joined hands in a noble effort to give liberty to the captive, food to the starving, balm to the wounded, light to the benighted.

America is the last to whom the appeal comes. Shall she be the only one to harden her heart and spurn pleading Ham? I hope not.

But what could and should America do in this matter?

PLAN FOR A PHILAFRICAN LIBERATORS' LEAGUE

A society with local branches all over the United States and Canada should be organized for the following purposes:

(1.) To secure first-hand information regarding African slavery and slave trade, the best means to mitigate and extinguish these evils, and the work that is being done in that line by governments and sister societies.

(2.) To disseminate this information through the press and the local branches among the public, and place it before parliaments and governments.

(3.) To watch over the faithful execution of good laws, and prevent the passing of bad laws touching slavery, especially laws tending to substitute forced contract labor for the old form of slavery.

(4.) To help ill-treated slaves to secure the emancipation to which they have a legal right.

(5.) To assist governments in the execution of their colossal humanitarian contract to care for the slaves they are bound to liberate by founding agricultural and industrial settlements of liberated slaves; all this in accordance with the provisions of the Brussels Act.

Here is the proposed

PLAN OF WORK IN AFRICA

(1) Obtain from European governments concessions of land in suitable regions.

(2) Settle on separate lots such liberated slaves as the governments may turn over to the station, or people whose legal emancipation has been secured by the society.

(3) Show these protégés how to improve their methods of agriculture, their house building, their native crafts, and introduce profitable cultivations and industries.

(4) Submit each settlement to a code of rules intended to keep out the chief causes of the African's miseries, namely, witchcraft and witch-doctoring, which is really poisoning, polygamy, rum, idleness, to enforce attendance on public schools and to encourage non-sectarian Christian education.

(5) Put the settlements in charge of an efficient staff of workers, including (a) a superintendent, (b) an agricultural or mechanical genius, (c) a teacher--the latter two to be assisted, wherever practicable, by hired native Christians from neighboring mission stations.*

* *Editorial Note.*--Such a league is being organized, and all persons who intend to join it, or desire more information, can address Mr. Chatelain at 118 East 45th street, New York.

ETNA HOLDERNESS

Native of the Bauca Tribe, West Africa

ETNA HOLDERNESS
Native of the Bassa Tribe, West Africa

Sketch of My Life in Africa

BY
ETNA R. HOLDERNESS
OF THE BASSA TRIBE, AFRICA

It was indeed a surprise to me when I was told that Dr. Thirkield wished me to appear before this assembly and tell the story of my past life. This story, though so simple, shows so plainly the love of Jesus for a poor, ignorant girl, and His wonderful care for me that, if I can honor Him in telling it, I am proud to show how He has dealt with, and used me thus for His cause.

It is supposed that I belonged to the Bassa tribe of West Africa, and that my mother fled from her people and sought protection with a civilized family of the name of Holderness, who lived near Brumley Town, and about fifteen miles from Monrovia. She gave to them her services for shelter and protection for herself and child. When I was not more than two years of age, my mother died, leaving me in the care of this family, who were very cruel to me, and often beat me until my little life became a burden. A little girl who pitied me, urged me to run away and live in the woods and be free from such treatment. This I did, but was hunted down and brought back to even a harder life. Not far away lived a good native missionary whom I had heard was the friend of even unfortunate and harmless little children; so I again ran away, but this time hid under the house of the missionary, where I spent the night.

These good people, the Rev. Anthony Watson and wife, already had several native children in their home, teaching and training them, and, pitying my forlorn condition, took me also under their care, and gave me a share in their hearts and home.

In the shelter of this Christian family I first learned what *home and kindness* meant, and was taught that I had a soul to save, and that Jesus had died even for a poor orphan girl like Etna. These Christian people took great interest in teaching and training us, not only to know the word of the Lord, but also to sew, to cook, to do general housework, and to cultivate and pick coffee, and make garden. The boys were also taught to care for the goats and hogs. I can see the garden now where we used to work, and sing together such songs as--

"Out on an ocean all boundless we ride,
We are homeward bound! homeward bound!"

This, with other sweet songs, we had learned at a mission school taught by W. H. Johnson, one of Dr. Blyden's pupils.

But I have not yet shown you my home and the garden behind it, and the swamp beyond, where the great berry trees grew which the monkeys loved so well, and where they used to feast and chatter. In our garden we raised ginger, coffee, okra, collards, corn, cabbage, potatoes and other vegetables; while around the stick fence were planted orange, banana, and lemon trees. In front of the missionary home was a great lemon tree, and on either side of the path from the door, were rows of coffee with flowers between. In the back yard were oranges, bananas, and lemons, and back of the garden a bread-fruit tree. How sweet a refuge was this to me, a poor, hunted child, and how happy was I there, where I first learned to know and love the Lord.

For a short time I attended the government school, and for another short time attended the mission school for Kru children, taught by Miss Mary Sharp, an American missionary, at Cape Mount; but most of my lessons were learned around the lamp-light at home, with my dear foster parents as the teachers.

At about the age of twelve, I was converted, out in the woods in the good old Methodist way. From this moment there came to my heart a burden of longing to help my poor people, thousands and thousands of whom know nothing of God, or the sacrifice of His Son as our Savior. Yet I realized that I was not prepared for this sacred mission, for my poor mind had as yet only little gleams of knowledge; so I felt that to be really useful I must have the necessary mental training. I took counsel of my Best Friend, and besought him to lead me to an open door. Three years of unanswered prayer passed by, and then in a most unexpected manner, the answer came, and the way opened for me to come to America, toward which land my longing heart had looked, hoping to receive there an education in the schools for the colored people.

The wife of a Presbyterian missionary in Monrovia died, leaving a babe of ten months. At her death she requested that the child be brought back to her mother in Charlotte, North Carolina. When I heard that the father wanted a nurse for this child, I believed that in his need I saw my open door. My dear foster-parents at first opposed my coming, but finally consented, believing that I was led of the Lord and that they must not hinder. So I offered to bring the baby home if Brother Perry would pay my passage. This he agreed to do, and about a week after, on the 28th of May, 1889, we, the baby and I a girl of fifteen years, took passage on the sailing vessel "Monrovia," and after a voyage of forty-two days we landed in Brooklyn, New York. Here we rested for two days and then started for Charlotte, North Carolina, where, after two nights and one day's travel, we arrived safely. In a few weeks the dear little one went home to the mother in heaven, and I was free to look about for work, that I might earn money for my expenses in some good school. I went to Maxton, North Carolina, and entered service, and lived very saving, laying by every penny I could spare for school money. After six months I had quite a little sum, thirty dollars ($30.00), and thought soon I could enter school; but exposure and the climate, to which I was not accustomed, brought on a fit of sickness, and soon the little savings were gone. I must commence again, this time weakened from prolonged illness; but my trust was in the Lord, who had brought me across the sea for some purpose and I did not lose faith or courage. I could not work as before, but canvassed for a book, hoping in this way to keep above want until my strength came again. But this work did not pay me, and I concluded to go to Asheville, North Carolina, hoping to secure better pay for my work. I had again saved $5.00, and with this I tried to enter one of our church schools, hoping for some assistance; but so many were before me, and I, a stranger, with no one to state my case clearly, failed to be understood.

I was afterward offered a scholarship in Shaw University if I would join the Baptist church; and later, a good Presbyterian friend offered to educate me provided I would go back as a missionary from that church. This I could not do, for was not my home in the dear old church of my honored parents? Almost discouraged, I was about to write my father to arrange for my return, for four years of failure had gone by. Then, providentially, I came to Asheville for work, which I soon found.

After I had been here some time I heard of the school at 249 College street, and thought I would make my last effort there. So I took with me two quilts I had commenced in Monrovia (hoping to sell them for my expenses to America), and also my little savings from my wages, and hurried away to the Teacher's cottage, and after telling my story offered my little all as part pay for my expenses in the school. I had asked the Lord to go before me and prepare the way, and He had not failed me, for here I found ready sympathy, and was told to come, and not only attend the day school, but enter the Home also. God was indeed good to me, and I praise Him for this school, which is saving and helping many of the girls of Asheville. My teachers say I am learning, and I hope in two years to go back as a "light bearer," and in the heathen village of Brumley Town establish a school for girls.

There are fifty acres near this town which can be purchased for $15.00 per acre, since most of those claiming it have either died or have gone to other places. My thought is to buy this and cultivate coffee and native fruit, and so sustain the home and school.

I am asking the Lord to give me this land for this work, and He will surely do it, for already, without the asking, some money has come in, and enough more will follow. The first money to come to me for this work was fifty pennies from the children of the primary grade in our school at Morristown, Tenn. They now intend to raise the balance of the $15.00 to buy one acre of the land.

The people of Brumley Town are totally uncivilized, have heathen feasts, devil's dance and grigra bush, a heathen society. But Christ died for them, and I believe they can easily be won for Him. And now my prayer is continually, "Lord, fit me for this work, and go with me to it." Will not you, kind friends and fellow-students, unite with me to ask for this?

JOSIAH TYLER, D.D.

Late Missionary to Africa ; Author of " Forty Years Among the Zulus," and of other valuable works on Missionary and African Topics

JOSIAH TYLER, D.D.
Late Missionary to Africa; Author of "Forty Years Among the Zulus," and of other valuable works on Missionary and African Topics

Missionary Experiences Among the Zulus

BY

JOSIAH TYLER, D.D. AUTHOR AND FORTY YEARS MISSIONARY IN
AFRICA

Mr. Chairman, Christian Friends:

To give you an adequate idea of the great work which has been accomplished in the evangelization of the Zulus of Southeastern Africa, the trials and successes, within the ten minutes allotted to me would be as impossible as to take the largest building in the Exposition grounds and pitch it into the midst of the sea.

The Zulu-speaking people in Africa are more numerous than is generally supposed. In the Natal colony there are about a half million. In Zulu-land, separated from Natal by a small river, there are nearly two hundred thousand. In Matabele-land, which has recently come under the domination of the British South African Company, the estimated population is three hundred thousand. In Gaza-land there is about the same number. In Nyassa-land there is an interesting tribe of Zulus called the Abangoni, which is not so large as the people in Zulu-land. The Free Church of Scotland have an interesting mission among them. Then there is another tribe living at the lower end of Lake Tanganyika which was found by Mr. Stanley, the explorer, when he went into Africa in search of Dr. Livingstone. The last time I saw Mr. Stanley I showed him my photographs of the people in Zulu-land, and compared notes with him. I was convinced that the tribe called the Amazitu was one of pure Zulus. They are cannibals; no missionary as yet has got a footing among them. There is still another tribe of Zulu-speaking people near "The Mountains of the Moon," discovered by Stanley in his trip through "Darkest Africa." Of the Bantu or Kaffir race, numbering at least fifty millions (one-fourth of the estimated population of Africa), the Zulu race stands at the head. They are intellectually bright, and strong of physique, and capable of carrying heavy burdens. They are of different shades of color, from light brown to black, but they prefer the former, or as they say, the black with a little red in it. They have a beautiful language, philosophically constructed and easily acquired. It has some clicks in it which young missionaries have to master in order to speak in it easily and fluently; it abounds in vowels, and is very euphonious, something like the Italian. I will give you the Lord's prayer in Zulu:

"Baba wetu ucsezulwini, mali dunnyiswe, igama lako, umbruso waho ma uzé, intando yako mayewziwe emhlabem lapa n'yeninga sezulwimi. U si pe nambla isinkwa setu, y si zekele izono zitu njeugo tiuna si za ba zekela ezono zabanya. U nga si ngenise ekulingweni, kodwa u si kulule ekwoneni, ngokuba umbuso u ngu wako uamandhla, uobukosi, ku be ngo npakadi." *Amen.*

It took me about a year to acquire the language, but for thirty-nine years I was employed in preaching in that beautiful tongue, and now, while speaking in English, Zulu words will often rush into my mind demanding utterance, and at times I find myself thinking in Zulu.

I would like, if there were time, to speak of the characteristics of the Zulus, and what has been accomplished among them by missionaries in the past fifty years. But I have only time to describe as briefly as possible, the *modus operandi* of raising barbarian Zulus from their barbarism to manhood and christianhood. Take, for instance, a young man as he comes for the first time to a christian station. He waits for you to salute him, the inferior always waiting for the superior to speak the first word. "Ujunanina?" "What do you want?" "Ngiyatanda beusabien jela imali." "I want to work for money." He does not want to become a christian. This is as far from his thoughts as the remotest star is from us. He wants cash to buy a blanket for himself, or a pick (a heavy hoe) for his mother, or to pay the annual hut tax levied by the English government. There he stands before you in his normal state, his head all stuck about with hen's feathers, porcupine quills and snuff spoons, the vertebræ of snakes, love charms, and pieces of crocodile skins and panther's teeth tied about his neck, and the tails of monkeys and other wild animals suspended from his waist. You say he looks like a savage! He is one, a heathen in his blindness. But, my friends, that noble form, that high forehead, those speaking eyes, that volubility of speech, indicating energy, emotion, show that he is a fine specimen of barbarians, one worth working upon. Strike a bargain with him, a pound (five dollars) per month with his food, consisting of porridge made of Indian meal, with a little salt or molasses in it. Set him at work in your garden, or taking care of your house, and you begin to work in him and for him. Take a porcupine quill and point out to him the letters of the alphabet,

[The above article was probably the last literary work of this distinguished author and missionary worker. Unfinished as it is, it has a significance that cannot be framed into words. After having spent forty years of his best life in Africa among the heathen, he is permitted to return to America and attend one of the most remarkable Congresses on Africa ever held here, and to see the beginning of a larger fulfillment of his hopes in the dissemination of missionary intelligence among the descendants of Africans and the preparation of trained missionaries for that benighted land. This unfinished article was accompanied with a letter, dated Asheville, N. C., December 19th, 1895, from which I quote two sentences: "Dear Mr. Thirkield: I took cold while at the Congress, which has terminated in the grippe, from which I am suffering." In a postscript to the same letter of December 20th, from a relative, we were informed that "Mr. Tyler died on Friday (20th) of congestion of the lungs and heart failure."]

[From the new Mt. Pisgah, this servant of God reviewed his journey of forty years in Africa, looked into the future of hope and the enlargement of the Redeemer's kingdom, and was translated from labor to reward.--SECRETARY OF THE CONGRESS].

ALEXANDER CRUMMELL, D.D.
Rector Emeritus of St. Luke's Protestant Episcopal Church, Washington, D. C.; Author of
" Africa and America ;" Missionary for Twenty Years in Africa

ALEXANDER CRUMMELL, D.D.
Rector Emeritus of St. Luke's Protestant Episcopal Church, Washington, D. C.;
Author of
"Africa and America;" Missionary for Twenty Years in Africa

Civilization as a Collateral and Indispensable Instrumentality in Planting the Christian Church in Africa

BY
ALEXANDER CRUMMELL
AUTHOR AND TWENTY YEARS MISSIONARY IN AFRICA

In considering this subject, we have, at the very first, to rid ourselves of an idle fallacy which not seldom has possessed the minds of many good people. For the notion has been held that the special aim of missionary zeal is to fit the soul of a heathen man for heaven, and that this was the finality of a missionary service. The errors of such a notion may easily be seen.

Let us take just here the case of a single heathen man, and I am speaking now from personal experience.

The missionary enters a pagan village. He addresses himself to the salvation of the pagan people around him, and ere long he rejoices in the gain of a convert. The man is a naked pagan. He lives in a rude hut. His clothing is a quarter of a yard of coarse cotton. He eats out of a rude bowl. He clutches his food with his naked hand. He sleeps on a floor, the floor of beaten earth.

By the dint of painstaking effort and assiduity, by careful teaching and solicitude, the missionary has succeeded in lodging the clear idea of God, the principles of repentance and faith in the Redeemer; and the heathen man receiving the great salvation is prepared for heaven.

Now, the question arises, "Is this service of the missionary a finality of duty?" Who here would maintain such a notion? The man, albeit converted, is hardly a quarter of a man. The fact that he has received the Gospel is evidence indeed that he has latent forces which may, under cultivation, raise him inwardly and outwardly to manhood; but as he stands before his teacher he is but a child! A crude, undeveloped and benighted child! A shadow of a man! Child, however, though he be, he is the head of a family. He is a husband. He is a father of children. He is a member of the community in which he lives. He is a laborer among his fellows.

What is to be done with this Christian man-child? Done, not, I mean, as to his inner spiritual condition. For the duty of the missionary in this particular is apparent. The missionary is to follow up the inculcation of divine truth and the flooding his soul with celestial light.

But what is to be done with this convert as to all the external circumstances of his life and being? Is he to be left in the rude, crude, half-animal conditions in which the missionary first found him? Surely not, for Christianity is, in all the ways of life, a new creation. This man-child is to be reconstructed. All the childishness of inheritance is gradually to be taken out of his brain, and all the barbarism of ages to be eliminated from his constitution.

Dropping for a moment the individual convert, let us take a wider view. The missionary ere long meets with other successes. Soon he gathers one or two score or a hundred converts; and a small church springs into existence. But, as in the case of the individual convert, so with this company. They are all nothing more than children, crude, raw, undeveloped, benighted children, nothing but the shadows of men. And in all temporal regards but a step beyond the lives of ancestral barbarism.

What is to be done with these rude, simple creatures? They are indeed to be fitted for heaven; but are they not to be fitted too for earth, for temporal elevation, for a resurrection from animalism? And has not the missionary been sent to them for this very purpose? They have received, it is true, the great salvation by repentance from sin and faith in the Lord Jesus Christ. They have been made, through grace, fit candidates for heaven. But are there not earthly duties and obligations which come home at once to them as members of Christ? Let us for a few moments rest this question just here while we attempt, in a very brief manner, an inquiry into the nature of the Christian system, and the aim and purpose of the Christian faith.

Let me interpose just here two or three principles which seem to me self-evident:

1st. Observe that Christianity is not simply and exclusively individualistic in its purposes.

2d. Christianity does not limit itself to celestial and external interests, but reaches out to temporal regards and achievements.

3d. Christianity in its full normal development implies the highest level of humanity amid all earthly relations.

If these are self-evident truths their bearing on the question would seem manifest. For the inference is quite direct that missionary effort reaches out beyond the conversion of the individual to the organisms of life.

By the organisms of life I refer to the family, to the school, to trades, to industries, to the State.

It seems then somewhat clear that, added on to the duty of personal salvation, comes the farther obligation of the reconstruction of society in its several forms.

For take either of these views of life, the individual or the social, in a heathen community it presents the same dark aspect. In either case it is humanity, maimed, crooked, low and degraded; falling short in every particular of that full development which is ever the aim of Christianity. The heathen convert, convert though he be, is a disorganized being, and needs reconstruction in every segment of his outer being and in every relation of his life. But while indeed the individual man is, in God's sight a large being, the family as an organism is a larger idea than he. And then, in its turn, albeit it is an important organism, yet society at large is greater and more important than the family. And then at a still further advance, the nation has a vastness of importance which is unequaled by either the individual, the family, or society.

The gospel of our Lord Jesus Christ is a grand and majestic economy, which, while taking in, indeed, the individual and his interests, stretches out, with divine and saving intents to the largest, widest circles of human interests below the skies.

But see how degradation dominates the features of these circles of interest in all heathen life!

The taint of heathenism has prostrated and degraded all family life in pagan lands; has debased all human industries to the level of animalism; has robbed the brain of man of every stimulus of noble thought; has shut out from the societies of circles of men the light of letters and the lamps of intelligence; and so, through long ages, ignorance, inferiority and superstition have had a universal and a degrading sway.

All these relations, however, are God's instruments, God's agencies for specific and noble ends on earth. But through ages of ignorance and superstition they have been debased to the level of bestiality! Hence, while the salvation of individual souls is the primal duty of the missionary, the obligation is manifest to lift up, as far and as fast as possible, the whole level of society into order, rectitude and excellence for the honor and glory of God and the progress of man.

It is manifest, however, that the rescue and conversion of individuals does not necessarily carry with it the uplifting and the renovation of the permanent organisms of social life. Godliness and culture, though somewhat related, are not natural correlatives. They have for centuries, in wide states and stages of advancement, stood far apart. Their union, in the progress of man, gives the assurance of reaching the highest planes of earthly superiority.

The aim of Christianity is to lift men up. It avails itself everywhere under right conditions of all providential appliances for this uplifting of degraded humanity.

Civilization is one of the grandest of God's gifts to man. And hence the adjunct of civilization is the needed factor to be added to the process of evangelization in a heathen community. It is only by this process that the grand transition can be made from the rudeness of barbarism.

The primary need, then, is spiritual existence. But then comes the immediate necessity--civilization. "What," it is asked, "do you mean by this word civilization?" I mean by it the clarity of the mind from the dominion of false heathen ideas. I mean by it the conscious impress of individualism and personal responsibility. I mean the recognition of the *body,* with its desires and appetites and passions as a sacred gift, and as under the law of divine obligation. I mean the honor and freedom of womanhood, allied with the duty of family development. I mean the sense of social progress in society. I mean the entrance of new impulses in the actions and policy of the tribe or nation. I mean an elevated use of material things and a higher range of common industrial activities. I mean the earliest possible introduction of letters, and books, and reading, and intelligence to the man, his family, and his social circles.

All this I maintain is the secondary obligation of missionary endeavor among heathen people. This obligation springs from the very nature of the Gospel. Look for a moment at the genius of the Christian faith. First of all observe how it puts upon every regenerate soul the obligation of progress and development. This progress is not simply progress in one section of the human being's nature, nor, on the other hand, is it individual in contrast with social progress. It is inclusive of both personal and organic progress. This progress is to take in the totality of his nature. It is to include the whole of his faculties and his powers. It is to sweep the entire circle of his relations In his heathen state he lived almost a bestial life. In dress, in domicile, in eating and drinking, in the stint and narrowness of his needs, in the low range of his wants and his desires, and in the limitations of his activities, in the relations of household and wife, of parent and children, there is in heathen society the narrowest line of division from the brute creation, the strongest assimilation in the whole trend and tenor of life to the animal.

But with the incoming of the grace of God, comes at once the command for an immediate revolution in all the modes of existence, both within and without. The revolution is to touch all planes of the man's existence. It is to change all the features of his living. Up he is to rise from the animalism of his living and to struggle to manhood. He is to prepare indeed for heaven; but he is to strive to bring somewhat of the heavenly order and excellence into his earthly life; he is to fit himself for the relations and the duties of life. He is to put on the inner garment of salvation; but he is likewise to get, as soon as possible, for himself and wife and children and house and household all the seemly garniture of a new creation, both inward and outward. He is to glorify God in his body as well as in his spirit, which God has given him. This change, moreover, is to reach every section of his personal being. Christianity is a gift for the "sanctification of the whole body, mind and spirit of a man" to the best and noblest purposes. He is to rid himself of the cobwebs of gross, material and degrading ideas. He is to strive after new and elevated thought. He is to get it by the processes of reading, thinking, and intellectual effort; and he is to get the very best possible training, culture, and appointments for the bodily and temporal existence, both of himself and his family.

There is natural obligation to just this productive use of the talents given us, for in the very possession of talents there is always included a commission to use them. In man's natural state this sense of obligation comes tardily and reluctantly. But when the grace of God is given men, then there comes a fiery stimulus to human souls to make our talents, whether two, or five or ten, bring a larger value and a noble fruitage.

Dissatisfaction is thus the very first result of spiritual life in a heathen soul; dissatisfaction with the past slavery of sense, dissatisfaction with the limitations of activity, dissatisfaction with the low planes of subsistence and of life.

The heathen man has no right, in his convert life, to be content with a degraded status and an abject condition.

The primary duty, however, in this wide range of change and transition is the missionary's. He has no right to tolerate content with low conditions. He is under obligation to put judicious but positive discontent into his soul. His duty is, to pioneer his converts into all these new exercises and elevating ventures. But, simultaneously with the unrest which he generates, he must give the spur and stimulus and the revelations which lead to somewhat more human and cultivated in the life of man.

Progress, not passivity, is the law of all evangelization. Heathenism is always morbid and persistent stagnation. Christianity brings a vital, a progressive, and a regenerating spirit to the souls, the homes, and the civil life of all peoples.

This, too, is the genius of the Christian religion in its bearing upon all the organism of human life. It takes hold, indeed, of the single man, but it lays its powerful hand also, and as its rightful possession upon the family, the industries, the community, the tribe, the nation, and all the trades and occupations of life. All these belong to God.

Heathenism has brought them down to degradation and to rot, but the mission of the Gospel is to lift them up from the mire to cleanliness, to order, to spiritual life, to human blessedness. The delusion is ever to be scouted that if the soul be saved, then the Gospel has fulfilled its mission. It is nothing but a delusion. The Gospel never truly takes hold of a man until it has not only mastered the central domain of his being, his soul, but has likewise shaped and regulated the several outer conditions of his life.

It is this mastery of the external as well as the internal state of heathen life which is the ultimate, the final end of missionary endeavor: for Christianity

173

implies the largest development of our faculties; Christianity signifies the uplifting of every craft and technique of industrial activity; Christianity is declaratory of the highest level of humanity.

This redemption, by the cross, of man's temporal condition as the accessory of his spiritual regeneration, is the testimony of history. The Lord Jesus has been everywhere in Christendom since the advent, the life of all souls, and the ransom of all pursuits. Everywhere where this faith of Christ has gone the barbarism of men has declined, and the cultivation of man has increased. Nowhere during these well nigh 2,000 years has the Gospel been divorced from the social and civil advancement of man. On the contrary in all the lands of its progress it has uplifted all the temporal incidents of human condition. It has breathed new life into the intellect of man; it has generated grand commercial activities; it has created most marvelous inventions; it has lifted nations out of the swamps of squalor and up to the highest planes of civility and refinement. It has now such a race of swift and agile glory that the peoples of all other religions of men have been left far behind in inglorious incapacity, so that now, in this year of grace, if you wish to find the imperial man he is the Christian man; if you wish to see the ideal nation, you must steer for the port of some great Christian nation. If you crave the influence and inspiration of some majestic and inspiring civilization, you must put yourself in immediate neighborhood to some grand people under the influence of Jesus Christ.

And all this is intrinsic. It is not casual. It is not the result of an accident. It is not historical coincidence. It is not miraculous intervention. It is that divine education of the great Redeemer which by the marvels of the Incarnation has touched and vitalized all the things of both the inner and the outer world, all the mysteries of the invisible spirits of men, and all the trades and businesses and material activities of human society, and so everywhere has "made all things new," to the glory of God.

Of course I mean nothing absolute in all this. This influence of Christianity has not yet reached its transcendent power in any land, and everywhere in Christendom one sees imperfection, and great limitations of Christian influence. What I mean is that, by comparison, Christianity is the most transforming agency upon the character of men, upon the order and the beauty of families, upon the glory and eminence of nations. The highest excellence in man, woman, races or nations, is Christian.

And this inherent and invariable characteristic of the faith is constantly manifesting itself to-day in all the fields of missions. In every fruitful and successful mission on earth civilization runs a parallel line with the processes of evangelization, and is one of its constant and immediate results.

The instances are many. I shall refer, however, to three well known cases.

(1) When the American Board 60 years ago sent its missionaries to the Zulus, their physical and material condition was on the very lowest plane of rude barbarism. Common sense and an enlightened Christian judgment guided the missionaries in their evangelizing policy. The missionaries saw that God's kingdom among these people was to come here on earth, as well as hereafter, in heaven. They recognized the earthly uses of the faith of Jesus, as well as the heavenly and the eternal. And so while bending every spiritual effort for the conversion of the souls of these poor people, they addressed themselves at the same time to a revolution of their low temporal state, and to the production of practical ends in their physical condition. And what has been the result? Why, the whole plane of their mental, physical and governmental life has been changed, altered, elevated. Schools have been established among them. Tribal rule has been altered to strong national and legal government. Civilized industries have become widely introduced. Mines have been opened, and the entire people, in the increase of its population, in the thrift and cultivation of family life, in the growth of wealth, as well as in the spread of missions, is on the ascending scale of a ripe and flourishing civilization.

(2) Sierra Leone, in West Africa, with its youngest child, the Colony of Lagos, is another conspicuous instance. The West African missions of the Church of England and the English Wesleyans are the direct parents of the grand civilization which has sprung up on that benighted coast. It was the entrance of the word in that whole region, the word preached by missionaries, which has introduced and built up schools, colleges, trades, fine and orderly cities, and that vast trade which commands the rivalry of England, France, Germany and Italy; and which sends from those West African ports almost daily a heavily laden steamer.

(3) Nor must Japan be passed by in this enumeration of the civilizing agency of the Christian faith. For it is a well known fact that the fine capacities and the subtle genius of this great race lay slumbering for ages beneath the spell of narrow paganism. But the missionary came. The divine word from the lips of

devoted men and from the page of sacred writ, was proclaimed; and at once a whole nation awoke to life, to animation, to fertile invention, to ingenious enterprise, to high martial valor. And now it looks as though a nation was born in a day.

Success and Drawbacks of Missionary Work in Africa by an Eye-Witness

BY
ORISHETUKEH FADUMA, B. D.
WEST AFRICA

We are now living in an age of intense missionary activity. The Christian church is realizing more than ever what is meant by "the kingdom of God." The Saviour's commission, "Go and disciple all nations," is studied more closely than it ever was before. From the church are proceeding men and women with consecrated zeal, and lips touched with holy fire, to publish the name of Christ at home and abroad. Where churches have been slow to move, individuals have gone out, depending on personal efforts and the strength of Jehovah. The missionary temperature of the church is rising every year. The spiritual system of that organism of the church whose temperature is not rising is in a bad condition, and needs spiritual life to quicken it to comprehend the commission, "Go ye."

There are now 561 foreign missionary societies obeying the call of the Master to win the world for Christ. Missionary work is no longer tentative. It has become a serious study, a science for all. Throughout the largest universities of the land, are to be found volunteer bands, and chairs on the philosophy of religion and comparative religion, besides annual lectures on missions from returned missionaries. Men and women are not expected to rush heedlessly into the foreign field; they are giving an intelligent study to their prospective fields of labor. There is much which is speculative in the study of the philosophy of missions. Nevertheless, missionary work in this latter end of the nineteenth century has passed, or is passing, from the region of speculation to that of reality, from the stage of uncertainty and experimentation to that of certainty and verification. "The art and the science of missions have been established. The main principles of management are settled; the one work is differentiated into its many branches; the definite aim of missions grows ever clearer to the view. There is no need of haphazard work. The missionary life is no longer a venture, a voyage of discovery, a groping for ways and means. It has become a business, a vocation, a profession."

Missionary work has its successes as well as failures. In attempting to carry out the Divine plan, sometimes the human element fails. The work of human salvation combines the human element with the Divine. As workers we are instruments in God's hand. These instruments are made of various materials, from the polished marble to the rough stone. So long as human instruments are used in the carrying out of God's plan, we need not expect perfection. In pointing out some of the drawbacks of missionary work, I do so in a spirit which is far from critical. I approach the subject with much sympathy, and crave of my hearers the same.

The student of Christian missions, if he approaches his subject in the right spirit, and as he stands confronted with the complicated machinery of the whole system, cannot but wonder at what has been accomplished through imperfect means. Nothing better proves the divine origin of Christian missions than the successes which have resulted from the feeble efforts made and imperfect methods used. The failures or drawbacks are reminders of our need of divine help. If this work of soul-saving were of man, it would have ceased long ago. Because the divine hand is guiding it, we are not discouraged at failures, but are willing to improve when better methods are found out. I regard it as already evident that there are drawbacks in missionary work. A few of these I shall attempt to enumerate and describe:

1. *The Languages of Africa.*--These are innumerable. In the British Colony of Sierra Leone, West Africa, not less than fifty native languages are spoken. In this respect, however, Sierra Leone is peculiar. Nevertheless, for almost every tribe, there is a language in Africa. The language of the Congos differs from that of the Yorubas, the Susus differ from the Yolofs, the Limbas from Fantis, the Eboes from the Houssas. In the northern portions of the continent, the Arabic language predominates. A knowledge of it enables one to travel and speak easily among the people. In the central portions, and reaching as far the Congo, we have the Soudanese, or Nigritic stock proper, whose languages and dialects of languages vary as the tribes. In these regions, the languages differ from those spoken in North Africa, which have a large infusion of Shemitic elements. From Upper Congo to the Cape of Good Hope in the South, we have a peculiar family of the Nigritic stock, the Bantu, with its dental, guttural and labial clicks, or with the letter R dropped off and substituted for L, as is found among the Congos. The missionary is almost tempted to replace these languages by his own, which is easier. He wishes to make a short cut of the languages. But all such short cuts will prove failures. When the disciples were gathered together in Jerusalem during Pentecost, waiting for the baptism of the Holy Spirit, the multitude which assembled out of every nation under heaven, was astonished to hear them speak, each one in the language of his people. Such a thing had never been heard. "How

hear we," they inquired, "every man in our own tongue wherein we were born? Parthians, and Medes, and Elamites, and the dwellers in Mesopotamia, and in Judea, and Cappadocia, in Pontus, and Asia, Phrygia, and Pamphylia, in Egypt, and in the parts of Libya about Cyrene, and strangers of Rome, Jews and proselytes, Cretes and Arabians, we do hear them speak in our tongues the wonderful works of God."--(Acts 2, 6-11.) The African people must hear the word of God in their own language. The English or other European languages are valuable aids in the evolution of the native mind from heathenism to Christianity. They contain treasures in philosophy and the natural sciences with which they cannot very well dispense. Let the white man's language be studied, but not to replace the native. None of the European languages is poetic enough, none is as euphonious, none touches the tender chords of the soul, and makes them vibrate in harmony with the music of heaven and the great heart of God, as the native language, spoken to a native. If God is to be seen, felt, and interpreted, let this be done by the eyes, the ears, and the understanding of the native. The aim and purpose of Christian missions is not to Anglicize, Americanize, or Germanize the world, but to Christianize it. The growth of the soul, in order that it may be fruitful, must be natural. What manifold blessings the English Colony of Sierra Leone and her sister colonies in West Africa would have been in the Christianization of their interior tribes, if, in addition to the study of the English language, the native languages were also studied and reduced to a system in all their schools. As far as I know, no native language is studied in any of the schools in the British Colonies in West Africa, not even in the mission schools. In most of these schools, the students, versed in oriental languages, cannot speak the language of their parents. It is often difficult to have natives as missionaries to the interior. They are as ignorant of the language of their country as the foreign missionary. The age of miracles has not yet passed. The linguistic acquisition in Pentecost may still be a possession of the modern disciples of Jesus. The missionary, in order to be heard and understood, must speak the word of God in the language of the people. Many have done it, and can do it. One of the tests of a call to a foreign field should be the ability to study and acquire languages. It is a natural as well as an acquired gift.

2. Another drawback to missionary work in Africa, is the inability of instructors to distinguish between the natural and the unnatural in the life and thought of the native. Coming into contact with Christian converts, especially along the West Coast, one is pained to see too frequently, an exact reproduction of the white teacher. Native modes of thought, and all those peculiarities of language and manner which ought to differentiate one race from another, are

suppressed. There are exceptions, as the Hon. Rev. James Johnson, a man of strong native individuality, and an excellent type of what is best in an African Christian. The general impression is, that in order to civilize and Christianize the African, he must be foreignized. Hence, one's native name, dress, and food must be changed in order that he may be ranked among the civilized portion of the community. It is too common when a native is admitted into the Christian church, to change his native name, which is not only euphonious, but historical and full of meaning, for a foreign one--English, American, German, or French. The idea is that all foreign names are necessarily Christian, and all native names necessarily heathen. The native Christian has been taught to venerate such names as Voltaire, Paine, Washington. He is baptized into the name of a foreigner instead of the triune God. One finds a long list of Smiths, Joneses, Cokers, and Johnsons in many families. They are names originally given to native converts by some white foreigner, and remind one of similar names given to the American Negro by his master during his enslavement. What is true of names is equally true of dress. The missionary teacher has a foreign dress, therefore his converts to be Christians, must be in the garb of the foreigner. Accordingly, that which distinguishes a heathen from a Christian is not moral character or allegiance to Christ, but outward dress. The stove-pipe hat, the feathered bonnet, the high-heeled shoes, the gloved hands, and all these under the burning tropical heat, make a man a Christian gentleman. The impression of the convert is, that in order to be a true Christian, he must do exactly what the foreign teacher does. For the past one hundred years, we have been confronted with such a training in Sierra Leone, and in all the British West African Colonies. We have had individuals point out these mistakes-Reforms have been started by natives and encouraged by some foreign missionaries, but with little or no effect. Habit has become second nature. Each reformer has left the field saying, "Ephraim has joined to his idols, let him alone." But as one bad seed sowed generates more than one, so in Sierra Leone, the oldest of missionary fields in West Africa, and where this foreignizing process is carried to its utmost extent, it has been productive of much evil. It is already a maxim that everything which is white and foreign is necessarily good. Now that missionary work in Africa is creating so much interest, may I, representing the few who believe in a native Christianity, raise a protest? What Africans need, and what all races need, is not what will denationalize or deindividualize them, not what will stamp them out of existence, but what will show that God has a purpose in creating race varieties. Christianity is a failure if it require a loss of race variety, loss of racial and national life, loss of racial and national thought. It is a failure if it require the native Christians of Japan or India to be the exact picture of their American or English instructors.

Let us have a Christian life and thought expressed in Africa, not after the manner of a Frenchman, an American, or Englishman, but assimilated into African. Let Christianity planted in Africa become native to the soil, growing from within and without, but losing none of its manhood and inherent vitality. I believe in race variety and development. If the Christian religion is not the white man's religion, but the religion of Jesus Christ, having life to support every race, let it have a trial on these ethnic races. There is a variety of life in the animal economy. All flesh is not the same. There is one of birds, another of fishes, and so on. Each is necessary in the organization of that system. In the spiritual life there is and should be a corresponding variety. Every race has a peculiar contribution to make to the sum total of spiritual and moral life. Christianity has not reached its highest achievement until all the races of mankind has brought in their contribution to the foot of the cross.

3. A third drawback in the work of missions is the difficulty of having self-supporting churches. In many cases dependence upon home churches has come to mean a life of parasitism. One of the causes of this dependence is found in a lack of foresight at the beginning of a mission. When natives are made to expect all supplies from outside, it is difficult to convince them that they are expected to support themselves. To begin a mission with large churches, fitted as they are in Europe or America, leaves the impression that the friends of missionaries are very rich. The natives are first astonished at the sudden grandeur and massiveness of their buildings. They pride themselves in them, but cannot keep them up. The best plan would have been to have a small beginning and gradually raise the standard. Begin with what the natives have, however small, and the time will come in the course of their training when they will be able to go up higher. Nothing is more destructive to the self-respect of a native than to place him in a position in which he is always a dependent. While it is true there are cases where praiseworthy attempts at establishing independent and self-supporting churches have been made, yet they are not as many as one would naturally expect. The author of "Modern Missions in the East," Dr. Lawrence, strikes at the root of the matter when he says: "But there has been on the whole, a great failure to attack the problem at the right point, and aim straight for this independence of the native church. Many causes have conspired to prevent this. Among these are:

(1) The necessary inexperience of the early missionaries.

(2) The failure to see that the aim of mission work is not simply the conversion of souls, but the founding of the native church.

(3) An exaggerated estimate of the poverty of the people, and of the difficulty of their supporting their religious leaders.

(4) The unconscious growth, in some cases, of a spirit of domination, which leads the mission too often to exalt itself above the native church."

The same author refers to specific cases of success in planting independent churches in the East, and commends the policy of the American Board, and the Church Missionary Society in India, China, Japan, and parts of Turkey. Writing on the Church Missionary Society's policy in settling the problem of independence and organization, he says:

"The plan is carried out in India, China, Japan and other countries, and has shown itself most efficient. Every church has a native church committee, consisting of the pastor as chairman, and at least three lay communicants. Not more than one-third of the laymen may be paid agents of the society or of the native church. This committee has charge of local affairs. Next above it is a district native church council, consisting of two lay delegates from each qualified church committee, of all the native clergy in connection with the council, and a chairman, usually a missionary, who has a veto on all proceedings. This council receives the funds of all the church committees and all other funds, and disburses from them the salaries of native pastors and other agents. It also makes grants for erection or repair of churches and houses. It sends into the parent society the estimates of expenses, receives report of all work, develops voluntary work, settles all salaries and allowances, and recommends new pastorates. When necessary there is a provincial council, similarly constituted by representation from the district councils. Here, then, is a complete system of native government. The missionary force is sufficiently represented by the chairman, with veto power. All the rest develops the native church. Grants-in-aid are made to complete the amount raised by the councils, but these grants are diminished a certain per cent. every year."

The same author enunciates what may be aptly called "axioms in the science of missions." They are and should be the foundation on which all methods of church organization rest. They are:

(1) "The native church in each country should be organized as a distinct church, ecclesiastically independent of the church in any other country.

(2) "The pastorate of the native church should be a native pastorate.

(3) "The principles of self-control, self-help, and self-extension should be organized in the very organization of the church. To postpone them to the days of strength is to postpone both strength and blessing."

Paternalism in government, whether civil or religious, is destructive to true manhood. It crushes self-respect and independence, and makes men become children. It pauperizes, belittles, and dwindles men into helpless suckling's. It wins thousands of adherents who are at best sycophants and cringers, men who will not dare express their thoughts for fear their missionary masters will be angry at them and cut off their means of living. Paternalism, in the working of missions, is rotten to its very core. "Make the tree good and its fruit good." What the church needs is not quantity but quality. A few independent churches, filled with enthusiasm for saving souls, and reproducing themselves, are worth a thousand times more than the innumerable host of suckling's with which most of our churches are filled.

4. It is a cause for regret that very little, comparatively speaking, has been done in Africa towards the industrial development of the natives by Christian missions. Lack of funds may be at the back of it. But, added to this, is a blindness to what I would term the spirit of the age. The spirit of the age is largely materialistic, not necessarily unspiritual. The church, by failing to introduce and develop the industries in mission fields, seems to be unwilling to recognize God in matter. It seems to think that a man's development is complete when he is religious. It has failed to appreciate the fact that body and soul are linked together in this mundane system. Industrial missions are necessary as a means to an end. For the following reasons they should be encouraged:

- (1) The development of natives.
- (2) The self-support of missions.
- (3) The self-respect of natives.
- (4) A cure to parasitism and sycophancy.

The need of Africa is a rounded Christianity, not a spiritual, nor a physical hypertrophy. The song of the church and of missions for the new century should be *Christ, Tools, and Man.* It should be Christ impressing himself upon the civilized man, ennobling his character, widening his horizon of life, and so transforming him that his sword shall be beaten into ploughshares and his spears into pruning hooks.

5. Another drawback to missionary work in Africa is an adulterated Christianity, a Christianity corrupted by the vices of the foreigner, and the heathen environments of the native converts. The millions of gallons of intoxicating drinks sent to Africa by the white races, often in the same steamer which conveys the missionary of the cross to his chosen field, are a serious hindrance to the spread of a pure civilization and Christianity. The missionaries of the cross take the Bible, the missionaries of Satan take barrels of whiskey and rum. When once the latter precedes the former, the mind of the native is so stultified that it is almost impossible to make any good impression upon him. In the civilized portions of West Africa there are natives engaged in selling intoxicating drinks, who justify themselves in the act because the distillers are men from Christian nations. European officials indulge in bacchanalian revelries with natives. Native chiefs and princes are approached by civilized foreigners, and tokens of friendship exchanged through the cup which poisons. The church, Christ's representative on earth, is not free from the vice. It is not uncommon to see members of the church who are drunkards. Throughout the villages of Sierra Leone there are private societies which convene on Saturdays. They are composed of men and women whose pastime is rum and whiskey. In marriage and burial ceremonies, and on the birth of a child, rum and whiskey crown the table. The priesthood is not strong in its condemnation of the practice. Many ministers cannot condemn it for conscientious reasons. In Sierra Leone, a bold and earnest champion of total abstinence is the Rev. J.C. May, principal of the Wesleyan High School, who with his late father is well known throughout the community as such. The bishop of Sierra Leone, Dr. Ingham, has rendered effective service in the temperance platform, and has set a worthy example to both native and foreign officials. For the interest of the Redeemer's kingdom, our foreign missionary boards should see to it that none but total abstainers are sent to the foreign fields. The Christian church is itself and ought to be a temperance organization, but experience has shown that even the church is weak in enforcing and teaching strict temperance principles as they relate to strong drink. Specific diseases require specific remedies. The readiness of natives to imitate foreigners because they are expected to be good, is a sufficient plea why, in addition to the qualification of a man for foreign missionary work, he should be a man who has a dislike to the wine cup and all narcotics.

Civilization has its virtues as well as vices. It is, therefore, not to be wondered at when I refer to the vices of the white man in Africa. In the French, German, Portuguese and English colonies, illicit relations with native women, and bastardy, are common. Polygamous white men are becoming too frequent. Sometimes alliances with daughters of influential heathen natives are made in order to get the trade of the people. Bastard children are sometimes sent to mission schools in the field, and sometimes educated abroad. The white fathers, representing as they do Christian nations, have thus placed mighty obstacles in the way of the gospel.

One more form of an adulterated Christianity deserves mention. It is the commingling of heathen and Christian conceptions. It is Christianity heathenized. Native converts just emerging from heathenism, seldom get rid of their heathen ideas. They make a kind of Christians. One hundred years of Christian missions in Sierra Leone have not entirely wiped off heathen notions from the minds of Christians. Some would, if they could, introduce polygamy into the church, just as the Mormons have tried to do in the United States of America. Secret charms and spells are believed to have some influence upon the lives of men. As with the people, so with the priests. It requires men of strong individuality to rise above their environments. There are few men who are scientific enough to see through the follies of heathen beliefs. It requires the work of more than one generation to do this. Men's minds are too conservative to quickly renounce the teachings and environments of their childhood. Paul, the Christian apostle, was tinged with Rabbinical thought. James was Christian, but he leaned toward Judaism. Some of the Pauline epistles contain Gnostic errors with which the air was charged, and which threatened to destroy the purity of Christian truth by amalgamating with it. Christian teachers in the early age of the church, could not escape the infection of Platonic thought, which is even traceable in our modern theology. Not that heathen thought is necessarily impure and antagonistic to Christianity, but that because it is heathen, it requires constant watching. In India, the weakness of Christians is caste feeling. In the United States of America, it is color prejudices, another form of caste. It requires time and persistent effort to educate men and get rid of these impediments. The native converts, therefore, need instruction and careful oversight. The leaders of the people should be men who are well-informed, and acquainted with what is best in Christian thought and life, but above all they should be men of sanctified common sense.

6. Another drawback to missionary work in Africa is denominational rivalry. In this we have a repetition of the mistakes of the home fields. It is a common sight in these United States to find from three to four kinds of the same denomination in the same field, all of them weak churches, when one would do better and be self-supporting and propagating. Not that these churches differ in creed or government, but each has something peculiar, which it means to emphasize at any cost. The co-operative system in foreign missionary work has not been sufficiently attempted. A careful division of fields, and co-operation when needed, would solve many difficult problems in native church government. When one looks at the extent of territory still untouched, it seems like ignorance of the mission of the church to go into places already occupied and attempt to oust another church. It does not seem like sincerity and earnestness to save souls, when one is confronted with such sights. There would be better native schools and organized churches if the Christian Church could be more economical in the distribution of its resources. Denominational rivalry with its opposing creeds is confusing to the native mind. It would certainly be a Day of Pentecost to the Christian Church when she can unite all her forces and do battle for the Lord; when narrow bigotry and religious intolerance will vanish because the Christ spirit has permeated the whole Christian life; when the disciples of Christ shall emphasize life and character in such a way that a man's creed does not become a hindrance to his usefulness; when societies will be large hearted enough to turn over their fields to others who can work them better, and betake themselves to regions beyond, where men and women are crying, "come over and help us"; when there shall be a return to apostolic church government, and we shall hear, not of the *churches,* but the *church* in Egypt, the church in Sierra Leone, the church in Lagos, the church in Natal, the church in Gazaland. Surrounded with all these drawbacks, we can triumph over them when there is a unification of all Christian forces, when the Christian church sets out to conquer the world for Christ, having one aim and purpose, because it has one Lord, one faith, one baptism.

PART II.--SUCCESSES.

We now turn our attention to some of the successes of missionary work in Africa. In making reports of missionary success, it is common to refer to statistics. The number of school and church buildings erected, the number of native and foreign missionaries, the number of converts and baptisms--all these give a bird's-eye view of what has been really accomplished. This quantitative method of estimating missionary progress is often too dry for the lay reader, and gives very inadequate and misleading accounts of the situation. Says Dr. Judson Smith, the foreign secretary of the American Board, in his report of October, 1893: "It must be remembered that much of the most significant results of missionary work finds no place in statistics. The heroism, and patience and indomitable hope and all-enduring love which marked the laborer in all these fields, and which shed undying luster on the Christian name, no figure or words can duly express. The patient and persistent inculcation of Christian truth, the gradual but widespread diffusion of the light and life of the gospel through the dense darkness of paganism and death, the slow emergence of the Christian home and the Christian society beneath the labors of the missionary and the brooding spirit of God--these are great and inspiring facts, though our statistics scarcely breathe a hint of them." Everyone who is acquainted with missionary work testifies to the truth of the above statements. I shall take the qualitative method, which refers less to figures, but more to men, leaving the statistical summary to other hands than mine. Missionary successes in Africa may be indirect and direct.

Indirect successes are often preparatory to Christianity. They are the John the Baptist crying in the wilderness, heralding the advent of the Saviour, and making rough places smooth. Some of these are:

1. Exploration. The modern study of Africa is interesting on account of the treasures of information which it contains. Some of these have been furnished by pioneer missionaries. The world is indebted to those explorers through whose labors Africa has come to be regarded as the continent of the future. The Landers, Speke, Grant, Cameron, Du Chaillu, Moffat, Livingstone, Stanley, Mrs. French-Sheldon and others are among the pioneers of Africa's redemption. It was when he was in Africa that Stanley understood what missionary work was accomplishing for the upbuilding of the natives. Hitherto he had been a skeptic. The conversion of many skeptics would be possible, if they could be influenced to cease speculating on the salvation of the heathen, for a face-to-face and hand-

to-hand experience, such as Stanley had. Foremost of all modern and indirect attempts to civilize and Christianize Africa, is the foundation of the Congo Free State by King Leopold of Belgium. The death of his son gave the occasion. The founding of a "Free State" in West Central Africa for the amelioration of the continent, was the best way he thought he could build a statue for his son. By this scheme, there was made a communication between the waters of the West Atlantic and those of the Upper Congo, roads were opened from the coast to the interior, interior lakes and rivers were made navigable by steamers of light draft. The leader of this scheme was Stanley, who sought the coöperation of civilized powers. At the international conference held in Berlin the object of the scheme was stated. It revealed the broad heart of Leopold. The object was "to open up into the interior of the African continent a broad road for the moral and material progress of its native races, and for the development of the general welfare of commerce and navigation." It also gives protection to all traders and missionaries without distinction as to creed, color or nationality. It makes it possible for the church to enter in and possess the land for Christ. Now may be found on the banks of the Congo the missions of the American Methodist Episcopal church, Bishop Taylor's self-supporting missions, the American Baptist, and others.

2. Commerce is another successful missionary agent which is preparing the way for Christianity in Africa. Foreign languages and modes of living are introduced among native tribes in a way which tends to remove the heathen a few degrees from barbarism. The arts of civilization are being introduced among the natives. Wearing apparel, household furniture, Birmingham wares, Sheffield cutlery, looking glasses, and beads are silent but true forces in preparing the uncivilized man for civilization. In fact, these articles of commerce are what Christian civilization is contributing in indirect ways towards the upbuilding of Africa. France, England, Germany, Spain, Portugal, Italy, and America are thus molding Africa for Christ. We are living in a materialistic age. The Christian merchant in Africa has proved to be a valuable adjunct to the missionary. The world was not created by leaps. It is a progressive plan of God's work. A *terra firma* was necessary for the habitation of man and the lower animals. Herbs were necessary before animals were created. The lower animals were before man, the masterpiece of creation. We see in his creation divine forethought. Christianity thrives most where Christian civilization has preceded it.

3. A third tribute to missionary success is the partition of Africa among foreign nations. The total area of land in Africa is estimated at 11,514,500 square miles. Of this amount, about one-tenth, or 1,500,000 square miles, is

appropriated by foreign nations. Of the three hundred millions of people, about one-sixth, or fifty millions, are under foreign influence. In many cases appropriation is merely nominal, yet to a large extent the power of foreign influence is felt. The civilization of Africa is therefore varied. Already may be seen native Africans who bear upon them the impress of the French. It is the result of the French colonies in Africa. In colonies such as Sierra Leone, Cape Coast, Lagos, Gambia, South Africa, the natives speak not only the English language, but read and write it, and imitate English manners. We are confronted in Africa with a multiform civilization. Liberia is America in Africa. Her government is American, her text-books are American. The civilized Christian nations have thus been contributing some of those forces which make a people Christian. This is practically a trial of Christianity. It is a reflection upon Africa of what Christianity has done to the white races. If the Christianity of the Old and the New World is pure and wholesome, its reflex life upon the natives of Africa will be the same.

4. The school house is also tributary to missionary success. Much has been said of the waste of money in mission fields in the training of men and women who are never employed as mission agents. It is a very selfish and narrow way of estimating success. Whether or not men are fitted in these schools for a preaching life, it will be found out on careful examination that these schools have furnished good leaven to native society. Exceptions may be found where men have become opposers of Christianity, but this is not due to the fact that they were trained in these schools, nor is it necessary to close these schools in consequence. Much more good than harm is done by education. It expands the intellect, and leaves men more prepared to receive the truths of Christianity. Christianity and the intellect are not enemies. They should never be divorced from each other. In the preparation of humanity for Christ the ancient nations of Egypt, Chaldea, Rome and Greece contributed. Philosophy, science and art have helped to expand men's minds. Plato, Seneca, Marcus Aurelius and Aristotle, heathen though they were, uttered truths which were not antagonistic, but preparatory, to Christianity. Roman law made it possible for the spread of Christianity for a considerable time. Christianity did not spring into the world of a sudden. In this work of the expansion of the intellect, the schools are doing much indirectly to make the gospel intelligible to the native mind.

But there are also direct agencies at work for the conversion of Africa.

1. The school house is both indirect and direct as an agent. It is like a two-edged sword, and cuts both ways. The mission school is often the training ground of the exhorter, prayer leader, and evangelist. From it the first lessons in Christianity are learned. It is not founded merely to expand the intellect, it plants the seeds of righteousness. Scattered over mission fields are schools of the latter type. They can be counted by the hundreds. Often the only education that can be had comes from the mission school. In Sierra Leone and along the West Coast, our native officials and merchants are invariably products of the mission school. From it the native school teacher and minister have their training which fits them for service.

2. The mission church stands first of all in importance. It is the nursery of the future self-supporting and self-governing native church. In the older fields the Church Missionary Society and the Wesleyan Methodists along the West Coast are leading the people to support, at least in part, their native churches. The American Board of Foreign Missions has already reported self-supporting churches in Benguela. The South African fields, both English and American, show encouraging results. Encouraging news comes from East Africa. There is an increased desire among the heathen to hear the gospel preached.

3. The translation of the Bible into the languages of the people is an encouraging sign of progress and success. The leading tribes in West, South and East Africa, are now reading the Bible in their own tongues. The printing press is speaking, though silently. The Yoruba, Eboe, Mendi, Fanti, Congo, Zulu, Tonga, Shutswa, and other African tribes, have the whole or portions of the Scriptures already translated. The work of translation calls for the best talent from Christian countries. The knowledge of other languages than the English, is often desirable in the translation of the Bible for the natives. It does not require less culture than the translation of the English Bible from Greek and Hebrew. Side by side with the translation of the Bible are reading books and catechisms for the use of schools. Thus, gradually, a native literature is evolved.

4. The Christian lives of natives show to what extent the gospel has been a success. Converts from heathenism holding firmly to their new profession, in the face of persecution and social ostracism, are trophies which many a mission field has produced. Christian heroism is as true in Africa as anywhere else. The life of Samuel Adjai Crowther, of the Yoruba Tribe, the first native bishop in West Africa, is a life of Christian devotion and courage, a life of Christian humility and sanctified common sense. There is to-day in some of our mission fields in

Africa a galaxy of native preachers, doctors, lawyers and artisans who are a credit to their people and to Christianity. For all these we exclaim, "Not unto us, O Lord, not unto us, but to thy name give we the glory."

Of Christian missions in Africa, I speak as an optimist and a believer in Africa's redemption. The next century will witness wonderful developments in most of the missions, if the church will continue to work and pray for the extension of God's kingdom. I repeat the soul stirring and prophetic words of Dr. Judson Smith, uttered at the annual meeting of the American Board at Worcester, Mass., two years ago: "These missions, small in themselves, some of them but recently planted, the oldest and most successful only in the morning of its productive life, all belong to a movement which is one of the most sublime in the world's history, the effort of the Protestant nations to make a Christian and civilized world out of the Dark Continent. Compared with what must yet be done to set the light of God on every mountain side, in every valley, by every lake and river, in every home and in every heart of this mighty continent, all that has been accomplished is but the beginning. But the march has begun and the goal is distinctly in view, and its meaning grows more clear with every wheeling year. Amid all the stir and activity, in politics and commerce, in exploration and occupation, by which the leading powers of the world are vying with one another to cover and appropriate to themselves the resources and power of Africa, this aggressive advance of evangelizing forces is the supreme movement of the times, and holds in plastic hands the long and glorious future of the nations that one day are to fill and adorn these lands with a varied and progressive life and with a Christian civilization."

The Absolute Need of an Indigenous Missionary Agency for the Evangelization of Africa

BY
Alex Crummell, D.D.
AUTHOR OF "THE FUTURE OF AFRICA," AND TWENTY YEARS A MISSIONARY IN AFRICA.

The planting of Christianity, by missions, is virtually the attempt to put an exotic element in a foreign and an alien field, and to make it indigenous therein. It is not exactly an act of grafting; for in that process the graft is the smaller agent, has the minor gift to make, and has to draw its major strength and vitality from the original stock.

Missionary work, on the other hand, is the endeavor to bring a high, noble and an eternal life into a region of stagnation and death. It is the attempt to introduce a divine and heavenly spirit into a province at once repellent and discordant. It is the endeavor to secure affinities between opposites of a most absolute nature. It is an undertaking to produce concord and harmony between elements of a most diverse and incongruous character. It is an aim after the adjustment of divine and human qualities, the one reaching upward to the heavens, and the other tending, with determined proclivities, to disaster and ruin.

The bare statement of the case discovers its prodigious difficulties. Consider the unnatural inherited ideas of heathen life; consider the master convictions which rule their being; consider the almost absolute animalism which has subjugated body, mind, and spirit; consider the crude springs of action which stimulate their general life; consider the dominant superstitions which master their spirit life; and consider the rude, uncouth language which is the vehicle of their narrow and stunted thought.

All this discloses somewhat the wide distance of the missionary from the heathen populace which surrounds him on his settlement in a pagan land, for the work of the gospel. Here, then, we see the bridge which, at the very start, the missionary has to cross. He wishes to enter the domain of the heathen mind; but the entrance is closed, the door is locked. Moreover, the pagan has no sympathetic desires for the spiritual message of the missionary. There may be curiosity, there may be surprise; but in the proclamation of the truth of the gospel these special hindrances are sure to arise:

First, the bar of settled custom and the prejudice which follows; second, the formidable barrier of language; and, third, the natural repugnance to divine truth and the opposition it always breeds. How is this immense barrier to be crossed?

1. It seems evident to me that, from the very nature of the case, the native man, as far as possible, is to be used as the agency for conveying the new truths to his fellows:

So soon as the faith has become a deposit in the souls of converts, these converts, simple though they be, will without doubt have the easiest access to the minds of their own people. For it is not theology which is the first gift of missions to the heathen. No multitude of dogmas are needed for them to lay hold of the salvation of the cross, to live a holy life, or to get to heaven.

The message of salvation is the simplest, plainest, most apparent of all things; easily understood, when put in clear, plain, apt words, in the vernacular. The message of the gospel is "repent" and "believe in Christ." All men, the rudest of men, have sinned and regretted or sorrowed over their sins; and hence they can take in, at once, the call to repentance. So, too, all men have believed. The exercise of trust or credulity is universal in all human society. Hence all men apprehend at once the requirement of belief, when the proper object is convincingly set before them, when the demand is clearly made upon them.

Whatever hindrances then, whether of ignorance, or inaptitude, or mental disharmony, or racial incongruity, or, more especially, of lingual divergence, may exist on the part of the missionary, and which, as a consequence, prevents his effective delivery of the great message, these, to a large degree, are neutralized by the use of the native language, from the lips of intelligent native converts. For the native convert knows his people; knows their mind; knows their modes of thinking; knows their prejudices and passions; knows their rude primal faith; knows its abiding roots and its normal elements; knows the tiny rivulets by which it chimes in, in some minor ways, with the new religion; knows the primitive moralities of his own people, which need no effacement, but simply the breath of renovation from on high; knows the springs of action which move and stir and stimulate the lives of his kinsmen; knows all this as well as the regenerative process and power which have made him a new creature in Christ Jesus; and hence, with his minute acquaintance and his lingual facility, he is fitted at once to carry the message of salvation to the hearts and homes of his people.

193

In fine, it seems manifest that by knowledge, by sympathy, by kindness and sentiment, by his ready tongue and his evangelical spirit, the simplest native man, if pious, is by far the most facile agent for the propagation of the faith, and cannot too soon be brought into the service of the Master.

This necessarily may be regarded as an almost universal condition. The exceptions most likely, from the very nature of the case, will be exceedingly rare. For these two things are manifest: (1) that most men know the spirit of their own race better than strangers do, and (2) that most people know their native tongue better than foreigners.

2. But now, casting aside theory, we get both prestige and assurance for our position from the policy of the apostles, and the methods of the first propagators of the gospel. That policy is disclosed to us in the Acts, and incidentally in the Epistles.

And here, first of all, it is to be noticed that the apostles strove, from the very first, to make Christianity native and indigenous. They used every possible device to plant the church in the sentiment and spirit of the people they preached to. They strove to put the terms, the formularies, and the dogmas of the faith into the vernacular of the new people who were willing to receive the gospel. Jews themselves, they rose up to the altitude of a sanctified self-abnegation. They made everywhere the endeavor to divest the new faith of the old and worn-out garments of Judaism, and to give it as much as possible the forms, features and complexion of native life, in the several countries where they preached the gospel.

St. Paul is the foremost exponent of this grand Christian statesmanship: "And unto the Jews I became as a Jew, that I might gain the Jews; to them that are under the law, as under the law, that I might gain them that are under the law; to them that are without law, as without law (being not without law to God, but under the law to Christ), that I might gain them that are without law." I. Cor., 9: 20-21.

Here we see the principle which guided the passage of the gospel from its Jewish environments into the Gentile world. The point of divergence was on the occurrence of the vision of St. Peter in the case of Cornelius. From that time the apostles went everywhere, preaching and founding churches; and in every instance where a group of disciples were converted, they took these crude, simple people, organized them into churches, and put all the several functions of the church into their hands.

They were but seldom people of the cultivated circles. Christianity ran its first course, and for a long period, among the outcast, the despised, the unnoticed people. It gathered its recruits chiefly from the common people. Turn to I. Cor., 1: 26-28, and see the description of the first disciples given by St. Paul:

"For you see your calling, brethren, how that not many wise men after the flesh, not many mighty, not many noble, are called; but God hath chosen the foolish things of the world to confound the wise; and God hath chosen the weak things of the world to confound the things which are mighty; and base things of the world, and things which are despised, hath God chosen, yea, and things which are not, to bring to nought things that are."

Up from such bodies of simple men sprung the first preachers of the gospel. On the very first persecution of the Christians, on the martyrdom of Stephen, these simple disciples became scattered abroad. They traveled abroad as far far as Phenice and Cyprus and Cyrene and Antioch, preaching the word, at the first to Jews only. But we are told that when they reached Antioch they spoke unto the Grecians. But it will be noticed that immediately, on the organization of the churches, they took the simple material and "ordained them" elders in every church; and with prayer and fasting commended them to the Lord on whom they believed. There was, as is evident, no time for formal, systematic, theological training. The organization of churches, the setting up of a ministry, were both extemporaneous, informal, conformable to immediate necessities.

The same fact shows itself most clearly in the charge of St. Paul to Titus:

"For this cause left I thee in Crete, that thou shouldst set in order the things that are waiting, and ordain elders in every city."

This principle of availability is visible almost everywhere in the Epistles. The apostles, under the direction of the Spirit, seized upon every useful power discoverable among their converts. This may be seen in the variety of offices and functions in the different churches.

In Ephesians 4:7 St. Paul declares: "But unto every one of us is given grace according to the measure of the gift of Christ." And to this he adds, in the 11th and 12th verses: "And he gave some, apostles; and some, prophets; and some, evangelists; and some pastors and teachers, for the perfecting of the saints, for the work of the ministry, for the edifying of the body of Christ."

Now turn to the First Epistle of St. Paul to Timothy, the third and fifth chapters, and also his Epistle to Titus, and you will see at a glance every indication of the fact that the elders, teachers, helpers of the apostolic church were men and women of the humblest position and of the greatest simplicity alike of culture and of manners and learning.

And from all this the inference is the clearest that, just the reverse of our modern system of missions, the ranks of the ministry were filled up from native sources. Instead of long continued supplies of new missionaries to the field, men were made to spring up from the bosom of the new Christian community; to assume ministerial duties, and then to carry the gospel to outer heathen provinces, and so spread the great salvation to benighted peoples.

The history of modern missions gives us facts of the most confirmatory nature in evidence of the position here taken. These facts are both negative, on the one hand, and positive on the other.

(1) We will take the negative first, and we shall find them full of light and instruction.

(a) Turn to the Roman missions in the Kingdom of Congo. The Portuguese entered that country in the 14th century. They baptized thousands of their converts. They built churches and cathedrals and monasteries. They secured the allegiance and submission of successive kings and princes and the great nobles of the land. They got complete control of all the interests of the country, both secular and religious.

They suffered no interference of other religionists. They had the clearest field conceivable for the working of their system.

What has been the fruit of Roman effort and Roman mastery? Nothing but utter and disastrous failure. The Kingdom of Congo is as much pagan to-day as it was 200 years and more ago! Their multitudinous baptisms have proven fruitless and empty effusions. Their numerous churches and cathedrals have either crumbled to dust, or become the abodes of bats and owls, of serpents and lizards.

And the children of their seeming converts, from generation to generation, down to the present, have remained naked pagans, devotees of fetichism, and the abject victims of degraded greegreism.

And the cause of this utter collapse of effort, this useless expenditure of force, is manifest. The Roman church has failed for the simple reason that she has been willing to remain an exotic in the land of the Congo! She has been satisfied with an alien life, amid a foreign population! She has been content to abide as an extraneous element in the rudest of heathen people. She has never had the wisdom to create a Congo church by entering into the thought, the sentiment of the Congo people; by raising up a native ministry, and lodging the Christian faith and the word of God in the native language of the people whom they had conquered.

What is true of the Church of Rome in Africa is true, though to a far less degree, of the Church of England in India.

The English church seated herself in the Indies at an early day, subsequent to the days of Clive and Hastings. No one can deny the grand eleemosynary and educational and civilizing work which, in conjunction with the state, that church and people have done in the abolition of suttee and Juggernaut; in the prevention of child-murder; in the deliverance of the Indian people from the terrible exactions of heathen kings, princes and rulers; in the enlargement of industrial activities; in the wide facilities for the education of children; in the introduction of colleges and learning and culture; in the creation of new and higher wants among the masses; in all these and several other respects, the church and people of England have uplifted the peoples of India to a plane of elevation never known before in all their histories.

All this is, without doubt, a glorious record. And yet, notwithstanding these large and pervasive benevolences, see on the other hand the sad limitations of the English church. For there stands the stark and naked fact that with the grandest opportunities, the Church of England has not succeeded in nationalizing the church of God amid the multitudinous populations. Missions abound, but they have no considerable native ministry; they organized no native church; they have not entered widely into the vernacular.

Work and service and sacrifice have been abundant, but the Christian faith has not reached the status and the strength of nationality, or the feelings of the people, in their sympathies. It is still the church of England; it has yet to become the church of India.

Now let us turn to a more pleasing aspect of this matter. Look, first of all, at the work of this same church of England in West Africa. It began this work but little more than a century ago, at Sierra Leone. The objects of its solicitude were the simple, naked re-captives from the holds of slave-trading vessels; but it began at once with the endeavor to reach the mind, the sentiment and inner spirit of these peoples by two simple processes, viz.: (1) The employment of native helpers, and (2) the translation of the Scriptures and the formularies of the church into the native languages of these re-captive people.

A large native ministry has been raised up from among them--deacons, priests and bishops--the church in its completest form. But long before this native catechists and readers and lay assistants were sent forth to teach their people; and the assistance of this indigenous agency is employed down to the present.

And the fruits of this national and common-sense policy is the creation of a native church and a native ministry in the native languages of the West Coast and in the interior, at Sierra Leone, at Lagos, in the interland, at Abbeokuta, at Ibadan, and for hundreds of miles along the banks of the Niger, in divers tribes and kingdoms, reaching out gradually but surely to the vast millions in the central quarters of the continent.

The work of missions in Natal, under the direction of the "American Board" of the congregational body, is equally suggestive and equally confirmatory.

Sixty years ago the Zulus were a savage people, dominated by idolatrous practices, living in miserable huts, roaming wild in the wilderness, low and degraded in personal and family habits, given to tribal feuds and sanguinary fights.

The missionary from New England came among them, and the native people in large numbers were converted. But the very first impulse of the missionary was to avail himself of the best resources and high capacities of his converts. And now, according to the reports furnished by the American Board for 1895, while there are but 32 foreign missionaries and teachers, male and female, no less than 408 teachers, pastors and helpers are engaged in spreading the gospel among these people.

The like practical wisdom is seen in the conduct of missions to Fijians. At an early day the native convert was made to assume the responsibility of a a missionary and a teacher to his own people. Care was taken to lift these people out of a stipendiary relation to a foreign missionary society. Immediately on their conversion they were taught the privilege and the duty of service to Christ, the obligation to labor for the conversion of their kinsfolk.

And so it came to pass that native preachers, native teachers, are the main agency in the evangelization of those Islands. The foreign element is hardly known among them. Among the ministers only *one* is a foreigner. Six ordained ministers, aided by 310 local preachers, carry on God's work in the entire circuit of the Islands.

M. C. B. MASON, D.D.
Assistant Corresponding Secretary of the Freedmen's Aid and Southern Education Society

M. C. B. MASON, D.D.
Assistant Corresponding Secretary of the Freedmen's Aid and Southern
Education Society

The Methodist Episcopal Church and the Evangelization of Africa

BY

M. C. B. MASON, D.D. ASSISTANT CORRESPONDING SECRETARY
FREEDMEN'S AID AND SOUTHERN EDUCATION SOCIETY

We live in a day of missionary enterprise and enthusiasm. Christian missionaries are found upon all shores, and the white sails of Christian commerce are spread upon all seas. Upon no land has the Christian thought of our day been so intensely fixed as upon Africa. Her salvation is the central thought of every Christian church, the burden of every Christian nation. Never before in the history of mankind has there been such widespread interest in this old land of the Sphinx and the Pyramid as there is to-day. Not even when Pharaoh enslaved Israel and Moses demanded their deliverance, when Hannibal's army crossed the seas to contest the power of the Cæsars, when Rome boasted of her civilization, and Cleopatra's barges floated the Nile, or when Christian culture and refinement in the days of Cyprian and St. Augustine sent a flood of light around her northern belt, and the world's scholars flocked to her great library at Alexandria, never before in the history of the world has there been such widespread interest in Africa as there is today. All the world, it would seem, recognizing her previous work for civilization and conscious of its indebtedness to her, is turning toward her with a helping hand for her uplift and evangelization. Robed in superstition and buried in ignorance today, she was not always thus. She was once the cradle of civilization, the mistress in the arts and sciences. Her sculptured maidens in the British Museum, hieroglyphics on Egypt's pyramids, inscriptions on tombs and monuments long since buried, now happily resurrected, these silent witnesses from the dust bear unquestionable testimony to her wonderful greatness and intellectual advancement. Sir Henry Rawlinson, in his great work on antiquity, in speaking of what Africa has done for the civilization of the world, says:

"For the last three thousand years the world has been mainly indebted for its advancement to the Indo-European and Semitic races, but it was otherwise in the first ages. Egypt and Babylon, Menes and Nimrod, both descendants of Ham, led the way and acted as pioneers of mankind in treading the fields of art, literature, and science. Alphabetic writing, astronomy, chronology, history, navigation, sculpture, textile fabrics seem all of them to have had their origin in one or the other of these countries." The inventors of any art are among the greatest benefactors of the race, and mankind at the present day lies under infinite obligations to the genius of these early ages. "Even Central Africa," says a noted writer, "boasted not only of its antiquity but of its intelligence as well, for if the legends tell the truth, while Orpheus was charming the forests into life and Hesiod was tracing the genealogies of the gods and weaving nature and time into song, and Homer was singing the wars of the Greeks and the wanderings of Ulysses, then the bards of Nigretia were celebrating the exploits of their heroes and publishing the record of their renown in the ears of listening kings and admiring nations."

The contention, in our day, of the civilized nations for the partition of her territory for commercial advantage, and the means and appliances necessary to the prosecution thereof, tend not only to revive her dormant life, but are indications of providential preparation for her salvation and enlightenment. And as intense as is this struggle for national supremacy and individual greed, more intense still will the church push forward with the insignia of the cross, and on the banks of her mysterious rivers and in the fastnesses of her benighted forests will yet be witnessed the greatest triumph of faith and self-denial in the spread of the Gospel and the redemption of her people.

The first Protestant missionaries sent to Africa were by the Moravians in 1736. The first missionaries sent to Africa on this side the ocean were by the Methodist Episcopal Church in 1833. Thus the church who helped Wesley into the fullness of a conscious personal experience of the new birth led the way in the old world, and the church which Wesley founded led the way in the new world for the evangelization of Africa. In 1822, just eleven years before the first missionary of the Methodist Episcopal Church reached Africa, the American Colonization Society, attempting to solve the vexed problem then before the American people, "What shall be done with the free Negro?" founded on the west coast of Africa a colony with Negro emigrants from America, and named it Liberia. On board the first ship carrying this company of Negro emigrants, a Methodist Episcopal Church with David Coker as pastor was organized, and this small company became the nucleus around which all our work has centered and the basis of missionary work and operation among the natives. Great privations were encountered by these early missionaries, but the work grew rapidly and in 1836, only three years after the first regular missionary arrived, the Liberia Annual Conference was organized with twenty-three members and probationers and a church membership of more than four hundred. In 1858, the same year that Livingstone was making his famous journey across the continent in search of the source of the Nile, Francis Burns, the first Negro bishop of the Methodist Episcopal Church, was elected and ordained bishop for Africa. In his election the church made no mistake. He was born in Albany, New York, in 1809, converted at fifteen, began to preach at seventeen, and, previous to his election as bishop, had spent twenty-five years in Africa as a missionary. By that manly bearing and exalted Christian character which ever distinguished him, he overcame many of the prejudices of his day and became the first Negro teacher of a mixed school in his native State. In July, 1834, just one year after the founding of the mission in company with Rev. John Seys, he went to Africa, joined the Liberia Conference, and was appointed principal of Monrovia Academy. In 1849, nine years before he was made bishop, he was appointed presiding elder of the Cape Palmas district, which work he prosecuted with vigor and success. In 1863, twenty-nine years after he first landed in Africa, overcome by the duties of his office and exposure in traveling by foot down the coast and in the interior, his health failed and he came to America for rest and recuperation, but died in the same year, in the city of Baltimore, soon after his arrival. His body, at his own request, was taken back to the scene of his early labors and triumphs, and he sleeps in the missionary burying-ground, at Monrovia, by the side of Cox and other brave heroes who, like himself, died that Africa might live. In 1866 John W. Roberts, another Negro, was elected his successor, and after nine years of unceasing labors, died during the session of the Conference in 1875. Bishops Levi Scott and Gilbert Haven visited the work subsequently, both of whom died from the effects of fever contracted there. At the General Conference of 1888, after a special season of prayer for Divine guidance, William Taylor, the hero of many a missionary field, was elected and consecrated bishop for Africa. With undaunted faith, almost superhuman endurance, and a missionary experience unparalleled in the history of the church, he still lives in a ripe old age to lead forth the hosts for the redemption and evangelization of the Dark Continent.

This work has steadily grown all these years, and the Liberia Conference now extends from Ports Roberts and Talla, its extreme northern point, to Cape Palmas, and from Cape Palmas up the Carella river to Baraboo. The Congo Mission Conference recently organized extends north and south from Cabinda to Banana, and in the interior from Banana and Boma up the Congo to Kimpoko on Stanley Pool. And in the Angola country from St. Paul De Loando through the interior to Purgo Andondo.

From 1834, when the first missionary appropriation was $2,164.00, to 1894, the church has expended, including gifts to Bishop Taylor's self-supporting fund,

$1,103,864.00. As an indication of the permanent growth of this work we note that from 1881 to 1894 the African Conference gave $53,273.00 for self support, and from 1875 to the present year $2,665 00 for benevolences. In 1894 the church membership amounted to 4,103 with church property valued at $73,538.00.

Among the many difficulties in the prosecution of missionary work in Africa is the unhealthy and deadly climate. The results of many missionary societies reveal the fact that white men cannot successfully labor in some portions of the territory. And the determined purpose of white missionaries in the very face of these facts to offer themselves to fight, if need be to die, that Africa might be redeemed, is one of the most positive declarations of the spirit of Jesus Christ in the world in our day and generation.

It is a fact tested by long and varied experience that Negroes become sooner acclimated and are better able to withstand the ravages of the African fever than the white man, and this, in addition to other reasons, places the burden, may I say the privilege, of African evangelization upon the Negro. For this very purpose I believe God has had him and still has him under preparation in this country for this work. Nothing is said here in favor of human slavery, and in this presence I am sure neither my words nor my spirit will be misinterpreted. I do not believe in the divinity of slavery. A system so cruel, so degrading, so inhuman, so barbarous was not God's, his hand never directed it, his eye never approved it. As well might I bow to the malicious wickedness of Joseph's brethren because of the results of his after life as to bow to that iniquitous traffic in human flesh because of the enlightenment that has come to the Negro in spite of it. The best that can be said on this wise are the memorable words of Joseph to his brethren: "As for you ye meant evil against me, but God meant it unto good to bring to pass as it is this day to save many souls alive." In spite of this evil then which God merely permitted, endured, great good has come. He has made the wrath of man praise him and now in this country after these years of trial, of severe persecutions and unusual hardships, a constituency is arising prepared in mind and heart to join with cultivated and consecrated men and women of all races to carry the light of the gospel to the Dark Continent, and when this remnant is fully awake to its privileges and responsibilities, earnestly and thoroughly consecrated to God and his work, we shall be ready to greet the rising sun of the twentieth century with the greatest movement for the evangelization of Africa the world has ever seen.

I do not plead here this evening for emigration to Africa. The time has not come, if indeed it ever will come, for the American Negro to emigrate to Africa. This is our home, this is our land, this is our country. The strong arm of our fathers cleared its forests, disemboweled its hills, and tunnelled its mountains. Their toil, their sweat, their tears, their blood have enriched its soil. Here our dead are buried. Here we are bound by the most sacred ties that ever touched or stirred or thrilled a human soul. We are American citizens, fully, completely-- denied rights, it may be, granted to other citizens of the republic--yet citizens withal. Citizens by birth, citizens by constitutional limit; citizens by special enactment; citizens, as these fields of the South once barren and bare, now by our labor made productive will attest; citizens because in every crisis of our nation's history, in every struggle for the perpetuity of the union of these States--from that memorable day when across Boston Commons the Negro Attucks lead the first patriotic band against British oppression, and became the first martyr for American independence, till the last black soldier shouted victory and freedom at Appomattox, citizens because in every crisis of our nation's history we have borne willingly and cheerfully a citizen's duty. But the obligation, my brethren, for African evangelization is nevertheless upon us--the obligation by racial affinity, by providential preparation, by special adaptation, by divine command, is upon us. Our lot has been hard, but our preparation correspondingly great. Into our lives during the last thirty years have been poured treasures of silver, of gold, of life itself. The most unselfish movement of the centuries for the uplifting of a people has been put forth in our behalf. Our hearts have been touched, our thought directed, our souls burnished, and God now calls us into the mount of higher privilege, enlarges our vision, places before us the crying needs of our brethren across the seas, and calls out from His throne in the skies, "Whom shall I send, and who will go for me." To this call I pray God a thousand earnest, consecrated souls may individually respond, "Here am I, Lord, send me!" Not emigration, but evangelization.

Our white brothers and sisters, be it said to their credit, have done much for the evangelization of Africa. Filled with the love of God, moved by the spirit of him first sermon at Nazareth announced his mission to be to the poor and unfortunate, they have willingly and joyously offered themselves for this work. From the very beginning, they were told, as they are told now, that the climate meant certain death to the foreigner; that white men could not live and labor there. But so intense was their interest, so deep their conviction, so determined their purpose, that they fought and died and conquered that Africa might be redeemed. Melville B. Cox, the first foreign missionary of the Methodist

Episcopal Church, filled with missionary zeal, as he stood on African soil, said: "It is the height of my ambition and the highest vision of my life to lay my bones in the soil of Africa. If I can only do this, I will establish a connection between Africa and the church at home that shall never be broken till Africa is redeemed." His vision became too soon a reality, for four months afterward he fell our first martyr for African evangelization, but left upon his grave an epitaph that for all these years has cheered and inspired the church: "Let a thousand fall before Africa is given up." Bishop Gilbert Haven of precious memory, who did more than any other man in his day to contend against the spirit of caste and prejudice, and to impress upon the hearts of men a Christianity that was essentially Christ's in spirit and life, fell asleep from the effects of a fever contracted in Africa, whither he had gladly gone in the course of his Episcopal work. Hundreds of others have fallen, but the work still goes on; and to-day, notwithstanding the unhealthy climate and deadly fevers, a mighty host--mighty in faith and love to God and humanity--is besieging her on all sides and marching through her gates for Christ and in his name.

The Negroes of this country, of all churches and denominations, are beginning to recognize their relation to the evangelization of Africa, and are satisfied that to longer remain indifferent to this work and leave it to God to use other means and other agents for the redemption of Africa, would be in every way criminal and wholly recreant to the most sacred trust committed to our care. And God is in many ways bringing this work to our thought and attention every day. The Methodist Episcopal Church has the organization of the Society of Friends of Africa in the schools of the Freedmen's Aid and Southern Education Society by Bishop Mallalieu, the establishment of an African missionary training school at Nashville by Bishop Walden, the Foundation for Africa in the Gammon Theological Seminary by the Rev. W. F. Stewart--this foundation out of which has come this congress which has attracted the attention of the whole country, and which it is hoped will do permanent good--these are but providential movements, indices of divine direction that we may see and hear and feel, that our eyes may be open in order that we may not be disobedient to the heavenly vision.

In consequence of these providential movements, I rejoice that a deep and increasing interest in the redemption of Africa is daily possessing the civilized Negroes of the world. They are going from the old world and the new, from Europe and America and the isles of the seas, from Barbadoes, Intigna, Jamaica, Demarara--going to join the grandest army in the world, to work, to suffer, if need be to die, that Africa may be saved. In our own country this awakening is most encouraging, this movement is most significant, and already across the seas some are hastening with the bread of life.

Finally, my brethren, a new era, with new ideas, with new and untried responsibilities is upon us. New conditions and environments have completely changed our position. The day of mere sentiment, thank God, has gone by never to return. We have reached the most critical period of our history and development in this country. A calm, dispassionate, critical, subjective study of present conditions, present obligations, and how to meet them, is the demand of the hour. This age calls for a new statement of the problem before us, a resetting of the whole question. The question now is not what shall be done with the Negro, but what will the Negro do with himself, his privileges and opportunities? Upon the answer to this question depends whether he shall be an insignificant figure in the world or whether he shall become a permanent factor in its life and civilization. Mere intellectual ability will not answer. Brilliancy unsanctified and unconsecrated to the highest possibilities of life fails and dies, as it deserves, by the sharpness of its own blade. Something great must be done, something wrought out by self-denial, by tears, by blood, by life itself--something great in its aims and purposes, great in its conception and achievement, thoroughly unselfish, altruistic, magnanimous--something that will challenge the attention and consideration of mankind everywhere. Let this be done, and a new day will dawn upon us; a new day for Africa in America and for Africa beyond the seas; a new day of moral, vigorous activity; a new day whose morn shall ever be bright, and whose sun shall never set.

Africa, there is hope for thee. All the world is turning toward thee and thy children from the four corners of the earth have come to bring thee light. A great army, composed of every kindred, tribe and tongue, is gathering upon thy shores and he whom thou didst shelter under thy palms and banyans leads forth the hosts for thy salvation and redemption. Drops from the coming shower have already fallen, but all around the heavens about thee clouds enlarge and descend with impending blessings. Thy idols shall be broken, thy idolatrous temples destroyed, thy people transformed, and Jesus the Christ shall reign throughout thy borders. Christian churches shall adorn thy hills and Christian school-houses abound in thy valleys. The rattling steam engine and the rumbling car of commerce shall be heard in all thy borders. Factories and mills shall dot the banks of thy rivers and steamboats and galleys float upon the bosom of thy waters. The music of the spindle and the tick of the telegraph shall be heard in all thy borders. Thy wonderful resources shall supply the world, thy storehouses once more feed the famished nations, and thy land become an asylum for the poor and oppressed of all mankind. All shall come and rejoice in thy salvation, and

"Shall drink at noon
The palm's rich nectar, and at eve
Lie down in the green pastures of remembered days,
And wake to wander, and to weep no more
On Congo's mountain coast, or Gambia's golden shore."

Self-Supporting Missions in Africa

BY
WILLIAM TAYLOR, D.D.
MISSIONARY BISHOP OF AFRICA, OF THE METHODIST EPISCOPAL
CHURCH.

The simplest form of self-support is that which embodies the principle of equivalents--value for value. "The laborer is worthy of his hire," to be paid by the people for whom he labors. "They who preach the gospel shall live by the gospel" they preach. The Lord Jesus sent His disciples forth, two and two, on this principle: "without purse, or scrip, or shoes," and they reported no lack of any needful thing. That method is practicable where the gospel messengers know the language and life of the people to whom they are sent.

If the people have adequate financial ability, not only to support their missionaries, but also to build and keep up all the houses, and provide all the appurtenances requisite, and will measure up to the high line of their possibilities, they will be self-supporting in the broadest sense. I have founded missions on both those lines in India and in South America, but neither is directly applicable to Africa. Not having the key to the understanding of the nations of the dark continent, we have to spend, in common with the missions to Asiatic countries and to the islands of the sea, many years of patient toil in mastering languages, printing the Holy Scriptures, founding schools and enlarging industries--preparing "the way of the Lord." The expense of most of this great preparatory work in foreign mission fields is provided by the missionary societies of Christian countries--the grandest charity in the world--till it can be developed into self-supporting and self-propagating churches.

To secure this result in what are known as barbarous heathen countries, the industries of such countries have to be reinforced. In India, Japan, China and Corea the people have the oriental type of civilization, and the industries suited to the requirements of oriental civilization, and fairly adequate to the demands of Christian civilized life.

In those countries missionary work is limited mainly to two lines of work, viz.: Educational and evangelical; the first comprising the whole range of school work required by Christian civilization, the second comprising all the appliances and agencies of the Church of Christ.

The industries of barbarous heathendom are, on the other hand, entirely inadequate to the demands of Christian civilization. The native people of Africa are accused of being lazy, but the result of my long and varied experience with them is that, with great natural physical force, they are quite willing to work up to the measure of their real necessities.

The work assigned to the men is pretty clearly defined, and that of the women equally so, and neither party is inclined to do the work of the other. To smelt iron ore and run it into metal, and convert the metal into iron and steel, and manufacture their own axes, hoes, swords, assegais, and spears is the work of the men. To collect the pods from the cotton tree, which is a huge forester, and spin their fine fiber into yarn, and weave it into thick cotton cloth on the same principle of the looms of our mothers fifty years ago, is the work of the men. They did not learn those industries from outside nations. They undoubtedly came down from the great shipbuilder, Noah, through Shem, Ham and Japheth, but sadly deteriorated through the heathenish demoralization of the ages. It is the work of the men to cut and carry building material and construct their houses, rude enough, but warm and waterproof. The men fell the forests and clear their farms. They aim to plant yearly in virgin soil, hence every man must clear a new field annually for each one of his wives, polygamy being one of their ancient institutions. If a man is found neglecting his axe in clearing season he is arrested and brought before the judges and fined a bullock, or its equivalent.

Most of the carriers that transport from the interior palm oil, palm kernels, ivory, beeswax, rubber, hardwoods, dyewoods, spices, etc., on their heads and shoulders, numbering an aggregate of about forty thousand carriers, supplying the commerce of about two hundred steamships plying between African and European ports; these patient, powerful burden bearers are nearly all men, with but few women in the caravans of commerce. Of course the man-stealers kill the men and work the women to death. Tribal wars seem to indicate the normal condition of the African nations, and it is, as a rule, the business of the men to do the fighting.

The legitimate work of the African heathen women is to make the pottery, which is of superior quality and in great variety, for all the purposes to which pottery can be applied, including cooking utensils. Near the sea the women boil down the sea water and make salt. The women do the digging, planting, cultivating, gathering, packing and storing, with the routine work of the house-- cooking and carrying wood and water for daily use.

It is an interesting fact that the natives of Africa not only provide for their own needs by the labor of their hands, but are "not forgetful to entertain strangers." When the men complete their task of clearing their farms they unite their forces and clear a farm for strangers, which is entrusted to the care of the chief wife of the king. She cultivates it with her own hands, and the rice, maize, beans and pumpkins are gathered by the queen and stored in her house, which, with the roots and fruits cultivated on her farm for strangers, are sacredly kept for that purpose. She gets her subsistence from those supplies for her industry, but no other member of her tribe, not even the king, would dare to use a grain of them. Even the wood required for a quick fire and a hasty meal for a hungry traveler is cut and seasoned and tied in bundles, and hung up in the house for strangers.

One forenoon, after a walk of twelve miles, from Cavalla river to the big town of the Gerribo tribe, we went directly to the house for strangers--three of us. It rained heavily all the forenoon, and the wet bushes bent over our narrow path so that we had not an inch of dry thread on us. The queen; majestic in symmetry and stature, received us cordially, and with dry wood all in readiness, we soon felt the genial warmth of a crackling fire near the centre of the round house, which was about twenty feet in diameter, and before we could half dry our clothing our dinner, consisting of boiled rice, fried chicken, sweet potatoes and bananas, was ready, served in large, deep dishes of pottery, made by queenly hands. There was no table, but a mat spread on the ground floor of the hut.

When we sat down to dinner the queen reclined quietly on her own mat on the opposite side of the fire. This is not an exceptional case, but is a sample of native hospitality generally beyond the lines of foreign innovations. In all such regions I should feel safe traveling alone without arms, and without any display of goods, and be fed without compensation. If I should have a visible supply of goods, the king would expect me to make him a present. If I should go into the interior of Africa with a caravan loaded with goods, with a thousand armed soldiers to protect my property, I would excite the cupidity and challenge the pluck of marauding tribes, and would have to fight. Hence the difference between the reports of Livingstone and those of Stanley.

The Lord has provided munificently for his colored children in Africa. The products which supply the two hundred steamships plying between African and European countries are nearly all indigenous and spontaneous, requiring simply the labor of gathering, preparing and carrying to the coast for steamship transport across the seas.

The food supplies, available through the industry of the women, consist of a variety and superior quality of rice, containing more glutin and more saccharine than the rice of other countries, and without irrigation; "Indian corn," which may probably be as justly called African corn; beans of best quality; cassada, or mandioca; eddoes, a good substitute for the Irish potato; yams, a good substitute for bread--a huge root, weighing as high as forty pounds; plantains, a species of the banana, but twice as large and more nutritious as food; the large, luscious fruits in great variety--oranges, lemons, limes, pineapples, guavas, loquats, sappadillos, butter pears, custard apples, mangoes, pawpaws, figs, etc., all cultivatable, and yield a rich harvest for the hand of the diligent: yet the heathen nations of Africa live on the low level of hand-to-mouth subsistence, and the industries requisite to that mode of life are entirely insufficient, as before stated, to meet the requirements of Christian civilization. Missionary work, therefore, comprising book education and gospel evangelization--so suitable to the old Asiatic civilizations, with their long established industries, is too narrow for broad, efficient work in Africa. This plan has been worked in Africa for more than fifty years by a majority of the greatest missionary societies in existence. The Basle missions of Acra, and other ports bordering on the Gulf of Guinea, supplement this regular Oriental plan by adding industrial education as a separate department. The boys in the workshops are taught mechanical industries, but not book knowledge, and those in the school-houses are not taught mechanics, yet the teachers in the business houses and workshops have the same missionary status as that of the regular missionaries. The industrial departments of those missions have supplied the West Coast and all the South Central African Coast with carpenters and coopers, brick and stone masons, boat builders, boiler makers, riveters, etc.--a means of adequate self-support to the operatives, and of incalculable value to their employers.

The Wesleyan missions of South Africa, covering more than a thousand miles of coast, south and east, with a regularly organized annual conference, containing more than fifty native Kaffirs as regular ministers of the gospel, and a vast and efficient church membership, have not incorporated into their plan of work any regular system of mechanical or other productive industries. The exception to this rule is the fact that when Sir George Gray was governor of Cape Colony he made liberal appropriations to supplement three large Wesleyan schools and the Scotch school at Lovedale, with each an industrial department.

212

The Natal government has made liberal appropriations also for an industrial department of the three Wesleyan schools, and for one of the schools of the American Board in that colony. It is true, also, that the Wesleyans encourage their converted people to learn and to utilize the industries of civilized life on their own account. Rev. Wm. Shaw, one of their early pioneer missionaries, induced King Kama to buy a big Dutch wagon, and train to the yoke sixteen of his big bullocks. The precedent thus established by Kama was followed in the course of years by hundreds of natives, so that Christian Kaffirs have long since become the principal carriers of the vast interior commerce of Cape Colony, Kaffraria, Natal, the Free State, Transvaal Republic, and the regions beyond; so, also, the missionaries of the American Board of Foreign Missions taught their Zulus agricultural and mechanical industries. The Lutheran mission, on St. Paul's river, Liberian coast, has been doing a good work of this secular sort; the Roman Catholics, also; but most of the other great missionary organizations, with their self-sacrificing, heroic missionaries, seem to have been so tied up by the exclusive sacredness of their high and holy calling that they seem to dread the secularizing tendency of "building tents with their own hands," or of teaching their pupils to build them. The orthodox thing was to build large school-houses and seminaries, and gather into them from one to two hundred children, who had reached "the school age," bordering on to their teens, and chock-full of heathenism, and drill them into a common school education, with catechetical recitations, and the routine of religious observances; all well enough in their way, but the pupils soon abandon the industries of their mothers, which, at best, are inadequate to their maintenance in the style of life into which they have been inducted. What is the outcome of all this?

I know of missions on the West Coast of Africa which have been worked on this plan for more than half a century. Besides many ordinary schools, they had large seminaries, and planted nearly a dozen missions among wild heathen tribes. Much good was done, no doubt, for many consecrated men and women devoted their time to that work and left their bones on the field of battle. A few of the pupils became ministers; the mass of them, not knowing how to dig, became very dependent non-producers. The missionary societies in charge became discouraged and cut down, down, down their appropriations; nearly all the seminaries were abandoned, and nearly all the stations among the raw heathen closed up.

The English-speaking work contiguous holds its own and is growing, but the purely missionary work among the native tribes has demonstrated, not delinquency on the part of the missionaries, but the ineffective narrowness of their plan of work.

The discussion of this subject by the General Conference of the Methodist Episcopal Church in 1884 brought out the discouraging aspects of their work in Africa, so that it became manifest that the conference would have given up the field but for the shame of defeat.

The next thing was to find a man to take the responsibility of that work, and become at least a respectable scapegoat to bear away their reproach into the wilderness, and probably die in the jungles of the Dark Continent. The conference was willing to risk my life on the venture, and I was thrust into the breach by more than a two-thirds vote, without discussion. They said: "We will turn him loose, and let him do as he likes."

As Missionary Bishop of Africa. I had the responsibility of administering for our missionary society in their old English-speaking Liberian work, which is prospering; but the forty new mission stations among raw heathen tribes, which I have opened, are not under the control of any missionary society, and receive no pay from any. These are all in tropical Africa, covering a coast line of three thousand miles; not a consecutive line of stations along the coast, but different chains of stations starting from the coast and extending inland.

My first chain is in Angola, south of Congo, extending inland nearly four hundred miles. I opened and manned five of those self-supporting stations in Angola in 1885. We now have seven, and are opening the eighth of that chain, all of which are self-supporting.

We have another chain, not so well developed, extending up Congo river to Kimpoko, on Stanley Pool; a chain of over one hundred miles on Cavalla river, and a chain of over one hundred miles on Kru coast. A number of my West Coast missions are now temporarily suspended by the wars now prevailing in that region.

All the funds required for opening the forty stations indicated come from the free-will offerings of the friends of the movement in America, England and Australia. On all our lines at the front we have regular church organizations, according to the disciplinary provisions of the church I have the honor to represent.

Going among wild heathen, as before stated, we have to master their languages, make books, teach the people to read them, and spend years in "preparing the way of the Lord," before the glory of the Lord can be widely revealed in the salvation of the people, but it is being revealed by the inauguration of simple, suitable methods. My plan first of all is to negotiate with kings and chiefs for mission sites in suitable centers and for a grant of land for a mission farm on each station, and from the start make industrial education an essential part of all our mission work; not the higher mechanics required by a high standard of civilization, but the agricultural and the simple mechanical industries essential to the independent self-support of the boys and girls whom we train and elevate to the plane of Christian civilization. Pupils thus trained will be prepared for all our variety of service as missionaries, or to select sites for farms of their own from any unoccupied portions of the public domain of the tribes to which they belong, and build their own houses after the model of the mission house in which they receive their education. By the land laws of African nations the land is held in trust by kings and chiefs for their people. Free selection and actual possession is a warranty deed. Our young people thus settled will found Christian communities, which will expand and develop into Christian empire.

The first leading feature of my plan of mission work for Africa, therefore, is industrial education which will develop and utilize indigenous resources and create self-support for all concerned.

The second, in common with all missions, is the impartation and drill of a good common school education in their own language and ours.

The third, as a distinct organic method of mission work, is unique. It is the establishment of a nursery mission on each station, under the management of a competent missionary matron, in charge of an adopted family of from ten to twenty little boys and girls, taken from heathen families before they become heathens. We thus put in "the ounce of prevention," and bring them near and teach them to come to the Great Physician and have Him "lay His hands upon them" --His saving power--"pray for them"--His priestly mediation, and "bless them." Thus coming to Jesus they submit themselves to His will, that is the *essence* and *act* of repentance; they lift their helpless hands and hearts to Jesus, and *receive Him* as their Savior; that is the saving *act of faith.* The blessing that infallibly follows these conditions comprises justification by faith and the inward "washing of regeneration and the renewing of the Holy Spirit." I demonstrated these verities before I graduated from the trundle bed, when about seven years old. "Verily I say unto you, whosoever shall not receive the kingdom of God as a little child, he shall in no wise enter therein." For responsible subjects of God's government, this is the only way into his kingdom and family. The measure of light involving moral responsibility involves the obligation of implicit obedience to God. The unconditional grace of God, which is adequate to all the exigencies of the irresponsible period of child life, living or dying, right up to the point of transit from the vale of infantile innocency to the plane of personal moral responsibility to God, is altogether inadequate to the demands of that higher plane. The choice is imperative--Yes or No--loyalty to God or rebellion against him. The only refuge and source of adequate loyalty and love is in Jesus, and the only way is to *submit* to Him and *accept* Him, as taught by His object lesson of the little children that came to Him.

There are about forty millions of little black lambs, belonging to the Good Shepherd, bleating over the hills and dales of the Dark Continent. Where are the pastors to guide their erring feet into "the paths of righteousness," and bring them to Jesus?

Under my nursery mission plan we have our adopted children adopted into the family of God by their simple faith, resting on "the Word of God and our testimony for Jesus," at the age of five or six years and upwards. As soon as they can handle a small hoe we put them to work on the mission farm three or four hours per day, with a drill of equal length in the schoolroom, and divide up several hours each day in a variety of religious worship and Christian work. A few months ago I counted forty-five little boys and girls of this sort kneeling at the sacramental altar at one time, intelligently partaking of the sacrament of the Lord's supper.

This road, tending directly from the nursery "into the kingdom of God," is the short cut, and the sure cut, for the development of muscle on the farm and in the workshop, of mind in the school room, and of Christian character in the paths of righteousness, and of soul-winners by daily witnessing for Jesus publicly to the masses, and personally to individuals. The testimony of our little ones has greater weight with adult heathen men and women than that of any other class of witnesses we can bring to the stand.

These simple, economical methods of missionary work, carried into effect on a scale commensurate with the demand of the stupendous undertaking in hand, and with a zeal to correspond with that of the rum sellers and man stealers, who are spreading death and desolation east, west, north and south, we might safely appoint the time, not fifty years from to-day, to celebrate the final conquest of the continent for God.

The results already achieved have demonstrated the wisdom of the plan. Such industries were introduced as were best adapted to the various sections of the continent where mission stations were planted, requiring, therefore, a greater or less time for their development. Coffee culture seemed the general line on the West Coast, and accordingly, our mission farms there have each from one to ten thousand coffee trees, now approaching the bearing age, which is about six years. These Liberian stations are now within one hundred dollars a year, on the average, of absolute self-support, outside of buildings. On the Congo the farms are of necessity smaller, but we have three self-supporting stations on the river, and the others nearly so, except buildings and heavy transport expenses. In the province of Angola, mainly on the commercial plan, all the stations and sub-stations, except the receiving station at Loando, are entirely self-supporting, and, to a considerable extent, self-propagating, annually increasing the number of sub-stations. Although those mentioned are the main lines developed, the natives are everywhere taught all the varied industries of the house, shop and farm; and the gain to them in developing a right spirit of independence, and acquiring a practical knowledge of useful avocations, has been far greater, in its beneficent effect, than the financial advantage of giving the mission a support. This higher motive of this part of the method of these missions should not be lost sight of. So satisfactory has thus far been this feature of the plan, that we gladly accept the general designation of "African Industrial Missions." The nursery missions are blessedly realizing the faith of their founder, not only in the happy conversion of nearly all of the little black lambs who have been gathered into the mission homes, but in each one becoming a spring of "living water" to many thirsty souls, an evangelist of salvation to their own people. By them heathen, from kings and petty chiefs to outcast "bushmen," whose adherence to various forms of witchcraft and polygamous complications defied the earnest efforts of the missionary, won by their clear testimony and happy songs of deliverance, have been led into the fold of Christ. These children, whom a high dignitary thought should not be "counted" with the native evangelists, into which some of them have already developed, are everywhere one of the largest human agencies in the work of salvation that is in progress in some of our mission stations, and has commenced in the others.

As the result to date of the addition to the usual method of school work and Gospel teaching of these *old* methods, in use by the Apostles of our Lord as recorded in the Acts, and set forth in the Epistles of St. Paul, what have we as a church in Africa to-day? New evangelistic life has been put into the old work of the Liberian Conference, which reported many conversions last year, and there has been introduced into it, as far as possible for an organization long drilled in other tactics, the methods which have been so successfully employed in planting and developing the new Industrial Missions in Africa, which is bearing fruit on a number of the charges, and three Methodist Seminaries, long abandoned to decay, have been rebuilt and schools opened in them. Two of them are in charge of our self-supporting missionaries, the third opened by the only two white missionaries the Missionary Society of the Methodist Episcopal Church has in Africa, and who were sent out last May [1894]. Under the authority of the General Conference, I have charge of this work of the Missionary Society in Africa, but the new missions I have opened and am developing, as authorized by the same body, are entirely distinct and separate. They comprise mission stations among purely native heathen on the West Coast and Cavalla river, Congo, Angola and Southeast Africa. In all these sections property has been acquired, from a few acres to hundreds of acres, either temporary or substantial mission buildings have been erected, and all is held by deeds from native kings and chiefs and from the different countries claiming "protectorate," either executed directly to trustees of the Methodist Episcopal Church or, where that has not been possible, to the Bishop *in trust* for said missionary uses. Thus, in West Africa large coffee plantations, on the Congo small farms and valuable mission sites, in Angola large farms and choice city locations, and in East Africa three large mission properties--aggregating many thousands of dollars in value--are inalienably devoted in perpetuity, or till poor Africa shall be redeemed from the civilized and savage curses that cling like blood-thirsty panthers around her "black yet comely" form, to the legitimate purposes of Christian Industrial Missions.

I once addressed a large concourse of natives, and my interpreter was a native boy about eight years of age, who in addition to the full-dress suit in which he was born, wore nothing but a cotton string around his waist; but he "passed the word" with such fluency and power as to melt the hearts of many hearers.

We do not simply train them in the industries of the home, garden, and farm, and the knowledge imparted by books; but in every instance the chief end in view is their personal salvation. When saved, they make the very best workers and witnesses for Jesus. We had one of these nurseries, for example, near the village of the above mentioned king. The missionary matron held her meetings under a bread-fruit tree, reading and explaining the Scriptures, and then giving her native children opportunity to witness to personal salvation. The crowd of natives would eagerly listen to these children, and ask them to tell it again and again.

Not a word of disrespect or doubt as to the reality of their experience is heard from the heathen. The king heard them, and in a few months he and one of his great chiefs were grandly converted to God: gave up polygamy and witchcraft; and with their own hands, assisted by native converts, built a Methodist church, native fashion, where the king himself now preaches to his people. The last time I was at Cape Palmas this same man arose in a fellowship meeting and testified to his salvation, and said: "Some of my people have been saved, but alas! many of them are still in darkness. Last night I prayed all night for my people, and I ask you to pray for them" We cannot do much with these old lions, but "a little child shall lead them."

The best workers for Africa are its own sons and daughters, not taken to a foreign land to be educated, but saved, trained and developed on their own soil. After a campaign of seven months in Africa, twenty-seven years ago, in which over seven thousand Kaffirs were converted, I said to the church among whose missions I was then laboring, that if they would ordain a native ministry, and give them full swing, they would sweep the country from south to north; but they were slow to see the situation; yet fifty native ministers of a single denomination of Christians have since been developed.

All that Africa needs from us is leadership--holy, skillful, self-sacrificing men and women, the best that we can furnish; and all that these leaders need is assistance to develop the indigenous resources of the productive soil, and the inherent capabilities of the black man. Teaching industries develops self-support, which we reach absolutely in from five to eight years, according to the location.

These methods are not experiments, but are demonstrated facts in our work in Africa; and we are pleased to observe that other societies in Africa are adopting these methods, though in a modified form. What we propose is to strengthen, develop and extend our work, in harmony with the methods employed by St. Paul and his co-laborers, until the midnight empire shall come into the light of gospel day.

To evangelize and civilize Africa is a stupendous undertaking, too great for any one man or generation of men; but the *present generation* of God's workers, with a leader He has appointed and trained for many years, have the blessed privilege, while they gather precious fruitage in the salvation of souls by the way, of helping to introduce and employ the methods which, under God, will be a guarantee of the final accomplishment of the whole work.

PART II

THE AMERICAN NEGRO: HIS RELATION TO THE CIVILIZATION AND REDEMPTION OF AFRICA

H. K. CARROLL, LL.D.

Editor of *The Independent,* New York: Superintendent of the United States Census of the Churches

H. K. CARROLL, LL.D.

Editor of *The Independent,* New York; Superintendent of the United States Census of the Churches

The Negro in the Twentieth Century

BY H. K. CARROLL, LL.D.
EDITOR *Independent,* NEW YORK CITY, AND SUPERINTENDENT
UNITED STATES CENSUS OF CHURCHES

What the Christian faith, Christian education and Christian example have done for the Negro in the United States, these influences can do for the Negro of Africa. It is natural that seven million Negroes, escaped from slavery, rising by culture, industry and economy to a high plane of civilization, should turn their thoughts to the Dark Continent, where untold millions of their race are living in a state of savagery, and that they should feel a strong desire to assist in the redemption of Africa.

The Negro is massed in no country in the world, beyond the boundaries of his own continent, as he is massed in the United States. Brought here originally for a wicked purpose, he has accepted the civilization of his late masters, and proved that he is capable of nobler uses than forced service under bondage. He has helped us to understand that no man, white or black, is good enough to be the master of slaves, and that the lowest savage, black or white, is too good for such base use.

We see in him as a free man excellencies and possibilities to which slavery made us blind. He has struggled against our doubts and fears, and has fairly conquered our long-lived, pertinacious prejudices. Many, even of those who wanted him to be free and gave him their sympathy, had grave misgivings as to his capacity for the highest duties of citizenship. He has had to prove, since the war, that schools and educational processes are of use to him. The first teachers who came South to instruct him were eagerly questioned as to his ability to learn. When this doubt was satisfied, another was expressed: Was not this ability to learn exceptional? Was the higher education possible to any of his race? We feel a sense of shame in simply recounting this historical fact; but it is a fact, and the greatest achievement of the Negro of the nineteenth century is in forcing from us the acknowledgment of his large capacity.

What he has done for himself under great difficulties and discouragements in the last third of the nineteenth century is a splendid prophecy of what he will be in the twentieth century. He has quickly learned that superior position is open to him on just the same terms as to any other citizen, and that if he would have his superiority recognized he must demonstrate it. Prejudice cannot withstand demonstration. It must yield, however slowly; and colored statesmen, merchants, bankers, lawyers, doctors, ministers, educators, will win their way by forces which are not an accident of race or color, but are developed by culture.

The strong, senseless, but galling prejudices which confront the Negro are by no means his greatest obstacles to success. These are ignorance and vice and shiftlessness, which, like their opposite virtues, are not confined to a particular race, but beset humanity in general. He has shown that he has the power to rise above the condition of a slave, and I look confidently forward to a brilliant future for him. I have no idea that he will leave this country. His greatest achievements will be here on soil that is as much his as ours. Here are found the conditions which are needed for his development, and here he will stay to contribute his share to the prosperity and glory of our great nation. I should expect to see a larger immigration from Africa in the twentieth century than emigration to Africa.

It is not his duty to evangelize Africa. The responsibility for that great work rests on Christians in every nation. He will simply take his part in it. We may expect it will be a large part. His zeal will be great, his qualifications unquestionable, and we may hope that the redemption of his own race in the Dark Continent will stimulate his heartiest endeavors and his largest sacrifices.

J. W. E. BOWEN, Ph.D., D.D.
Secretary of the Congress

Professor of Historical Theology in Gammon Theological Seminary; Ex-Field Agent of Missionary Society of the Methodist Episcopal Church; Late Professor of Hebrew Howard University, Washington, D. C., and Professor of Church History in Mo College, Baltimore, Md.

J. W. E. BOWEN, Ph.D., D.D.
Secretary of the Congress
Professor of Historical Theology in Gammon Theological Seminary; Ex-Field
Agent of the Missionary Society of the Methodist Episcopal Church; Late
Professor of Hebrew in Howard University, Washington, D. C., and Professor of
Church History in Morgan College, Baltimore, Md.

The Comparative Status of the Negro at the Close of the War and of To-day

BY
J. W. E. BOWEN, PH.D., D.D.
PROFESSOR IN GAMMON THEOLOGICAL SEMINARY

History is history, and fact is fact; what has been written is written, and cannot be unwritten. We are afflicted in this day with a brood of ready, flippant, but inaccurate writers, white and black, who are disposed to misrepresent the past and understate the present as these times appertain to the American Negro. To charge them with ignorance makes them fit subjects for the pity of clear-thoughted men; but to charge them with bias and want of intellectual integrity makes them jugglers, incapacitates them as witnesses, and throws their testimony out of court. No bold stroke of pitiless logic and no rhetorical flourish or mystification of language can change one item of fact or erase one scintilla of truth. To tell "the truth, the whole truth and nothing but the truth" is at times unpopular and distasteful, and the fool or venturesome youth who is thus audacious in public speech will find that prudence and sophistry are no mean virtues and accomplishments.

The American Negro is the American Sphinx and, like his ancient kith and kin upon the plains of Gizeh, his history has not been fully deciphered. His nature, like the forests of his aboriginal home, is a "terra incognita." To understand the Negro of today one must study his past, for the fruitage of today was rooted in the past. Therefore, nothing short of a careful and honest study of past history can explain adequately the things of today. Lament it never so much, and do what we will to suppress it, the Negro question still lives and it will be a disturbing element until it is settled upon biblical lines. To present the status of the Negro at the close of the war makes imperative a review of the system of slavery, for the Negro at the close of the war was what slavery had made him.

Just at this point, two questions arise, viz.: First, what was American slavery? Second, what did this slavery do for the Negro? An editor in the Methodist Episcopal Church South has given us, in a recent railroad article, written "on the wing," a modern semi-original and gratuitous definition of slavery in these words: "a mild and humane system of bondage, almost misnamed slavery." The flippancy of this definition is only equaled by its boldness and it would not merit a passing notice from sensible men, were it not for the fact that this new Noah Webster assumes to speak in his official role. Other writers have made bold to declare that American slavery was educative to the heathen African. A distinguished writer casts into a negative form the nature of American slavery thus: (1) It was not apprenticeship. (2) It was not guardianship. (3) It was in no sense a system for the education of a weaker race by a stronger. (4) The happiness of the governed was in no sense its object. (5) The temporal improvement or the eternal wellbeing of the governed was in no sense its object. See "Key to Uncle Tom's Cabin," page 233.

Every slave State, and as well the United States, had settled and decreed in law that slaves were deemed, sold, taken, reputed and adjudged in law to be chattels, subject to the will of their masters, belonging to them, a part of their personal property, as beasts, animals, furniture and real estate. Judge Stroud, in his "Sketch of the Laws Relating to Slavery," declares: "This maxim of civil law, the genuine and degrading principle of slavery, inasmuch as it places the slave upon a level with *brute* animals, prevails universally in the slave-holding States." "It is plain that the dominion of the master is as unlimited as that which is tolerated by the laws of any civilized country in relation to brute animals--to quadrupeds, to use the words of the civil law." "The cardinal principle of slavery--that the slave is not to be ranked among *sentient beings,* but among things, as an article of property, a chattel personal--obtains as undoubted law in all these States."

Inhuman and horrifying as are these records of slavery, and they have not been denied with proof, a better conception of American slavery is reached when we describe the system in its social, moral and religious aspects and actual doings. To the unprejudiced observer, at thirty years' distance, the whole system, as a system, was "the sum of all villainies," one universal harem that, at the emancipation of the slave, had swept to the vortex of tyranny, degradation, fornication and diabolism of the most vicious character.

Read with me a few nauseating paragraphs for truth's sake, and also that we may see the horrible pit from which the Negro was digged:

"In the case of Harris *vs.* Clarissa and others, in the March term, 1834, the chief justice, in delivering his opinion to the court, said: 'In Maryland the *issue (i. e.* of female slaves) is considered not an accessory, but as a part of the use, like that of other female animals. Suppose a *brood mare* be hired for five years, the foals belong to him who has a part of the use of the dam. The slave in Maryland,

226

in this respect, is placed on no higher or different ground.'"--*Slave Code, Goodwin, p.* 30.

But it remained for a Mr. Gholson, of Virginia, to shock the modesty of those halcyon days by his speech in the Legislature of his State, January 18, 1831, when he said: "Why, I really have been under the impression that I *owned* my slaves. I lately purchased *four women* and ten children, in whom I thought I obtained a great bargain, for I really supposed they were my property as were my *brood mares."*

"Slaves," shouted Mr. Vanderpool, of New York, "had no more right to be heard than horses and dogs." Judge Stroud declares that "a slave cannot even contract matrimony, the association which takes place among slaves, and is called marriage, being properly designated by the word *contubernism,* a relation which has no sanctity, and to which no civil rights are attached." It was Daniel Dulaney, the attorney-general of Maryland, who affirmed that "a slave has never maintained an action against the violator of his bed. A slave is not admonished for incontinence, or punished for fornication or adultery; never prosecuted for bigamy, or petty treason; for killing a husband, being a slave, any more than admitted to an appeal for murder."

The slave Negro was taught by precept and authoritative commandment as well as trained by example and driven by the merciless lash to commit adultery and fornication, and to live in the murky and unrestrained passions of the flesh that rush on through the open sluices of libertinism and shame down through the gates of hell. Who dare deny it and will buttress that denial with fact? A thousand trustworthy witnesses will confirm it, who carry in their minds and souls the imprint of that lustful period and who can speak that which they do know and testify to what they have seen and felt. Nay, let the South herself speak. President Dewey, of William and Mary College, in Virginia, speaking of the slave trade, says: "It furnishes every inducement to the master to attend to his Negroes, to *encourage breeding* and to cause the greatest number of slaves to be raised." "Virginia is, indeed, a Negro-raising State for other States." "The noblest blood of Virginia," says Paxton in a letter to Jay, "runs in the blood of her slaves." The slave had no marriage or family rights. Dr. Taylor, in his "Elements of the Civil Law," says: "Slaves were not entitled to the conditions of matrimony and therefore had no relief in cases of adultery, nor were they the proper objects of cognation or affinity, but of quasi cognation only." And the Louisiana reports quoted by Wheeler in his "Law of Slavery," page 199, declare: "It is clear that

227

slaves have no legal capacity to assent to any contract. With the consent of their masters they may marry, * * * * but while in a state of slavery [it] cannot produce any civil effects." "No slave," says Jay, "can commit bigamy, because the law knows no more of marriage of slaves than it does of the marriage of brutes. A slave may indeed be formally married, but so far as legal rights and obligations are concerned, it is an idle ceremony."--*Jay's Inquiry.*

This serpent had wound its slimy body of death not only around the State but also, about the very neck of the church. The church recognized that the system was vicious, immoral and ruinous, but because of her complicity which had tarnished her character, she had not power to shake herself loose. She had played at the den of the unholy cockatrice and was held spellbound by the deceptive glare in her eye. The Presbyterian synod of Kentucky felt the remorse of conscience enough to say in its address: "The system produces general licentiousness among the slaves. Marriage, as a civil ordinance, they cannot enjoy. Our laws do not recognize this relation as existing among them, and, of course, do not enforce by sanction the observance of its duties. Hence all marriages that could ever be allowed them would be a mere contract, violable at the master's pleasure. Their present quasi marriages are continually thus voided. They are in this way brought to consider their matrimonial alliances as a thing not binding, and they act accordingly. We are then assured by the most unquestionable testimony that licentiousness is the necessary result of our system." The complicity of this branch of Christendom with slavery may be seen in another incident. In 1836 the fever for buying slaves ran high, and banks and corporations extended their loans and took risks unheard of in the business world. "Then it was that the trustees of the General Assembly of the Presbyterian church, lured by these high rates of interest, *though well knowing, as everybody did,* the purpose for which their capital was wanted, withdrew their funds, to the amount of $94,692.88, from a Northern institution, where they were drawing the usual interest, and invested them in the southwestern banks, where they would be loaned to the speculators in the bodies and souls of men, women and children. In the reaction and general bankruptcy which followed, the Presbyterian church lost $68,893.88 of their funds."

The deplorable condition of the slaves was well known to slaveholders and abolitionists. The legally closed school house and church, and the cupidity of master, as well as his inhumanity and brutality, were bringing forth fruit of the blackest kind and in prodigious quantities. Human reason hesitates to accept, without convincing proof, the horrible tale of woe, and when this tale is well authenticated it sits dumb and speechless in its presence. These are not the fancies of verdant youth, nor are they the ravings and discolorations of an unbalanced brain, neither are they the highly colored tales of the Arabian Nights; but they are the statements of honorable slaveholders, the careful compilations and observations of the white ministry in the South during slavery, and the unvarnished accounts of the actual sufferers themselves. It is safe to say that mediævalism, with its Inquisition and *auto da fé,* in comparison with the treatment of the American Negro slaves, would be counted humane and a blessing to mankind.

Let it be borne in mind that these facts are not written to feed the almost quenchless fires of prejudice. I would walk, *face forward,* in the presence of that harrowing and nameless shame and cover it with the garment of Christian charity; but my only apology for uncovering this pit of seething, reeking and nauseating corruption is to show from whence we came, and to refute the statement that slavery was the halcyon days of purity and moral power for the Negro, and to show the absurdity of the claim that the slave-driver's whip and bloodhounds are superior moral teachers for MAN to a sympathetic, consecrated and humanity-loving teacher with a spelling-book in one hand and the Bible in the other. And again, these words are written to show to the Negro himself the black heritage he brought with him from slavery, and to impress him with the thought that heroic treatment, patiently and persistently administered, will ultimately develop in him those moral qualities that are necessary to a happy life.

On the 5th of December, 1833, a committee of the Synod of South Carolina and Georgia, to whom was referred the subject of the religious instruction of the colored population, made a report which has been published, and in which this language is used:

"Who would credit it that in these years of revival and benevolent effort in this Christian republic there are over 2,000,000 of human beings in the condition of heathens, *and in some respects in a worse condition?* From long continued and close observation, we believe that their moral and religious condition is such that they may justly be considered the HEATHEN of this Christian country, and will bear comparison with the heathen of any country in the world. The Negroes are destitute of the Gospel, *and ever will be under the present state of things.* In the vast field extending from an entire State beyond the Potomac to the Sabine river, and from the Atlantic to the Ohio, there are, to the best of our knowledge, not *twelve men exclusively devoted to the religious instruction of the Negroes.* In the present state of the feeling in the South, a ministry of their own color could neither be obtained nor tolerated. But do not the Negroes have access to the Gospel through the stated ministry of the whites? We answer, No; the Negroes have no regular and efficient ministry; as a matter of course, no churches; neither is there sufficient room in white churches for their accommodation. We know of but five churches in the slave-holding States built expressly for their use; these are all in the State of Georgia. We may now inquire if they enjoy the privileges of the Gospel in their own houses and on our plantations? Again we return a negative answer. They have no Bibles to read by their own firesides; they have no family altars; and when in affliction, sickness, or death, they have no minister to address to them the consolations of the Gospel, nor to bury them with solemn and appropriate services."--*Jay's Inquiry,* 138.

This is the language of Southern Christian ministers who preached to slave-holders, and occasionally to slaves.

I ask, were there no exceptions to this unnamed treatment? An answer will be found in the humane and novel act of Bishop Wm. Capers, of the Methodist Episcopal Church, in South Carolina, who became superintendent of missions to the plantation slaves in 1829. His missionary labors among these unfortunates are a bright spot in the sky of that gruesome day. In every State there were masters who were kind-hearted and genuinely sympathetic, who treated their slaves with consideration, and some of them taught their slaves to read; had them to marry according to the requirements of the church; did not allow them to violate with impunity, nor did these masters them-selves violate the marriage vows of the slaves; took them to their churches and had them to share in the benefits of pulpit ministrations, and thus acted towards them in the capacity of fathers and mothers towards their children. There was genuine affection between them, and these slaves were the favored ones in the South, and the ex-slaves of today who had such masters never cease to sing their praise.

But it must be borne in mind that such slave-masters were exceedingly few and far between, and what is still more remarkable, such moral, intellectual and spiritual care of the slave by these few noble spirits was contrary to the letter and spirit of the law in every slave State. The designed product of the slave system, which Dr. Steel calls "a mild and humane system of bondage," was a dehumanized and bestialized thing, and there was no stone left unturned, no vigilance was deemed to exacting, no privations and cruelty too heartless, and no punishment too severe and diabolical to compass the end desired. The law of certain States forbade the use of the Bible or any other book, and also religious meetings to the Negroes, unless a majority of whites were present. All prohibited the impartation of instruction, while Virginia unequivocally forbade all evening meetings. "In the House of Delegates of Virginia, in 1832, Mr. Berry said: 'We have *as far as* possible closed every avenue by which light might enter their [the slaves'] minds. If we could extinguish the capacity to see the light our work would be completed; they would then be on a level with the beasts of the field, and we should be safe! I am not certain that we would not do it if we could find out the process, and that on the plea of necessity.'"

Can language be made stronger? Only Kentucky and Maryland of the slave States did not prohibit learning to the slave, but of the slave in Kentucky the Presbytery declared: "Slavery dooms thousands of human beings to hopeless ignorance."

The claim that the Negro received a knowledge of the English language, of Christianity and of handicraft as the special gifts and blessings of slavery is substantially true, but is devoid of ethical significance to the masters, because of the absence of purpose and motive in securing these ends. True, the slave did get a workable knowledge of the English language, but this acquirement was perforce of necessity to enhance the value of slave property, but intelligence in the slave was considered a vice to be dreaded. In religious matters the conception of the Negro of those sacred duties is easily explained. Dr. Blyden, in his "Christianity, Islam and the Negro," says: "The highest men in the South, magistrates, legislators, professors of religion, preachers of the gospel, governors of States, gentlemen of property and understanding, all united in upholding a system which every Negro felt was wrong. Yet these were the men from whom he got his religion, and whom he was obliged to regard as guides. * * Saints, no doubt, there were among the bondmen, but they became so not in consequence, but in default, and often, we may say, in defiance, of instruction." The sacredness of the marriage relation, the punishments for fornication and adultery, ethical integrity, the glories and rewards for faithful service, and the duties, privileges, and opportunities of the Christian life, were never discussed before and unfolded to the slave. Where he was permitted to hold meetings he was trained in the most grotesque types of worship; his emotions and wildest eccentricities were cultivated, and his motives for life were drawn from no higher source, in the main, than this temporary, enthusiastic and emotional worship.

He was trained in certain handicraft for financial considerations. The lash was his taskmaster, and from him he received no view of the dignity of labor. A man may learn mechanics by force, but not ethics. The lash may make (?) a good blacksmith but not a good conscience.

There was no thought among the slave-holders of improving the slave in any element for the slave's sake. Take as an illustration the apparently humane action of the Legislature of South Carolina, Act 1740, in which it declared that slaves should not be worked more than fifteen hours in the long days and fourteen in the short, under penalty to slave-holders. This act had as its purpose, not the comfort and well being of the then dumb-driven cattle, formerly called men, but it had a shrewd business purpose in view, namely, to keep this property as long as possible in good working order. If, however, this property should become useless as a strong mule or a patient ox, the slave-holder might dispose of him at a discount to a medical institution for scientific purposes. See *Charleston Mercury,* October 12, 1838.

Thus when the famous edict of freedom went forth on January 1, 1863, the Negro, instead of being born into a state of liberty and freedom, was damned into it. For well nigh eight generations he had been worked like dumb, driven cattle, and punished like a brute, crushed with the iron hoof of oppression and repression; whipped, torn, bleeding, in body, mind and soul; day after day, year after year, he had toiled, sweated, groaned and wept, but there had been no hope of reward to lighten his burdens. He had no wife, no children, no altar; no home, no hope, no purpose; no motive, no aspiration, no thought, no life, *but he had a God.* He was a thing, a dog, a brute, an animal. His notions, even among his preachers, were crude; he had seen her whom he had desired to call wife torn from his side, insulted, degraded, banished; he had looked upon his fondlings with an indescribable heart-ache as they were sold from under his eye; he had been trained in theft, dishonesty and duplicity; he had drank deeply from the bitter waters of crime and lewdness. He was ignorant of the duties and even privileges of Christianity, and of the responsibilities and possibilities of the family life. Thus he walked forth on that famous morn, out from the tomb of his living and torturing death, with absolutely nothing in his hands, his head, his heart, his pocket, and he went forth to try his fortunes in a new world. Freedom gave him his hands and his wife to start with, two great boons; with the hand to chip out his place and to work with a royal will and a wife to build his altar and weave his destiny. He is endowed as never before. Hence the Negro, at the close of the war, was all that American slavery would make any people, viz.:

bestialized and animalized; ignorant, poor, crude, rude; helpless, moneyless and thoughtless. American slavery was not a blessing; it was a curse. The good that came to the Negro (and there was good even in so baneful contact) came in spite of slavery. "Endeavor, then, to combine the whole in one view--to take in the full idea of this mighty mass of evil, in all the sufferings of mind and body which it inflicts, in all its brutalizing effects and demoralizing tendencies on the slave and on his master--the miseries which it entails on man, and the guilt which incurs in the sight of God--and you will have some conception of the multiplied and horrifying evils of slavery."

This view represents the status of the Negro at the close of the war. No other slavery in all history has ever succeeded to so great extent as has this American slavery in degrading the women of a race and in corrupting the fountain of every virtue; and were it not that the gospel is all conquering and all purifying, we would be hopeless, but turn to another picture and consider

THE STATUS OF THE NEGRO OF TODAY.

In discussing the Negro of today, it has come into general method to gauge the man by his possessions. In other words, his avoirdupois in property accumulation, stocks, bonds and landed interests are taken as the measure of the man and the sum total of his moral power. This method of calculation is in some respects a good one, for the power to accumulate wealth and to amass a fortune by wise and skillful investments is no mean power; but, on the contrary, it reveals an element of character necessary in these practical days. Civilization in these latter days is taking an unfortunate turn in its measurements, but it must be remembered that dynamics are not ethics, and that financial avoirdupois is not necessarily character; they may be far apart in essentials and life. With this in view, I shall give a picture of the Negro of today as he is in himself, and not as he appears in the census report or in the tax lists of cities and States, for a man's life consistent not in the things which he hath.

The Negro, as was seen in the survey of slavery, began his life of freedom with certain moral deficiencies of character that are at the very root of civilized life and moral strength, viz.: self-reliance, self-control and self-command, and to this day, in addition to his intellectual lack, as a mass, of those very faculties found wanting in criminals, the logical, the deductive and analytical power, he is still wanting in many of the fundamental virtues of a highly civilized and Christian life. He is a child; these powers come with years of training in full

233

maturity. The sins of his barbarous state have only been surpassed by those of his semi-barbarous state in slavery. Let it be understood that he is not an angel in purity by a long distance. His moral sins in many cases are shockingly cruel.

Let us ask the question, has the Negro improved intellectually? The answer to this question will be considered the first item of Negro character of to-day. In the first place the outlay of money and means for the education of the Negro during the last twenty-five years has exceeded that of all the centuries of his enslavement. It is estimated that the Southern States have expended for his education $45,000,000 and the Northern States $19,000 000, making a total from the States of $64,000,000. Among the public and private institutions set apart for this purpose there were in 1891 fifty-two normal and industrial schools maintained by the States and by various religious denominations, having 10,000 students; twenty-five sectarian and non-sectarian universities and colleges, having 8,000 students; forty-seven institutions for secondary instruction, having 12,000 students; twenty-five schools of theology, having 700 students; five schools of law, with 100 students; five schools of medicine, with 240 students; all, with two exceptions, located in the States formerly known as slave States. Besides these, there are in the South sixteen schools receiving both State and Federal aid and offering to the colored youth industrial and agricultural training, having about 2,500 students. "In educating and evangelizing among the Negroes, the various religious bodies have been specially active. Among these bodies the Congregationalists claim to have spent $11,000,000 for the Negro, and spend now nearly $400,000 a year. The Methodists have spent since emancipation $6,000,000 and is now spending annually through the Freedmen's Aid and Southern Education Society $350,000 a year; the Presbyterian Board of Missions for Freedmen in twenty years have spent $2,400,000, and in addition to this contribution founded Lincoln University, Pennsylvania, in 1859. The Baptists since 1865, $3,000,000; the Southern Presbyterian church $55,000 between 1878 and 1894; the Christian church $100,000. This vast outlay has produced a result known and read of all men. No man has attempted to deny the statement that the Negro has improved intellectually. Not even the bitterest of enemies have denied this statement, and it may be said modestly that there are a few men and women among the Negroes who can compare favorably with some of the best of the other race.

The intellectual development of the race is no more in question. The revelations of history are indeed a reflective commentary upon the so-called intelligence of those who went so far as to affirm the impossibility of intellectual improvement to the Negro. Had they turned back the pages of history for one century they would have seen the names of Wm. Anthony Amo, a genuine Negro, educated at the University of Wittemberg, with the degree "Doctor of Philosophy," and who could write and speak Latin, Greek, Hebrew, French, Dutch, and German; Gustavus Vassa, a learned Englishman; Abou Brer Sadiki, a versatile Arabic Negro scholar; James E. J. Capetieu, of the Universities of Hague and Leyden, who was familiar with Latin, Greek, Hebrew, Chaldee, and German; his poetry is written in Latin; Geoffrey L'Islet, a mathematician, botanist, physicist, geologist, and astronomer; Benjamin Baneker, the Maryland slave, and mathematician and astronomer, and a host of others who were recognized in the world of letters, in art, science, philosophy, and philology. There has been a decline and apparent retrogression, but the movement forward has again set in, and today there may be found many brilliant scholars in all the disciplines of learning. Ignorance of these historical and present day facts is inexplicable, except it be that American prejudice has decreed what should be known and what left unknown. These adverse views must be treated with the deference that extreme antiquity, without the adjunct of intelligence, deserves. The truth remains, seen or unseen, that the Negro has a right and title to the citizenship of the republic of thought.

But the pivotal point that is determinative in this discussion, and that which is considered the conclusion of the whole matter, is the moral and social question as well as the domestic virtues of which woman is the queen. The accumulation of property and achievements in the world of letters, admirable as they are in themselves and for purposes of civilization, are secondary and and valueless in the final analysis. if there is no moral development and social power. The evolution of the family, based upon monogamy, is one of the chief glories of Christianity over against the libertinism and polygamous practices of paganism.

Speaking of the woman of our race, "we cannot but speak the things which we have seen and heard." With Dr. Crummell, "in her girlhood all the delicate tenderness of her sex has been rudely outraged. In the field, in the rude cabin, in the press-room, in the factory, she was thrown into the companionship of coarse and ignorant men. No chance was given her for delicate reserve or tender modesty. From her childhood she was the doomed victim of the grossest passions. All the virtues of her sex were utterly ignored. If the instinct of chastity asserted itself, then she had to fight like a tigress for the ownership and possession of her own person, and ofttimes had to suffer pains and lacerations for her virtuous self-assertion. When she reached maturity all the tender instincts of her womanhood were ruthlessly violated. At the age of marriage--always prematurely anticipated under slavery--she was mated as the stock of the plantation were mated, *not* to be the companion of a loved and chosen husband, but to be the breeder of human cattle for the field or the auction block."

Has this condition of affairs changed? I answer unequivocally, yea, a thousand times, yea. A negative answer would be the quintessence of ignorance. From a recent careful survey of every Southern State through nearly one hundred trusty observers, I have the testimony that the young women are pure in large numbers, and are rapidly increasing in an intense desire and determination to preserve themselves chaste and pure from the lustful approaches of the sinner; and that the number of legally and lovingly married families purely preserved in the domestic and social virtues among husbands and wives, sons and daughters is so far beyond the days of slavery that a comparison would minify the difference. The marvel is that the Negro had sufficient moral vitality left to make his way through the whirlpool of licentiousness to the solid rock of Christian character. From the harem-life of the promiscuous and unnameable sins of slavery, some of which were the natural and fatal growth of pagan vices, others the fruit of prostitution, to the making of one clean, beautiful, noble and divine family and home covers a period of intense moral, spiritual, and intellectual development, more significant than the geologic transformation of ages. Be it known that this one family can be duplicated by a hundred thousand and more.

The moral and social darkness has not been increased either in quantity or intensity. The splendid results of philanthropic effort have served only as a small tallow candle which has been brought into the darkness of this Egyptian night, and the darkness has thickened relatively only because the light has been brought in. That faint and flickering light reveals how great the darkness has been and is. Some think that the shadows are lengthening into eternal night for the Negro, but that flickering light within has upon it the breath of God, which will some day fan it into the white and penetrating blazes of the electro-carbon search-light that shall chase away the curse of slavery.

It has been the boast of the defenders of slavery that it was a restraining influence upon the vicious, pagan Negro. It is hardly possible to believe that such a statement was accepted by sensible men as a justifying clause for the existence of slavery. A school boy's effort at thinking would reveal the untruth of such a view as a determining factor in character-making. Character is not developed by *restraints* but by *constraints*. Restraints and repression merely dam up the passions, smoulder the fires, stunt the growth, warp and consume individuality. It has no proper place in a moral system of of training. It suits the horse that must be directed with bit and whip, or the ox that has to be goaded unker the yoke; it does not suit man, that must be educated and trained by living examples and positive precepts, and inspired and ennobled with lofty sentiments. By its system of repression and oppression, slavery refused to set before the Negro one decent, clear-cut sentiment or to give him one unmixed divine idea to awake the deepest and purest instincts of his unsophisticated African nature. Therefore, when liberty came at the mouth of the cannon, this poor, ignorant, deluded, falsely trained and pent-up creature quickly read, not in words, but in deeds of unconscious activity that liberty meant libertinism. This was the inevitable extreme to which the pendulum would swing. But it is now finding the happy mean of power and life.

Another vital question in this consideration is, has the character of the Negro Christian ministry improved? The bald statement of truth is that the distance between the ministry of to-day and that of slavery days, or the days immediately following freedom, cannot be measured in words. Again, we had no regularly constituted Negro ministry. A few of our fathers in whose heart the "woe is me if I preach not" burned with an unquenchable fire, were permitted to speak occasionally to the slaves, and that under the freezing gaze of an overseer's eye, and to this day it is a miracle unsolved how God preserved a knowledge of the truth through the broken vessels of nought amid the dervish worship of the ignorant slaves.

Since that day there has been a constant stream of educated and consecrated ministers flowing into the ranks of the Negro population. These have been trained in the great universities of the North. Besides these, there have gone forth from the institutions established in the South for colored people large numbers of genuinely consecrated ministers of every denomination. Whether it be accepted or rejected, the fact is that there are in Negro pulpits all over the land and in the South some Negro preachers who, in intellectual ability, in moral power and purity, and in spiritual insight and breadth of vision, are the equal of some of the best of the Anglo-Saxon race.

These schools of the South had, in their early days, Biblical departments. These departments in three instances have developed into full theological institutes and seminaries. The chief ones are the Richmond Theological Institute, the Theological Institute connected with Fisk University, and Gammon

Theological Seminary. Out from the Gammon Theological Seminary have gone seventy-six well-trained ministers in twelve years. They are in nearly every State on this side of the Mississippi, and in six denominations. Their moral life, as well as their intellectual, was under the careful training of picked men, and they stand as monuments of grace and power and purity among their people, and as constant rebukers to the villifyers of their race. Nay, the existence of this one Theological seminary, the largest and best equipped for Negroes in the South, is a perpetual argument that the stream is purifying and rising higher.

Let us hear the conclusion of the whole matter. Before the war the Negro was a dumb-driven and a dumb-used cattle for work and for breeding. Shame, the virtue that Eve brought out of the Garden with her, that belongs alike to heathen and to Christian, was mocked, insulted and trampled under merciless hoofs. The women were the tools for lechery and leechery. The whole head of the race was sick and the heart was faint, bruises and putrifying sores covered the body of the race. Today, in education, in morals, in spiritual power, the Negro is far superior. He marries according to law, rears his family in a home of culture and morality, and reaches up with divine aspirations to the ideal perfections of human nature. *The women are women.* And while it is true that as a mass the race has not yet attained unto all perfection, yet they press with vigor toward the mark and are far removed from that dark age. They are purer, their preachers have improved and are still improving in all the elements of moral power.

THE MORN COMETH.

J. W. HAMILTON, D.D.
Corresponding Secretary of the Freedmen's Aid and Southern Education Society; For nine years Pastor of People's Church, Boston, Mass.

J. W. HAMILTON, D.D.
Corresponding Secretary of the Freedmen's Aid and Southern Education Society;
For nine years Pastor of People's Church, Boston, Mass.

Occult Africa

By
J. W. HAMILTON, D.D.
CORRESPONDING SECRETARY FREEDMEN'S AID AND SOUTHERN
EDUCATION SOCIETY

Africa has been the world-long riddle of the race. It has puzzled the geographer no less than the historian; it has been the Dark Continent of geography, the Dark Forest of history. There could be no philosophy of its development or envelopment, for its story has been only a charade, in which the most important syllables of its word have been acted out alone far away; out of sight and out of hearing of the few persons who have been interested to study it. What has been known of it has been an enigma, parts of which have been guessed at through the curiosity of sight-seers like Mungo Park and other like travelers, or the selfishness of traders and slavers like the Arabs and Portuguese, or indeed Englishmen and Americans. It has been an occult Continent inhabited by an occult people.

The Aristotelians, according to Newton, gave the name of occult qualities not to manifest qualities, but to such qualities only as they supposed to be hid in bodies and to be unknown causes of manifest effects. This definition accurately defines the kind of occultness the world has attributed to Africa. The things which are seen in Africa, which come from Africa, or are in any sense African, are not believed to have been made of things which do appear. They are believed to have come about in some way different from that in which all things elsewhere have come about. An air of mystery hangs about the origin and procedure of everything that is African. The discovery of the continent is veiled in the dim and nebulous distance of pre-historic times; and as for the people, they never were created--like Topsy, who said, "I never was born, never had no father, nor mother, nor nothin'. I spect I grow'd; don't think nobody never made me." This is the way the world, from time out of mind, has looked at Africa.

"While yet Europe was the home of wandering barbarians, long before Abraham left his father's field or the Phoenicians had settled on the Syrian coast, one of the most wonderful civilizations on record had begun to work out its destiny on the banks of the Nile. It enters into the oldest traditions and the most ancient history." But whence came the Egyptians? Whence their civilization? Was it of purely indigenous growth, or did it pour in with older peoples from

Asia? The knowledge of Africa possessed by the ancients was very limited, owing principally to its great size, physical configuration and construction. Africa contains about one quarter of the land of the globe, which is more than three times the area of Europe, or nearly as much as that of North and South America combined. It is 5,000 miles long from north to south, and 4,500 miles long at its broadest part. The great desert, which in a broad belt stretches quite across the continent, forbade every attempt to cross it until the introduction of the camel by the Arabs. The want of any great known river except the Nile that might conduct into the interior; contributed to confine all movements to the habitable belt along the northern coast. The great river Nile itself was as much a mystery as the desert of Sahara. It has puzzled a hundred generations with the mystery of its source, which has been solved only within our own time. Moreover, it was a prevalent belief among the first geographers, and even down to the time of the Arab occupation, that the torrid zone of the earth, and especially of Africa, was uninhabitable on account of its heat. Africa has a story unprecedented in the case of any other continent.

It is said in the First Book of the Kings that Solomon, about a thousand years before Christ, made a navy of ships in Ezion-geber, which is beside Eloth, on the shore of the Red Sea, in the land of Edom. And Hiram sent in the navy his servants, shipmen that had knowledge of the sea, with the servants of Solomon. And they came to Ophir, and fetched from thence gold, four hundred and twenty talents, and brought it to King Solomon. But where is Ophir! Volumes have been written on the subject, and it has been identified with at least a dozen localities of the present day.

The Phoenicians are known to have formed establishments on the northern, coast of Africa probably not less than 3,000 years ago. They are credited with having circumnavigated the continent in the time of King Necho, about 610 years before Christ. It may have been that Homer and Hesiod derived their knowledge of the Mediterranean from them. But Thebes was about the limit of Homer's knowledge of Africa on the south, though he had heard of the Ethiopians and the pigmies. Unfortunately there is no literature come down from the Phoenicians.

The Egyptians, with all their wonderful civilization, were not great navigators. It was not until the time of the Ptolemies that they possessed a fleet of any great importance. One of the Ptolemies, the famous Alexandrian astronomer, summed up the knowledge of the world concerning the continent for four thousand years, but he was no traveler; he has sometimes been called an armchair geographer.

The Greeks had great curiosity concerning Africa. Hecatasus of Miletus, one of the earliest Greek geographers, made a map of the world, but it was lost. Herodotus fifty years later made another map, and it would have been more to his credit if that had been lost.

The Romans, succeeding the Greeks, took possession of Egypt and the northern borders of Africa, but their acquaintance with the other parts of the continent was vague and unsatisfactory.

Most modern history, like ancient, has been able to give only a mythical account of the impenetrable interior of Africa. Jonathan Swift did not describe so very inaccurately the results of much of the explorations down to his day when he said:

> "So geographers in Afric maps
> With savage pictures fill their gaps,
> And o'er unhabitable downs
> Place elephants for want of towns."

Only half a century ago the map of Central Africa was a blank from ten degrees north latitude to the confines of Cape Colony. It is about thirty years since we obtained any certain knowledge of those great lakes which from an early period were rumored to exist in the center of the continent. A little more than twenty-five years ago the Rev. F. D. Huntington wrote in the introduction to a little book on the Home Life in Africa as follows: "Beyond a little strip a few miles wide running all around it next to the seas and oceans that roll their waves against its coast, like the variegated border of a black shawl, almost nothing is known; the names and appearance of a few rivers and mountains and lakes and rude kingdoms, or tribes of negro savages, are all." It is now not more than fifteen years since the course of Africa's greatest river was traced out by Mr. Stanley. It is not yet ten years since we saw "the powers" scramble for the nearly (12,000,000) twelve millions of square miles of area and parcel it out among themselves just as if there were no (210,000,000) two hundred and ten millions of people inhabiting the country.

The continent has been invested with mystery no more than the millions of people who inhabit it have been invested with myth or fable. The oldest inhabitants whose civilization dated back to more than four thousand years before Christ, are believed by many scholarly persons to have been like Melchisedec without father, without mother, without descent. The Egyptians appeared strange and incomprehensible to the educated among the Greeks who really tried to understand them. The Greek populace regarded them with the same timid wonder which our people feel for the "pigtailed Chinese" or Japanese. To them, they were a subject for cheap wit, and "they made jokes about their worshipping oxen instead of sacrificing them, revering eels instead of eating them, and mourning for dead cats instead of skinning them. Yet in spite of their mockery they had a feeling of respect for this people who, with their ancient civilization, looked upon the Greeks as children; there might be a deep hidden meaning in these strange deities and temples."

They were conquered but not any better understood by the Romans. The people from whom we derive the first information concerning the interior of Northern Africa, whose people were the first to be known, were the Arabs, who by means of the camel, were able to penetrate across the great desert to the very center of the continent and along the two coasts as far as the Senegal and the Gambia on the west and Sofala on the east. But what satisfactory account of the natives have we ever derived from the Arabs?

The fifteenth century produced a new era in maritime discovery. The Portuguese were the first to circumnavigate Africa, and from various coast points, they penetrated toward the interior. But the Portugese began the lowest and worst humiliation of the Africans that has ever cursed them as a people.

With Mungo Park, strictly speaking, it is said, begins the era of unceasing endeavor to explore the interior. The first actual crossing of the continent that has been recorded was accomplished no earlier than between the years 1802 and 1806 by two Pombeiros or mercantile traders in the employment of the Portugese, who passed from Angola eastward. But there is great difference between traveling as tourists or traders and as explorers. African exploration did not really begin until Dr. Livingstone in 1840 began those remarkable journeys in the interior of Southern Africa which have continued until the present time and have given him first place among African explorers.

Greatest among the mysteries of this mysterious Continent has been the language which has written and concealed most of its history. Considered as one of the most ancient languages, it is said the Egyptian throws great light upon comparative philology, the relative antiquity of various words and locutions, the general construction of language itself, and the development of picture writing into the abstract cyphers of sound called letters. But the literature of the Egyptians for thousands of years was a hermetically sealed library. To foreign nations the hieroglyphics always remained a mystery. Although Moses was versed in the knowledge of them, the Greeks appear not to have possessed more than a colloquial use of the language. I remember with what profound feeling I stood, a few years ago, in the British Museum, before a slab of black basalt having inscribed on it, first in hieroglyphics, second in demotic or enchorial (a cursive popular form of writing extant at the period), and thirdly in Greek, a decree of the priests of Egypt assembled in synod at Memphis in honor of Ptolemy V. That black slab was the keystone in the doorway to Egyptian literature. It was the famous Rosetta Stone, discovered by the French savans of Napoleon's army in 1799, and which furnished the first clue to the decipherment of the hieroglyphics.

From every view point Africa has seemed, until now, to be the world's greatest secret. The very origin and meaning of the word Africa is veiled in mystery. Compared with the other continents, its story, as I have said, is unprecedented. It was indeed a land of dark forests--so dense as to be impenetrable. The few explorations and decipherments before the discoveries of the present generation only aggravated curiosity and inquiry. Dr. Livingstone, in describing the density of the dark tropical woods, said: "In these primeval forests, the sun, though vertical, cannot penetrate, excepting by sending down at midday thin pencils of rays into the gloom." Some such penciling was all that the great geographical and other learned societies had been able to do through the explorations they had promoted. Curiosity and inquiry had only conjecture to guide them, and what they had discerned was only a balance of probabilities. It was not surprising that the world had come to believe the black man was consigned to the "circle of perpetual occultation."

In the absence of reliable information, it was natural for the rest of the world to go to guessing at Africa. Possibly it was not unnatural for the guessers to arrive at some very inconclusive opinions. It would not be incredible that the African people had been relegated to and made victims of the occult sciences; those imaginary sciences of the middle ages which related to the supposed action or influence of occult qualities or supernatural powers, as alchemy, magic, necromancy and astrology.

The popular notions which have prevailed concerning African slavery have shaped imaginations and controlled opinions concerning the origin and destiny of the African races. Men have asserted boldly and arrogantly that the African people were designed in the very first cosmogony to be hewers of wood and drawers of water. Slavery was their natural relation. As the slaves in America within the recollection of the present generation have been Negroes, most persons have thought that all slaves have been Negroes. As Negroes have come from Africa it has been commonly believed that all Africans were Negroes. As the sons of Ham in the dispersion went into Africa to live, it has been supposed that all Negroes were the sons of Ham. And as Ham is said in the book of Genesis to have looked on the nakedness of his drunken father, and so incurred his anger that he visited the sin of the father on the son of Ham, and in his anger cried out "Cursed be Canaan; a servant of servants shall he be unto his brethren," it has been claimed Scriptural warrant is found for the enslavement of all Negroes.

Of such knowledge and such argument it is pertinent to affirm, in the language of Mr. Josh Billings, that it would be better not to know so many things than to know so many things that are not so. The trouble with this mode of argument has been that it was characteristic of Mr. Kremlin, and "Mr. Kremlin was distinguished for ignorance; for he had only one idea, and that was wrong." The phrase "hewers of wood and drawers of water" was not applied to the African people, but to the Gideonites by the children of Israel. The first slaves were not Africans. The monuments of Egypt, it is true, contained frequent representations of files of captives, but they were both Asiatics and Negroes. The monuments of Nineveh exhibit crowds of captives, men, women and children, taken in the warlike expeditions of the Assyrian sovereigns, and they were of all the nations about there. Slavery existed in Persia, China and India. Parents sold their children to be slaves. There was slavery among the Hebrews. "In the Old Testament," says Ewald, "slavery makes its appearance abruptly in the history of Abraham, as a fully-developed institution, without any earlier mention of it, except its prediction by Noah at the commencement of the history of the present race." As war was one of the earliest promoters of slavery, the captives who were enslaved were as likely to be white persons as black. All Africans are not Negroes. Of the whole number of inhabitants on the continent, probably less than 1,000,000 are recent immigrants from Europe, settled chiefly in the extreme

North (Egypt and Algeria) and in the extreme South (Cape Colony, Natal and the Boer States). About 34,000,000, all of Semitic stock, are intruders from Asia, some in remote or pre-historic times (3,000,000: Himyarites in Abyssinia and Harar from South Arabia), some since the spread of Islam, over 30,000,000 nomad and other Arabs, chiefly along the Mediterranean seaboard, in West Sahara, and Central and East Soudan. All the rest, numbering about 175,000,000 altogether, may be regarded as the true aboriginal element. But these are classed by Lepsius in two great physical and linguistic groups: Hamites in the North, Negroes in the South, meeting and intermingling in the intermediate region of the Soudan. "But this broad grouping is inadequate to explain the present conditions. * * *In general it may be said that, viewed as a whole, the Negro family presents as profound deviation within itself as do the Caucasic and the Mongolic,--that is, the two other great families of the Eastern Hemisphere. The deviations are even greater." So the "Cursed be Canaan" never was the father of the Negro and Negroid peoples, but of the Jebusites, Amorites, Gergasites, Hivites, Arkites, Sinites, Arvadites, Zemarites and Hamathites--but never the Afracites. In the latest book on Africa the author writes of the Congo people whom he had visited, and who belong to the great Bantu family which has been classed among the Negro peoples, to say, "These natives are entirely distinct from Negroes. They are generally of a chocolate color, are finely developed physically, have thin aquiline noses, small hands and feet, slight beard and moustache. The popular notion that all Africans are Negroes is entirely erroneous." Whatever may have been the ethnological classification hitherto, this author finds sufficient dissimilitude between the types and images to invoke at least more careful study.

It is not Noah, nor Ham, nor Canaan, nor Africa, but sin and slavery that have cursed the Negro. It is positive ignorance of the influences of both sin and slavery that creates prejudice and fosters caste. It is this occultism that is responsible for the occultation of both Africa and the Negro.

> "How few think justly of the thinking few;
> How many never think, who think they do!"

Sin is a reproach to any people, and slavery has cursed the white people as well as the black.

The declension and dwarfing of Africa is more a matter of sin than sovereign decree. God never determined against the Negro: The Negro determined against God. His apostacy accounts more for his lapses than his prognathism or his projecting heel. Like all paganism, "it was of an occult kind, and so insensible in its advances as to escape observation."

But it has not obliterated human affinities, nor utterly concealed the human relations. "Between the receding forehead, projecting cheek-bones, the thick lips of the Negro of Guinea and the more straight configuration of the head of a Galla in Abyssinia there are still many striking analogies; and modern philology having traced still greater analogies, denoting a common origin among the only apparently disconnected languages of so many thousands of tribes, whose color presents all the hues between the deepest black and the yellow brown, it is no longer doubtful that the Negro, the Galla, the Somali, and the Kaffir all belong to the same ethnological stock." They are all mixed readily with the Arabs, as the English are mixed with the East Indians in the Eurasians, and the Americans with the Negroes in the mulattoes. The Hottentots bear resemblance to the Chinese, Malays, or their original stock, the Mongols. The half-naked barbarians of Abyssinia claim descent from King Solomon and the Queen of Sheba, and boast that all other kings are but upstarts and pretenders compared with theirs. The lowliest native of the farthest interior exhibits enough self-consciousness and complacency with which to start, and our of which to build a lofty and noble race.

Mungo Park, while traveling in Africa, once entered a region until that time unexplored by civilized man. His escort of Guinea Negroes carried him to witness a gala day jollification. The sable chief was sitting on a stump in the center of a cleared half acre, his face tattooed, trinkets dangling from his nose, ears, chin, etc., and his subjects were dancing around him. Having sold Negroes, captured in war, to the slave-traders on the coast, the chief had learned to speak a little outlandish English. When the visitor approached his majesty (the dance suspended), he exclaimed: "English?" "Yes," said Park, "I am an Englishman." "Way over yonder?" said the chief, pointing westward. "Yes," answered Park; "three thousand miles off." "What folks say about me dar?" was the eager inquiry of his African majesty.

Dr. Drummond, writing from Tropical Africa, says: "Here, as elsewhere, every fresh investigation tends to establish more and more the oneness and simplicity of nature." In the light of the latest intelligence from over the earth science never adhered more firmly to the unity of the human race.

The argument against the differentiation of the race in the races is met irrefutably in the possible and actual assimilation of all the races in the one man. The unity of the race is demonstrated with emphasis in the personalities and careers of men like Benjamin Banneker, Frederick Douglas, and Alexander Dumas.

It was slavery made Africa what Livingstone called "the open sore of the world."

"In 1442," says Mr. Ingram, author of the "History of Slavery," in the Encyclopedia Brittanica, "when the Portugese under Prince Henry, the navigator, were exploring the Atlantic coast of Africa, one of his officers, Antam Gonsalves, who had captured some Moors, was directed by the Prince to carry them back to Africa. He received from the Moors in exchange for them ten blacks and a quantity of gold dust. This excited the cupidity of his fellow-countrymen, and they fitted out a large number of ships for the trade, and built several forts on the African coast. Many Negroes were brought into Spain from these Portugese settlements, and the colonial slave trade first appears in the form of the introduction into this newly discovered world of children or descendants of these Negroes." There began the cruelties which cursed a race in the thought and feelings of the American people. We will not follow it in its descent, but will say with the eloquent Castelar, whose voice, pleading for the lowly in Spain, was like one crying in the wilderness, "Let there be no more accursed races on the earth." There are hereditary influences which have come down with the slave-holder and sons of slaveholders; there are marks of oppression which have come down with the slaves and the sons of the slaves. In the very nature of the case it could not have been otherwise. But slavery itself is dead, and the doom of all the ages has trodden the grass on its grave--pledge that there shall be no resurrection of the dead. Even the sons of "Cursed be Canaan" are now freemen, or will be when the Turk is dethroned. The vials of the wrath of God have long been full. O thou Angel of the Altar! hasten thy coming, when the sons of earth may hear thy voice saying, "Even so, Lord God Almighty, true and righteous are thy judgments."

"It is Christianity alone," said Max Muller, "which, as the religion of humanity, as the religion of no caste, of no chosen people, has taught us to respect the history of humanity as a whole, to discover the traces of a divine wisdom and love in the government of all the races of mankind, and to recognize, if possible, even in the lowest and crudest forms of religious belief, not the work of demoniacal agencies, but something that indicates a divine guidance, something that makes us perceive, with St. Peter, 'that God is no respecter of persons, but that in every nation he that feareth Him and worketh righteousness is accepted with him.'"

"There is a principle," said John Woolman, "the man who," it is said, "in all the centuries since the advent of Christ, lived nearest to the Divine pattern." "There is a principle," said that Christian man, "which is pure, placed in the human mind, which in different places and ages hath had different names; it is, however, pure, and proceeds from God. It is deep and inward, confined to no forms of religion nor excluded from any, when the heart stands: in perfect sincerity. In whomsoever this takes root and grows, they become brethren."

There are "low-down" white people just as there are "low-down" black people. But both will come up and by the same set of stairways. They will come one by one, and by just so much will the races be brought up with them. Bishop Simpson, in the last sermon he preached, narrated the following incident: "I was in a Western city, and was visiting a school, or rather an exhibition of a school for the education of imbeciles. A young man had conceived the idea that it was possible to educate idiotic children--perfect imbeciles. He went over to Europe to ascertain the best methods of teaching. He returned and opened a school not far from Philadelphia, the first started in this country. After making experiments, he published a note, asking that the most imbecile child in all the land should be sent to him, and that he would test the possibility of educating him. A number were sent to him and he was engaged constantly, but among others sent him was a little boy five years of age. *It* was so perfectly helpless it had never spoken, never chewed a hard substance, never seemed to recognize a single human being; it had no power to turn itself over; it seemed like a mass of purely animate flesh. That was the child of five years, sent to the young man to be educated. He made various experiments and failed for a long time to make any impression. Weary with the toil of teaching in the forenoon he adopted the plan of going in about noon and lying down on the parlor carpet with the child beside him; and, failing to reach its attention at all, he simply read aloud from a book, and he continued to do so daily for six months without ever gaining one look of apparent recognition from the child. One day at the end of six months he was very weary; and lying down beside the child he did not read. Directly he discovered that the child was restless; it was not able to turn over but it could make slight motions; it had never been able to raise its fingers with apparent power, and yet it had some little. The teacher thought to himself, the child misses the noise of my reading.

249

Taking that idea, he got down very closely by the child, put his face almost to its hand and noticed that it was trying to move its fingers. He put his lips down very close, and the child, after various efforts, succeeded at last in putting its fingers on his lips, as much as to say, 'make that noise again.' The teacher said from that moment he felt that he had that child. He commenced working with him, developing the muscles by pressing upon them, and working in various patient ways. At the time when I saw him, five years after that, the boy stood on a platform, made a little address, named over the Presidents of the United States in their proper order, told over little things in our national history, and appeared to be like a boy about five years of age. The teacher had worked with that boy until he had developed the little spark of intellect, and the little force that was in the child and made it somewhat of a power. I looked at him with perfect astonishment and my heart was stirred, and I said to myself "was there ever such a case?' " That was a white child.

There are black children, and there will be black children, victims of privation--"privation more of light and absent day," that will be a long time rising and who will not rise very high. But all may try, and some will try, and the world will wait. It will be long before all the lowly ones rise very high, but all will rise above the lowest. "There is nothing so powerful as truth--and often nothing so strange." But it will require great patience for truth to conquer; truth is direct; "the advance of the world is by a spiral movement, not direct; not a quick movement of ideas, but a slow and almost a hopeless process." It is not hopeless, however.

Slavery did much to dethrone man-likeness, but the slave was left a man. His anthropology vindicates him. I know a book was printed over here in Richmond two or three years ago which was written to prove that the Negro was not a man; was not of Adam's race. In this book it is said "The non-Adamic races are not adapted to, nor intended for, the spiritual religion of the New Testament, because without the spiritual nature which was given to Adam, and are not men in any true and proper sense." This book was written by a clergyman, but even the clergyman, when a defender of human slavery "perverts the prophets and purloins the Psalms." The spiritual movement and progress of the Negro answers this Richmond "Anthropology for the People."

The movement and progress is demonstrated. The willful or stubborn unbeliever who may deny the fact because his theories and traditions will not permit him to understand the process, could, with equal authority, deny that the sun shines, when he is warmed by its rays. "Fraternity," says Joseph Mazzini, "is undoubtedly the basis of all society, the first condition of social progress; but it is not progress, it renders it possible--it is an indispensable element of it--but it is not its definition." Robert Browning has said:

> "Progress man's distinctive work alone,
> Not God's and not the beasts'; God is, They are.
> Man partly is, and wholly hopes to be."

This is as it ought to be, and what ought to be is true. There is struggle; must be struggling. But out of the contest comes the upward movement. It is in leaving the low and earthy that the high and heavenly appear. It is thus the beauties of earth are resplendent. The contrast increases the estimates. For this transition things beautiful and spirits excellent seem to have been formed. "Out of mud," say the Orientalists, "springs the lotus flower; out of clay comes gold and many precious things; out of oysters the pearls; brightest silks, to robe fairest forms, are spun by a worm; bezoar from the bull, musk from the deer, are produced; from a stick is born flame; from the jungle comes sweetest honey. As from sources of little worth come the precious things of earth, even so is it with hearts that hold their fortune within. They need not lofty birth or noble kin. Their victory is recorded."

There is no inferior race. There are races with inferior conditions; they may be white or black; they are at times both. There is nothing in race to ruin the man for this world or the next one. "There is no absolute or essential superiority," said Dr. Blyden, "on the one side nor absolute or essential inferiority on the other." Man is a unit in the plan of salvation. He is the individual when he is saved. We are all saved by ones. All races were lost. But Christ came to recover the lost--all lost. The salvation of this world is the salvation of God. The uplift of the races must be something of an evolution, but it is more; it is revolution, and revolution first of the one man. Too long have we confined the redemption of this world to the work only of grace within the pales of the Christian Church. The world is the subject of redemption, and the world must embrace the whole race of mankind. "Whatever makes men good Christians," said Webster, "makes them good citizens." There has been too much of masquerading for one's funeral on earth and one's home in heaven. It is this world that is to be redeemed. It is the heaven below that is to antedate the heaven above. We are to be all one here, one race, of one speech, and one color. We are to be all one, even as Christ in God is one.

No man is too inferior to be saved. The message of Christianity is, go to him first who needs most. Let every man go with lighted candle to find his nearest neighbor or most distant brother. How towering the watchman and how thrilling the watchcry of Melville Cox, "Let a thousand die before Africa be given up."

But the whole earth must be filled with the light before the last man can be found. "Knowledge is the only fountain both of the love and the principles of human liberty." It is the only safeguard of human rights. I recall the little shop of a jeweler which stood in the post village where I lived when a boy. The town is described in one of the geographies printed fifty years ago as "noted for its numerous churches and gross immorality." I remember with what admiration I was accustomed to look on the possessions of this goldsmith, who spread on a board, covered with black cotton cloth, here and there, a ring that had been repaired, a few watches, silver and gold, and some other small pieces of jewelry. In the evening he would lift the board from its place in the window and carry it with the treasures to a little wooden box in the back part of the store. There he would deposit it for the night, turn down the lid, fasten a padlock in the staple, and then close a heavy wood shutter over the window, fling an iron bar across the shutter, hold it in its place by a couple of screws, secured by a nut at each end on the bolts which came through from the outside. The heavy wooden door was then closed and locked, with the store as dark within as if Phoebus were dead. He went to his home as complacently as if his treasures were in heaven. The darkness quite as much as the windows and door were his defense.

You and I know, secure as he deemed his little stock in the store to be, that the boy burglar of our time would have taken it as only a bit of pastime to carry away the jewelry before the jeweler had sat down to his supper. Thus the protection of half a century ago could have been thwarted.

But I went into the city of Boston a few nights ago when the clock was striking twelve--midnight--I stopped on Tremont street to wait for a car. While waiting I discovered that I was standing in front of one of the largest jewelry establishments in New England. Not only on Tremont street, but down the side street, I noticed that the two brick walls of the building had been removed, both in the front and on the side, to the height of the ceiling, to make room for plate-glass windows. I walked about the windows, and saw that great showcases were stretching through the store from the front to the back, in which were displayed costly gifts that could not have been bought with all our fortunes. Then over each case, the whole length of the store, blazed an electric light, which revealed in sparkling splendor everything contained in the cases. I said: "Here is the defense of our times; the darkness has given place to the light."

Then turn on the light. Let every mind flash with intelligence and truth. Let every man who can see be guide and guardian of him who is blind.

> "Shine all around you,
> By day and by night."

Vice and crime will flee away with the darkness, and virtue and innocence will sleep in the surest defense of the light. Your sons and daughters will grow up angels of God, if pilgrims of the night. So will the lances of light go before them to pierce the thick darkness of demons and shatter the blind bucklers of caste. The occult lines, with all their occultation, will go out in the face of the sun. What a heavenly morning!

"I have opened the door," said Livingstone; "I leave it to you to see that no one closes it after me."

Africans--Afro-Americans! Ye are no more strangers and foreigners, but fellow-citizens with the saints and of the household of God; and are built upon the foundation of the apostles and prophets, Jesus Christ himself being the chief cornerstone. In whom all the building, fitly framed together, groweth unto an holy temple in the Lord. In whom ye also are builded together for an habitation of God through the Spirit.

The Study of Folk-Lore

BY
ALICE M. BACON
SECRETARY HAMPTON FOLK-LORE SOCIETY

The folk-lore of any people is the body of unwritten knowledge that is handed down from generation to generation. It contains the beginnings of all arts and sciences, and ceremonies and religions. It is the source from which the earliest history of any people must be drawn. As a race advances from the unlettered to the lettered stage of civilization, it trusts more to the written record and less to the unwritten tradition, and so, as education in letters spreads, this unwritten knowledge grows less and less important in popular estimation, until at last the searcher after these beginnings of literature and art and science, finds them only in the rural districts among the ruder classes of the population, in the shape of old stories told by the winter fireside, old ceremonies continued after the meaning of the rites has been lost, old songs and games commemorating long forgotten events, but still sung and played by the children, who keep unconsciously the traditions which their elders have outgrown. In these places the folk-lore of each race and nation survives unchanged by advance in civilization and learning and forms, if patiently gathered and rightly read, one of the few links that connect each one of us today with our remote pre-historic past, with the time when our ancestors looked out with the wondering eyes of childhood upon the strange world about them and began the reasoning from observation of natural phenomena, the reaching out after beauty of thought and expression, the groping after the infinite behind the finite, which have resulted in the science, the literature and art, and the religion which are the world's proudest boast to-day. If we would rightly know our past, we must study our folk-lore. If we would come into sympathy with what our ancestors have thought and suffered, as well as with what many of our fellows are thinking and suffering to-day, we must go into the cabins and talk with the old folks and the unlettered country people; and with all reverence, knowing that these things are the stuff from which all our present advance has been made, we must gather together and preserve what still remains of the ancient stories and beliefs and songs and customs of our people.

The American Negro is the resultant of many forces. His history is a complex one and as yet mainly unwritten. His past begins in the barbarism of African tribal life, continues through the horrors of captivity and transportation, moves on through the hard but effective school of slavery into close contact and large participation in the most complicated civilization that has yet arisen. Each of these forces has moulded and shaped his character and belief, and what he is to-day, or what he will be in the future can be discovered only through a careful examination and study of the effects produced by each of these forces upon his mind and character.

In the study of his own past through his folk-lore, the American Negro has his peculiar advantages and his peculiar disadvantages. The first obstacle that he will meet arises through the circumstance that the original languages--the evolution of the African life of the race--have been wholly laid aside, and the tongues of the new countries in which his lot was cast have been substituted. By this change of language a considerable body of folk-lore has undoubtedly been lost, and one of the important links between the past and present is lacking. Again, the breaking up of family ties, so common in slavery, has interfered seriously with the transmission of traditions from father to son and from mother to daughter, and especially with the preservation of legends of ancestors or heroes or tribal ties such as may be found among the American Indians. These disadvantages are, however, more than balanced by the great advantage to be found in the close proximity of the culture of the present with the primitive beliefs of thirty years ago. In this fact lies the great and unique opportunity for the colored collector of his own folk-lore.

It is only thirty years since all the learning of his race was embodied in its folk-lore, when the written literature of the white men among whom he lived was sealed to him by the compulsory ignorance in which he was kept. The Negro, in the old days, must spend his time in hearing and thinking and talking, where the white man by his side spent it in learning through the medium of books; and thoughts and beliefs must be perpetuated by him in stories, songs, rythmic utterances and rites and ceremonies which could by the whites be committed to paper, to survive or be forgotten as the case might be. In consequence of this short distance in time that lies between the Afro-American and the unwritten learning that belongs to the childhood of his past, he may look back with ease and gather up for himself and his future history the small beginnings of learning which preceded literary attainment. What would not the Anglo-Saxon give if he could study today from the life, the customs, and thoughts, and beliefs of his barbaric ancestors, if he could visit them in their wild tribal life among the German forests, could follow them to the slave markets of Rome, could talk with those who had, through slavery and conquests and all the stern teachings of the earlier days in Europe, worked their way out into heirship in the civilization of Egypt and Phoenicia and Greece and Rome? But this is denied him. He must search in musty, dusty libraries for what contemporary historians have written of his people's childhood. He must gather from remote corners and out-of-the-way places the little that remains of the pre-historic savage and barbarian in the ruder specimens of his race. The American Negroes, however, are today passing through so curious a crisis in their history that these conditions, impossible for any European race, may be realized by them. There are along the line of two great railroads that cross our continent places where the way lies through high mountain passes, winding in and out, ever higher and higher, toward the summit of the "Great Divide;" and the engineer, directing and urging the train onward and upward, may find himself looking at times in at the windows of the last cars of his train. In this same way the colored people, traveling towards the summit of the great divide that separates the past of slavery and ignorance from the future of civilization and citizenship, find that the leaders are now in full view of the men on the last car. One generation is all that separates them from each other-- the unlettered past from the cultured present. In many homes, by the firesides, in the softest chairs and the warmest corners, are still sitting the old folks who have come out from slavery, who have preserved in memories, strengthened by the necessity of remembering what could not be committed to paper, the traditions and beliefs of the old days, and who will give out to those whom they love and trust, and to those only, the many thoughts over which they ponder as they sit and watch the young folks who have had so many opportunities that they sometimes think that the old folks can teach them nothing. Do not let these of the older generation think that the young people care nothing for the past. Do not wait until the toil-hardened hands are folded for the last time, till the dim old eyes have looked their last upon the glowing fire, till the soft crooning voices, with their quaint words and expressions, are stilled forever, before you begin to want to know what they might have told you. Do not believe that the learning of the white man is all that the black man needs; do not suppose that Africa and slavery have no part in the past of the American Negro citizen any more than that the Mayflower is a matter of no importance to those whose ancestors it brought from England. If the Negro would be not a mere imitation white man, but the kind of a man that God, who has guided his past, meant him to be, he must take an honest pride in those things that belong to himself. He must study his own history, not in the light of what white people have said about him, but from the abundant material for history embodied in the folk-lore of his race, whether in the transplanted stocks of America or in the aboriginal tribes of Africa.

At Hampton a beginning has been made in this direction--a beginning that can amount to comparatively little without the cooperation of as many as possible of the cultivated colored people on both sides of the Atlantic. A Folk-Lore Society has been formed, and through the *Southern Workman* some of the matter collected is published monthly with a view to creating and keeping up an interest in this branch of study. At the monthly meetings of the society, papers are read and discussions held on topics announced a month in advance, and the secretaries of the society, by means of these papers, and notes on the additional matter brought to light in the discussions, collect and arrange all material contributed, under classified heads, with a view to its ultimate publication in book form. The society to-day is working almost alone; it needs coöperation with workers in all parts of the South; it wants correspondents also in Mexico, in the West Indies, in Africa, for the proper carrying out of the plan. Only by comparison of the folk-lore of widely differing localities can what is local and recent be separated from what is universal and ancient, a true outgrowth of the race character of the Negroes and not the result of recent changes of environment.

Persons desiring to become corresponding members of the society will receive, on payment of $1.00 a year the *Southern Workman* and all circulars, bulletins and other publications of the society, and will greatly aid the work by contributing from time to time any facts along lines already opened up, or any hints as to new lines of investigation that may occur to them. Whenever enough persons are interested in the work to form a local society, the interest many be vastly increased and the work of each member doubled in efficiency by monthly meetings for papers and discussions, and comparison of data collected.

The topics originally outlined for study and inquiry are as follows. (I quote from our first circular issued in November, 1893:)

1. Folk-tales. The animal tales about Brer Fox and Brer Rabbit and the others have been well told by many white writers as taken down from the lips of Negroes. Some of them have been already traced back to Africa; many are found existing, with slight variations, among Negroes and Indians of South as well as North America. These, with other stories relating to deluges, the colors of different races and natural phenomena of various kinds, form an important body of Negro mythology. Any additions to those already written out and printed, or variations on those already obtained, would be of great value.

2. Customs, especially in connection with birth, marriage and death, that are different from those of the whites. Old customs cling longest about such occasions. The old nurse who first takes the little baby in her arms has great stores of old-fashioned learning about what to do and what not to do, to start the child auspiciously upon the voyage of life. The bride receives many warnings and injunctions upon passing through the gates of matrimony, and the customs that follow death and burial tend to change but little from age to age. What was once regarded as an honor to the dead, or a propitiation of his spirit, must not be neglected, lest the dead seemed dishonored, or the spirit--about which we know so little after all--wander forlorn and lonely, or work us ill because we failed to do some little thing that was needful for its rest. And so the old ways linger on about those events of our lives, and through them we may trace back the thoughts and beliefs of our ancestors for generations.

3. Traditions of ancestry in Africa, or of transportation to America. Rev. Dr. Crummell, in his eulogy of Henry Highland Garnett, says of that great man: "He was born in slavery. His father before him was born in the same condition. His grandfather, however, was born a free man in Africa. He was a Mandingo chieftain and warrior, and, having been taken prisoner in a tribal fight, was sold to slave traders, and then brought as a slave to America." If this tradition was preserved for three generations, may there not be others that have been handed from father to son, or from mother to daughter, through longer descents? The slavery system as it existed in the United States tended to obscure pedigrees and blot them out entirely by its breaking up of all family ties; but even if only here and there such traditions are still found, they are worth preserving as tending to throw light upon the derivation of the American Negroes.

4. African words surviving in speech or song. Here and there some African word has crept into common use, as *goober* for peanut, which is manifestly the same as n'gooba, the universal African designation for the same article of food. Are there not other words less common which are African? Do not children sing songs or count out in their games with words which we may have taken for nonsense, but which really form links in the chain that connects the American with the African Negro? Do not the old people, when they tell stories, use expressions sometimes that are not English, and that you have passed over as nonsense? Are there songs sung by the fireside, at the camp-meeting, or at work, or play, that contain words, apparently nonsensical, that make a refrain or chorus? If there are, note them down, spelling them so as to give as nearly their exact sound as possible, and send them in with a note of how they are used.

5. Ceremonies and superstitions. Under this head may be included all beliefs in regard to the influence of the moon or other heavenly bodies; superstitions in regard to animals of various kinds, and their powers for good or evil, as well as all ideas about the medical or magical properties of different plants or stones. Here also may be noted all that can be learned about beliefs in ghosts, witches, hags, and how to overcome supernatural influences. How to cork up a hag in a bottle so that she cannot disturb your slumbers; how to keep her at work all night threading the meshes of a sifter hung up in the doorway and so escape her influence; how to detect or avoid conjuring, or magic in any form; how to escape the bad luck that must come if you turn back to get something you have forgotten, or if a crow flies over the house, or if your eye twitches, or if any of the thousand and one things occur which, in the minds of the ignorant and superstitious, will bring bad luck if the right thing is not done at once to avert the evil influence.

6. Proverbs and sayings. From the time of King Solomon until now there have always been embodied in proverbs many bits of sound wisdom that show the philosophy of the common people. The form that the proverbs and sayings take depends largely upon the habits and modes of thought of the people who make them. Thus a collection of the proverbs of any people shows their race characteristics and the circumstances of life which surround them. Joel Chandler Harris, in his "Uncle Remus' Songs and Sayings," has given a series of plantation proverbs that show the quaint humor, the real philosophy, and the homely surroundings of the plantation Negroes. (In Mr. Harris' book the Georgia Negro dialect is carefully preserved, but that is not necessary for our work, though adding to its value where it can be done well.)

7. Songs, words or music, or both. Hampton and other schools have been at some pains to note down and preserve many of the "spirituals" which are probably the best expression so far attained of the religious and musical feeling of the race, but there are innumerable songs of other kinds which have never been taken down here. One of the earliest methods of recording and preserving historical or other knowledge is through the medium of rythmic and musical utterance. The Iliad of Homer, the great historical psalms of the Hebrew poets, the Norse sagas, the Scotch, English and Spanish ballads, were but the histories of the various races moulded into forms in which they could be sung and remembered by the people. In the absence of written records or of a general knowledge of the art of reading, songs are the ordinary vehicle of popular knowledge. A few years ago I was listening to the singing of some of our night

students. The song was new to me, and at first seemed to consist mainly of dates, but I found as it went on and interpreted itself that it was a long and fully detailed account of the Charleston earthquake, inwhich the events of successive days were enumerated, the year being repeated with great fervency again and again in the chorus. Are there not songs of a similar character that take up older events? Are there not old war songs that would be of permanent value? Are there not songs that take up the condition and events of slavery from other than the religious side? Are there any songs that go back to Africa, or the conditions of life there? What are your people singing about--for they are always singing at their work or their play, by the fireside or in social gatherings? Find out and write it down, for there must be much of their real life and thought in these as yet uncollected and unwritten songs.

There are many other lines along which observation would be of value for the purpose of gaining a thorough knowledge of the condition, past and present, of the American Negro. Are there any survivors of the later importations from Africa, or are there any Negroes who can say to-day, "My father or mother was a native African?" If there are, talk with them, learn of them all they can tell you, and note it down. Are there any families of Negroes, apparently of pure blood, characterized by straight or nearly straight hair? If there are, do they account for it in any way? What proportion of the colored people in the district where you live are of mixed blood? Give the number of pure and mixed blood. What proportion having white blood have kept any traditions of their white and Negro ancestry so that they know the exact proportion of white to Negro blood? How many have traditions of Indian ancestry? Reports on all these subjects would be in the line of our work.

Along these lines of research we have tried to proceed, but have found work in some directions much more difficult than in others, and our choice of subjects has been determined largely by the special interest or knowledge of those who have brought in papers. Of tales, we have gathered enough to make sure that Uncle Remus has not yet exhausted the possibilities of that field. Recent publications by the American Folk-Lore Society, of Angola, Louisiana, and Bermuda Folk Tales, render the work of comparison more easy than it has hitherto been, and have added a new interest to collections along that line. We should like to gather more stories of heroes and ancestors, reminiscences, if such there be, of African life or of local celebrities, whether slave or free, runaway, or conjure doctor, preacher, or leader of any kind.

Of customs we have collected a few. The line that we have been at most pains to follow out is an investigation of courtship customs and questions. The numerous riddles and figurative speeches in use among the young people of the plantations form a body of folk-lore of distinct and peculiar interest. That they have their parallel in Africa seems quite certain, and that they have no relation to any custom that has survived among the white races seems equally certain. The study of these customs among the Negroes of both continents is a most promising field for investigation. Correspondence bringing in further investigation along this line is earnestly solicited.

Of words which are of African origin, we have so far been able to discover very few. There seems no reason to doubt that the word gomber-work, often used for conjuring or divination, comes direct from the African *ngombo,* the spirit who reveals the unknown through the medium of his servant, the ngombo man. Other words we have noted, of which the origin is doubtful, and it is probable that in the parts of the South where the colored people live much by themselves on the great plantations, a larger proportion of words from the original tongues of the race would be found than in our section of Virginia.

Of superstitions of various kinds, we have gathered many. Almost the first work that we did was the collection of quite a body of hag-lore, and the development in as much detail as possible of the gruesome particulars that make this night-riding horror one of the most uncanny products of the human imagination. Considerable attention has been paid to the belief in conjuration, the powers and peculiarities of conjure doctors, their charms and spells, and the results which are expected from them. Of signs, omens and portents, we have also collected many. Of proverbs and sayings, comparatively few have been gathered, though there is little doubt but that a rich harvest lies open to the investigator of that field.

For many years the Hampton School has been making an effort to preserve and collect the spiritual songs of the Negroes in America, and to give to its students so great a love for these beautiful utterances of the emotion of an enslaved and deeply religious race, that they would strive as they went out to gather up and preserve a form of emotional expression only too likely to pass away in the transition period through which the colored people are now passing. So impossible is it to reproduce this music under changed conditions that there is danger lest even where both words and music are preserved, the spirit which gives it its peculiar charm may be lost forever. The educated Negro can not sing

261

the old songs as his father sang them. He may yet evolve a higher and nobler music of his own, but the old spirituals, squeezed, as it were, out of the human heart by the pressure of slavery, are a part of his history that he cannot afford to lose--a breaking forth from bondage of that thing which could never be enslaved, the genius of a race.

Of great help in interpreting both words and music would be some account of the origin or use in worship of particular songs. Even now the question of the origin of the whole body of music, so long attributed to the peculiar race genius of the Negro, is in dispute. Would we save to the race a part of its heritage we must find out all that can be discovered of the source of these songs. Each one has arisen, either on some special occasion or to fill some want in devotional service. Thus a study of the present uses, and, so far as possible, of the past history of each song should be made at once.

Closely connected with the religious music is that other form of religious and rythmic utterance found in the prayers and sermons heard still in many of the Negro churches. These sermons and prayers, with their rythmic form, their musical intonation, their pauses for the deep chanted responses of the audience, are poetry rather than prose, and should be classed with the utterances of psalmists and prophets rather than with the plain matter-of-fact teaching of the nineteenth century preacher.

The fact that these sermons and prayers are handed down from older to younger preachers, and are used again and again by the same man, increases their resemblance to poetic rather than prose utterance, and gives them a place in the true folk-lore of the race. Every effort should be made to collect and preserve all sermons, prayers and religious songs, for through these means much of the emotion that was repressed in other directions found its noblest utterance.

One other direction there is in which our collection of folk-lore should be extended, and that as quickly as possible. We have had it in mind for some time to establish a folk-lore museum, in which to preserve as complete material evidence of the transition from Africa to American citizenship as can be obtained. Specimens of all those implements, furnishings and manufactures that belonged to the plantation life should be there collected, with a view to showing to the student of past conditions exactly what were the material surroundings of the old days. Of especial interest as establishing connection between Africa and America would be the contrivances in common use for the capture of fish and game, specimens of basket work, weaving and iron work and other industries, a part of the knowledge of which might have been brought from Africa. Household furnishings of domestic manufacture would also be of value, for it is often the most common article of every day use that retains longest its distinct characteristics.

Such a museum should contain also a collection of charms, "bands," conjure bags, and roots and bulbs commonly believed to possess medical or magical properties. To a full collection from American sources should be added as rapidly as possible a collection of African implements, etc., that by comparison of the two the connection between the Negroes on both continents might be traced. Such a museum can only be established through the coöperation of workers all over the South; for the things that we seek to gather are the rude contrivances and manufactures that are being rapidly supplanted, even in the remote country districts, by the better implements and more showy products of the great industrial centers. But the fact that they are hard to obtain now makes it more than ever necessary that we should set about obtaining them at once, for such is the perishable nature of most of the things desired, and the little esteem in which they are commonly held, that the lapse of a few years only will sweep away all such material relics of the old days.

This then is the work that the collector of Afro-American folk-lore has to do--the work of gathering up patiently and in a spirit of scientific inquiry the rapidly vanishing memorials of an humble but fruitful past. As every circumstance of that past has left its trace upon the character of the men and women of today, so is each circumstance a part of the life history of the race. Whatever there is remaining today to point out the path over which your people have traveled to their present position, is of great value, not only to you but to the whole human race--for we are all one. We have all alike come up out of barbarism, heathenism, slavery and superstition to citizenship in this free republic. What is of importance to the Afro-American is also of importance to the Anglo-American, is a part of the history of this great country in which we are all working together today for the freedom, the enlightenment and the Christianization of the world.

BISHOP H. M. TURNER, D.D.
Of the African Methodist Episcopal Church: Editor of the *Voice of Missions,*
Atlanta

Essay: The American Negro and the Fatherland

BY
THE REV. BISHOP H. M. TURNER, D.D.
AFRICAN METHODIST EPISCOPAL CHURCH.

It would be a waste of time to expend much labor, the few moments I have to devote to this subject, upon the present status of the Negroid race in the United States. It is too well known already. However, I believe that the Negro was brought to this country in the providence of God to a heaven-permitted if not a divine-sanctioned manual laboring school, that he might have direct contact with the mightiest race that ever trod the face of the globe.

The heathen African, to my certain knowledge, I care not what others may say, eagerly yearn for that civilization which they believe will elevate them and make them potential for good. The African was not sent and brought to this country by chance, or by the avarice of the white man, single and alone. The white slave purchaser went to the shores of that continent and bought our ancestors from their African masters. The bulk who were brought to this country were the children of parents who had been in slavery a thousand years. Yet hereditary slavery is not universal among the African slave-holders. So that the argument often advanced, that the white man went to Africa and stole us, is not true. They bought us out of a slavery that still exists over a large portion of that continent. For there are millions and millions of slaves in Africa to-day. Thus the superior African sent us, and the white man brought us, and we remained in slavery as long as it was necessary to learn that a God, who is a spirit, made the world and controls it, and that that Supreme Being could be sought and found by the exercise of faith in His only begotten Son. Slavery then went down, and the colored man was thrown upon his own responsibility, and here he is today, in the providence of God, cultivating self-reliance and imbibing a knowledge of civil law in contra-distinction to the dictum of one man, which was the law of the black man until slavery was overthrown. I believe that the Negroid race has been free long enough now to begin to think for himself and plan for better conditions than he can lay claim to in this country or ever will. *There is no manhood future in the United States for the Negro.* He may eke out an existence for generations to come, but he can never be a *man*--full, symmetrical and undwarfed. Upon this point I know thousands who make pretensions to scholarship, white and colored, will differ and may charge me with folly, while I in turn pity their ignorance of history and political and civil sociology. We beg here to itemize and give a cursory glance at a few facts calculated to convince any man who is not biased or lamentably ignorant. Let us note a few of them.

1. There is a great chasm between the white and black, not only in this country, but in the West India Islands, South America, and as much as has been said to the contrary, I have seen inklings of it in Ireland, in England, in France, in Germany, and even away down in southern Spain in sight of Morocco in Africa. We will not however deal with foreign nations, but let us note a few facts connected with the United States.

I repeat that a great chasm exists between the two race varieties in this country. The white people, neither North nor South, will have social contact as a mass between themselves and any portion of the Negroid race. Although they may be as white in appearance as themselves, yet a drop of African blood imparts a taint, and the talk about two races remaining in the same country with mutual interest and responsibility in its institutions and progress, with no social contact, is the jargon of folly, and no man who has read the history of nations and the development of countries, and the agencies which have culminated in the homogeneity of racial variations, will proclaim such a docrine. Senator Morgan, of Alabama, tells the truth when he says that the Negro has nothing to expect without social equality with the whites, and that the whites will never grant it.

This question must be examined and opinions reached in the light of history and sociological philosophy, and not by a mere think-so on the part of men devoid of learning. When I use the term learning, I do not refer to men who have graduated from some college and have a smattering knowledge of Greek, Latin, mathematics and a few school books, and have done nothing since but read the trashy articles of newspapers. That is not scholarship. Scholarship consists in wading through dusty volumes for forty and fifty years. That class of men would not dare to predict symmetrical manhood for the Negroid race in this or any other country, without social equality. The colored man who will stand up and in one breath say, that the Negroid race does not want social equality and in the next predict a great future in the face of all the proscription of which the colored man is the victim, is either an ignoramus, or is an advocate of the perpetual servility and degradation of his race variety. I know, as Senator Morgan says, and as every white man in the land will say, that the whites will not grant social equality to the Negroid race, nor am I certain that God wants them to do it. And as such, I believe that two or three millions of us should return to the land of our ancestors, and establish our own nation, civilization, laws, customs, style of manufacture, and not only give the world, like other race varieties, the benefit of our individuality, but build up social conditions peculiarly our own, and cease to be grumblers, chronic complainers and a menace to the white man's country, or the country he claims and is bound to dominate.

The civil status of the Negro is simply what the white man grants of his own free will and accord. The black man can demand nothing. He is deposed from the jury and tried, convicted and sentenced by men who do not claim to be his peers. On the railroads, where the colored race is found in the largest numbers, he is the victim of proscription, and he must ride in the Jim Crow car or walk. The Supreme Court of the United States decided, October 15th, 1882, that the colored man had no civil rights under the general government, and the several States, from then until now, have been enacting laws which limit, curtail and deprive him of his civil rights, immunities and privileges, until he is now being disfranchised, and where it will end no one can divine.

They told me in the Geographical Institute in Paris, France, that according to their calculation there are not less than 400,000,000 of Africans and their descendants on the globe, so that we are not lacking in numbers to form a nationality of our own.

2. The environments of the Negroid race variety in this country tend to the inferiority of them, even if the argument can be established that we are equals with the white man in the aggregate, notwithstanding the same opportunities may be enjoyed in the schools. Let us note a few facts.

The discriminating laws, all will concede, are degrading to those against whom they operate, and the degrader will be degraded also. "For all acts are reactionary, and will return in curses upon those who curse," said Stephen A. Douglass, the great competitor of President Lincoln. Neither does it require a philosopher to inform you that degradation begets degradation. Any people oppressed, proscribed, belied, slandered, burned, flayed and lynched will not only become cowardly and servile, but will transmit that same servility to their posterity, and continue to do so *ad infinitum,* and as such will never make a bold and courageous people. The condition of the Negro in the United States is so repugnant to the instincts of respected manhood that thousands, yea hundreds of thousands, of miscegenated will pass for white, and snub the people with whom they are identified at every opportunity, thus destroying themselves, or at least *unracing* themselves. They do not want to be black because of its ignoble condition, and they cannot be white, thus they become monstrosities. Thousands of young men who are even educated by white teachers never have any respect for people of their own color and spend their days as devotees of white gods. Hundreds, if not thousands, of the terms employed by the white race in the English language are also degrading to the black man. Everything that is satanic, corrupt, base and infamous is denominated *black,* and all that constitutes virtue, purity, innocence, religion, and that which is divine and heavenly, is represented as *white.* Our Sabbath-school children, by the time they reach proper consciousness, are taught to sing to the laudation of white and to the contempt of black. Can any one with an ounce of common sense expect that these children, when they reach maturity, will ever have any respect for their black or colored faces, or the faces of their associates? But, without multiplying words, the terms used in our religious experience, and the hymns we sing in many instances, are degrading, and will be as long as the black man is surrounded by the idea that *white* represents God and black represents the devil. The Negro should, therefore, build up a nation of his own, and create a language in keeping with his color, as the whites have done. Nor will he ever respect himself until he does it.

3. In this country the colored man, with a few honorable exceptions, folds his arms and waits for the white man to propose, project, erect, invent, discover, combine, plan and execute everything connected with civilization, including machinery, finance, and indeed everything. This, in the nature of things, dwarfs the colored man and allows his great faculties to slumber from the cradle to the grave. Yet he possesses mechanical and inventive genius, I believe, equal to any race on earth. Much has been said about the natural inability of the colored race to engage in the professions of skilled labor. Yet before the war, right here in this Southland, he erected and completed all of the fine edifices in which the lords of the land luxuriated. It is idle talk to speak of a colored man not being a success in skilled labor or the fine arts. What the black man needs is a country and surroundings in harmony with his color and with respect for his manhood. Upon this point I would delight to dwell longer if I had time. Thousands of white people in this country are ever and anon advising the colored people to keep out of politics, but they do not advise themselves. If the Negro is a man in keeping with other men, why should he be less concerned about politics than any one else? Strange, too, that a number of would-be colored leaders are ignorant and debased enough to proclaim the same foolish jargon. For the Negro to stay out of politics is to level himself with a horse or a cow, which is no politician, and the Negro who does it proclaims his inability to take part in political affairs. If the Negro is to be a man, full and complete, he must take part in everything that

belongs to manhood. If he omits a single duty, responsibility or privilege, to that extent he is limited and incomplete.

Time, however, forbids my continuing the discussion of this subject, roughly and hastily as these thoughts have been thrown together. Not being able to present a dozen or two more phases, which I would cheerfully and gladly do if opportunity permitted, I conclude by saying the argument that it would be impossible to transport the colored people of the United States back to Africa is an advertisement of folly. Two hundred millions of dollars would rid this country of the last member of the Negroid race, if such a thing was desirable, and two hundred and fifty millions would give every man, woman and child excellent fare, and the general government could furnish that amount and never miss it, and that would only be the pitiful sum of a million dollars a year for the time we labored for nothing, and for which somebody or some power is responsible. The emigrant agents at New York, Boston, Philadelphia, St. John, N. B., and Halifax, N. S., with whom I have talked, establish beyond contradiction, that over a million, and from that to twelve hundred thousand persons, come to this country every year, and yet there is no public stir about it. But in the case of African emigration, two or three millions only of self-reliant men and women would be necessary to establish the conditions we are advocating in Africa.

T. THOMAS FORTUNE
Editor *New York Age*; Author of " In Plain Black and White "

T. THOMAS FORTUNE
Editor *New York Age;* Author of "In Plain Black and White"

The Nationalization of Africa

BY

T. THOMAS FORTUNE EDITOR NEW YORK *Age,* NEW YORK CITY

Mr. President, and Ladies and Gentlemen of the Congress:

"The proper study of mankind is man." Man is the simplest and yet the most mysterious mechanism in nature. His physical, mental and spiritual attributes have been the most interesting of his studies in all ages. He has been and he is now, in large part, as much of an enigma to himself as the sphinx, in the sands of old Egypt, reared by black giants of Africa when the world was young, and when color was not the test of manhood or of genius, is now to the students of ethnology and philology. He who contributes in any way to the enlargement of our knowledge of the supreme subject of moment and of interest is a benefactor of his race. That we know as much of the temple in which the Creator has placed the image of himself--grand, mysterious, magnificent--that we know as much of his past history as we do, and of the empires he has reared, and which have long since relapsed into the dust from which they proceeded; that we have been able to follow him from the tower of Babel on the plains of Shinar through the blackness and the mists that envelop human hope and aspiration before we possessed "the letters Cadmus gave," into the remotest corners of the earth, placing metes and bounds, and to his rise and to his decline and fall, is due as much to the patrons of the arts, the sciences and of letters, as to those who have toiled in the darkness and in the light, weaving the long chain of ratiocination which links the remotest past to the living present, clinching the poet's thought that "All are but parts of one stupendous whole."

As "the heirs of all the ages," as the legatees of the accumulated wealth of sacrifice and of labor which have built up our splendid consensus of knowledge, we stand here to-day with the map of the earth unfolded before us, upon which there are but few black spots into which the explorer has not penetrated and which the philosophical historian has not illuminated as to its people and as to what they have done and have not done. Where our ancestors groped in ignorance and doubt we now walk in the fullness of knowledge and the self-assurance that it gives.

The unity of the human race is no longer a disputed question. That "one-touch of nature makes the whole world kin" is as universally accepted, as the

271

theory that the sun is a stationary orb and that the earth is round. Color of the skin, texture of hair, differences of language and of habitation avail nothing against the demonstration that all mankind proceeded from the same cause and will ultimate in the same effect; that their origin and their destiny are as interlocked and as inseparable as life and death. When so much has been ascertained, when so much has been accepted, when so much shall have become the rule of conduct of individuals and of aggregated societies, of man to man and of government to government, we may rest in the assurance that the dreams of Edward Bellamy, in some remote æon of time, become facts in the intercourse of mankind. The dreams of genius often become realities in "the wreck of matter and the crush of worlds," in the discoveries of science and of philosophy, in the passing away of old beliefs and of old forms, and in the establishment, as a result of such transformations, of higher ideals of living and of government. All being is but the aspiration of the human soul after perfection. In the savage and in the highest type of civilized man, this philosophy will be found to have been, and to be, exemplified. It has been the touchstone of all the progress which has been made in every department of human effort, from the Chaldean of old, reading the stars, to Benjamin Franklin, harnessing the lightning and Robert Fulton compressing the steam, so that the twain have become the Archimedean lever that unlocks the doors that conceal the treasures of the earth and of the heavens.

The map of Africa is no longer a Chinese puzzle. Its geographical mysteries have been solved. Its mighty lakes and rivers have been traced to their source, and fiction and cupidity have unlocked hordes of treasure by the side of which that of King Solomon's mines was as the vastness of the Atlantic's waste of waters to the smallest stream that, like a silver thread, wanders down the mountain side and sighs itself away into the sands of the desert. Railroads are spanning its immense distances, steam boats are navigating its water-ways, and the electric wire has brought it into talking distance with Europe and America. Its limitless agricultural and mineral resources are being developed for the comfort and the happiness of mankind. Vast States have sprung into being, as if by magic, controlled by European colonists, so that already a South African confederacy has worked its way into the brain of Cecil Rhodes, whose empire is cemented with more human blood and tears than the East Indian empire wrenched into the British Government by the crimes of Lord Clive and Warren Hastings.

Never in the history of mankind has a continent been so rapidly subdued and its waste places made the habitation of civilized governments and its savage inhabitants brought into contact and under the control of civilization. More has been accomplished along these lines in Africa in the past quarter of a century than was accomplished by European colonists in America in the first one hundred and fifty years of their desperate struggles here to subdue the aborigines. Steam and electricity and gunpowder are responsible for this phenomenon. They are conquering forces against which no other forces can prevail. The savage, with his primitive weapons of defense, falls before them as the mists vanish before the all-powerful and all-searching rays of the sun. He must relinquish his sovereignty and his wealth of all sorts when these forces confront him. The heroism of the Ashantee or the Zulu warrior, fighting in defense of his fireside and his country, is wasted when his assagai is opposed to the maxim gun or winchester rifle, or even the old Colt's revolver. We have seen this in the subjugation of the North American Indians, and we are now witnessing it in the case of the Africans.

The extent to which the continent of Africa has been spoliated and delimitated by Europeans is shown in the fact that of 11,360,000 square miles of territory, all of it has been absorbed or is claimed except the 9,700 square miles controlled by Liberia on the west coast. France and Great Britain have already made efforts to absorb this residium, and we have no reason to suppose that when they get ready to absorb it and resolve it into a colony they will not do so. In the philosophy of our civilization might makes right in practice, however much we may disclaim it in theory. In this, as in many other of the Christian virtues, our precept and our example are radically at war.

If the conquest of Africa shall proceed in the next seventy-five years as it has done in the past twenty-five, the whole continent will be as completely under European control, after the lapse of a century, physically and mentally and morally, as it is possible for conquerors to impose their conditions upon the conquered. The vast population of Africa will be brought under Christian influences in new forms of government and habits of thought and of conduct. The whole life of the people will be revolutionized. Ancient beliefs and superstitions and tribal relations and dissimilarity of vernaculars will, in the course of time, be transformed entirely. The demoralizing heterogeneousness which now prevails over the whole continent will give place to a pervading homogeneity in language, in religion, and in government.

WHAT WILL BE THE RESULT IF AFRICANS ARE BROUGHT UNDER CHRISTIAN INFLUENCE?

The physical and mental forces now dissipated in tribal wars, in savage methods of industry, will give place to peaceful administration of government and to concentrated methods of industry. The nationalization of the continent will proceed along these lines as naturally and as surely as did that of Great Britain and Ireland, and as did the Germanic States under the masterful direction of Kaiser William, Prince Bismarck and Count von Moltke. Experience, as the great Virginian proclaimed, is the only light by which we can be guided in a matter so speculative. We can reason only by analogy. Human development proceeds along a straight line.

A common habitation, a common language, a common religion, are the necessary bases of homogeneous citizenship and of autonomous government. They are not possible without these. No government has successfully prevailed without them. It may be that Rome, whose legends overran the world, failed in the end because of the too rapid absorption of alien races possessing dissimilar languages and religions. Absorption was too rapid for proper assimilation, and the mistress of the world perforce died of strangulation. And what a fall was there when "the Niobe of nations," borne down by the massiveness of its own strength, torn by dissensions from within and surrounded by barbarous hordes from without, her proud eagle, which had circled over the nations of the earth, plucked of his pinions, lay prostrate in the dust, even as Milton's arch fiend which had braved the host of heaven. When so great a giant among the nations of the earth can fall to so low an estate as to furnish the nations of the earth with bootblacks and fruit-venders and organ-grinders, what nation, what people can hope to escape the handwriting on the wall however vaunting their pride, however herculean their strength? Pride goes before a fall, and death lurks in the frame where health is accounted a heritage. "Oh, why should the spirit of mortal be proud!"

The surface of the earth is capable of sustaining so many people. The population of the earth to-day is very little greater than it was a century ago. It will be but a little greater a century hence than it is now. The pressure of population upon subsistence is insistent and relentless. The supreme struggle of mankind is one of life, of subsistence, of preventing death by starvation or exposure. All other objects of life are subordinated to this one. It is the sleepless agent of colonization. It has penetrated the utmost bounds of the globe. It has wrenched from the weak their fertile valleys and luxuriant hillsides; and when they have protested, when they have resisted, it has enslaved them or cut their throats. It has invented all weapons of defense and of offense. It has invented all the machinery to increase the productivity of effort at a minimum cost, of whatever sort.

It was, therefore, but natural that the congested population of Europe should seek an outlet in North and in South America and the islands of the sea and in Asia and in the Australias; and it is but natural that the same congested population, in the desperate pursuit of something to eat and something to wear, should now be seeking an outlet in the virgin continent of Africa, whose vast areas of territory and hordes of population have been the despair of geographers and ethnologists and philologists and antiquarians alike. The book of mystery having been unlocked, mankind has made indecent haste to master its contents. No fear of burning sun and expansive wastes of deserts and savage beasts and black men, the fabled genii of the Arabian Nights' entertainment, has deterred them. They are plunging into the forests and the sandy deserts, braving the deadly miasmas, more fatal than "an army with banners," fearful that the pearl of great price shall escape them. If we are to give credence to the doleful croakings of many ravens in this country, we should stand in wonderment and awe at the spectacle of caravan after caravan of white men and white women, the flower of Europe's children, winding in a long procession into the black continent, ultimately to impose their civilization upon the continent and to mingle their blood with that of the 300,000,000 children of the sun, the despised black children of the family of races. Their conduct should be inexplicable to these ravens, who insist that black blood and white blood will not mix, although it has so far done so in the West Indies and the United States, that these countries have a yellow streak running through them so thick and so long that only those hopelessly inflicted with blindness fail to see it and to properly account for its existence and to deduce from it the fact that reason, sympathy, affection, and not the color of the skin or texture of the hair, are the tests of the brotherhood, of the unity, of the human race.

> "Skins may differ, but affection
> Dwells in black and white the same."

Europe will continue to pour its hungry and ambitious and adventurous children into the continent of Africa in the future as in the past, but there will come a time when self-preservation will dictate a restriction or cessation of the infusion. But even before that time shall have been reached, the white races of Europe who are now subduing savage tribes and laying the foundation of empires upon the ruins of savage villages and imposing their yoke upon the natives, their language and their religions and their forms of governmental administration and their system of commerce and industry--even now the European minority in Africa are beginning to be absorbed and assimilated by the vast black majority. This is inevitable. A minority race in contact with a majority race is doomed to absorption and assimilation. It is the primal element of nationalization. The minority race must exterminate the majority or be exterminated or absorbed by it. This is an iron law. It has been verified in the history of every race and of every nation. It will be verified in the history of Africa. It will be impossible for France to recover Alsace and Lorraine because the population has become Germanized in blood and language and religion. The minority Frank has been absorbed and assimilated by the majority Teuton, even as the invading and conquering Saxon minority was by the conquered Angle majority, and even as the imported and enslaved African black is being absolved by the heterogeneous white races of the United States. The inevitable destiny of the European whites in Africa is absorption and assimilation by the African blacks as surely as the ultimate destiny of the African blacks in the United States is absorption and assimilation by the American whites. I know that to many this is an abhorrent view of the question, but we are dealing with the philosophy of recorded history and the invariable laws of human conduct and not with the prejudices of men. Men are governed by the laws regnant in their environment. They do not make the laws; they cannot control them. If they do not like them, they are free to take themselves into a more congenial atmosphere. If the whites of America did not want to absorb the blacks, they should have left them in Africa; if the European whites do not want to be absorbed and assimilated by the blacks they should remain out of Africa. The matter is a very easy one to decide before the first step is taken; beyond that point it is controlled by "the divinity that shapes our ends, rough hew them as we may." The rigid laws and rules and regulations already adopted by the English, the Germans, the French and the Belgians in Africa to keep the natives in their place will prove as ineffectual to their purpose as such laws and rules and regulations now prove in the United States. The amalgamation of the European in Africa will proceed as surely towards the development of a national type of man as the amalgamation of alien races has proceeded in the United States for two centuries towards the same end.

276

Here we absorb and assimilate the Indian, the European, the Asiatic and the African and grow strong in mental and physical prowess in the process. Indeed, our national strength is to be found in the homogeneity of its heterogeneous race elements, in its common language and in its common religion. The nationalization of Africa will proceed along the same lines as that of the United States is proceeding. What manner of man will be evolved from the process, what sort of national power he will represent, we are already able to judge, inferentially, by the results being worked out in the nationalization of the people of the United States. The intermingling of so many race elements must work for national and spiritual and material strength in Africa as it has done in all the instances with which history has concerned itself.

I believe that the nationalization of Africa will be along English lines, as that of the United States, in its language, from the basic point of view, in its system of government and in its religion. The English language is the strongest of all languages, the most elastic in its structure, the most comprehensive in its use as a vehicle of human thought and expression. The English system of civil government is the best that has been devised, because it allows the greatest possible freedom to the citizen consistent with the safety of the state. The Christian religion is destined to supplant all other religious systems of belief, because it is the best code of moral philosophy ever given to man as an inspiration or as a development, an evolution of the social life of a people.

The English-speaking people are to-day the strongest force in Africa, from the European point of view. They will disappoint the truth of history if they do not ultimately effect a confederation of all the other European forces, including the native forces comprised in each of them. They will be forced into this federation in self-defense, as the American colonists were. History repeats itself. The nationalization of the African confederation which is a foregone conclusion from the facts in the case, will be the first step toward bringing the whole continent under one system of government. Language and religion may not produce a homogeneous people, as stated by the Hon. John H. Smithe yesterday, but habitat, language, and religion will do it in Africa, as they are doing it in the United States.

It is written in the Holy Book that Ethiopia shall stretch forth her hand to God. Is it in the power of men to make of no effect the divine prophecy? Perish the thought. There shall yet be evolved out of the conflicting race elements on the continent of Africa a civilization whose glory and whose splendor and whose strength shall eclipse all others that now are, or that have gone before into the shadows, locked in "the double night of ages," from which no traveler returns in gladness or in sorrow.

E. W. S. HAMMOND, D.D.
Editor of the *Southwestern Christian Advocate*, New Orleans, La.

Africa in Its Relation to Christian Civilization

BY
E. W. S. HAMMOND, D.D.
EDITOR *Southwestern Christian Advocate,* NEW ORLEANS, LA.

By civilization, we mean a condition of human communities characterized by political and social organization and order; by advancement in knowledge, refinement and the arts, and progress in general. When we speak of Christian civilization, we mean that condition of human society which results from the establishment of the truths of the Christian system, as they are found in the doctrines and teachings of Jesus Christ. This gives emphasis to every human purpose and aspiration, and furnishes the inspiration to the work of the mental, moral, and social uplifting of humanity. And so far as those agencies are dominant in effecting the necessary changes in the conditions, habits and lives of the people upon whom they are brought to bear, so far do we behold the triumphs of those great principles which underlie all human happiness.

I am in full accord with the statement that "The main progress of mankind lies in the development of the ethical idea, which, existing in our nature as a form of the mind, an element of human personality, has ever more and more unfolded itself in history, as the vivifying principle of those ordinances and institutions whereby we live as civilized men, as the justification of the common might, which, without it, would be mere brute force."

The pages of the world's history are replete with the story of the conquests of civilization. Too often has mere human selfishness turned its splendid victories into defeat. That there has been unnecessary bloodshed, that the more powerful nations have spoiled the weaker, will not be denied. Yet, out of the great struggle for human aggrandizement, God has brought light and order; and the time is near at hand, if it is not even now at our doors, when no civilized nation will dare to trample upon the rights of the weakest.

The trend of sentiment indicates growth in favor of the settlement of all international disputes, not by red-handed war, but by the more humane methods of arbitration. In no other way is it possible to counteract the influence of those nations who seem to be actuated only by a desire to increase their territorial acquisitions.

In some way or other the more highly civilized powers should protest against the high-handed seizure of territory from weak and semi-barbarous people, and more especially so since the conquerors have too often left the aboriginal owners of the territory under a system of bondage far more appalling than the heathenism in which they were found.

But we rejoice to know that brotherhood is in the very air, and the time is surely coming "when men shall beat their swords into plowshares and their spears into pruning hooks." The victories of civilization will be the victories

of peace; the gospel of Christ and humanity will be regnant, and the banners of Christian civilization will carry the inscription, "To the fatherhood of God and the brotherhood of man."

The echoes of the "Macedonian Cry" have been reverberating down through the centuries, with ever-increasing pathos, and with irresistible importunity. And I am profoundly grateful to say, that the disposition of the friends of the blessed Master to respond to this call can be measured only by their lack of facilities with which this work is to be accomplished.

It is a glorious privilege to be living in this progressive age, in which there is so much that conduces to the broadening of our ideas with reference to the vastness of the work to be done, and with such enlarged facilities by which it may be successfully accomplished.

It will not be disputed that nations, as well as individuals, are under the most solemn obligation to the Giver of all good, for the inestimable privilege of enjoying the benefits of these conditions, which will put them in touch with the forces which He would use for the salvation of men.

It is no surprise that Christian people the world over are working in harmony with the plans of God for the accomplishment of his great purpose. It is in his great plan to better the condition of the human family through human agencies and instrumentalities.

Thanks to the progress of Christian civilization we have fallen upon times when we can perceive a determined disposition to recognize divine obligations, human relationships, and brotherhood; to redress grievances and to institute plans that will ameliorate conditions less favorable, and make this whole earth pay tribute to the advancing civilization of the age.

The Bible, the school-house, and the printing press are the corner-stones of this imposing structure which stands for the temporal and spiritual supremacy of the world. They are the underlying principles which give inspiration to the manifold energies of the increasing multitudes who shall come under their beneficent influence. We can form at best a very feeble conception of the results of this most magnificent providential arrangement.

If the future may be judged by its past achievements, when we consider the rapidly multiplying facilities for the increase of knowledge, the aggressive and progressive Christian spirit manifest in all lands, we may be justified in the prediction that Christian civilization will march into the twentieth century the mistress of the entire world.

Nor will high walls, powerful navies, or well-drilled armies repress the steady and increasing purposes of the sons of men to look into each others faces, and to help lift their weaker brother up to higher planes of thought and action.

Literature, science, and philosophy have called into action innumerable agencies by which the successive steps in the world's progress have been noted and marked. God moves in a mysterious way, and his purposes will more and more flash upon human hearts and consciences.

> "There's a fount about to stream,
> There's a light about to gleam,
> There's a midnight darkness changing into day.
> Men of thought and men of action,
> Clear the way!"

Yes, clear the way, for it has come to pass in this year of our Lord, in this the brightest era of the world's progress, that the continent of Africa has become not only the center of geographical and scientific attraction, but the greatest field for missionary activity and zeal and interest that the world has ever witnessed since the dawning of the Christian era.

But what of Africa?

My heart kindles as I catch a shining shaft from this age of spiritual dynamics. I seem to hear the Master as he utters his great, irrepressible "Go!" and the answer of millions of the blood-washed, "Here am I, send me, send me." "This gospel of the kingdom shall be preached in all the world for a witness." How the promise has tarried! Nineteen hundred years have almost passed. But these are only as a day with the Lord.

I hazard nothing when I say that Africa is now the most practical enterprise open to Christian civilization. It is no longer an insurmountable barrier in the pathway of the progress of geographical science. Its darkness is melting into a glorious sunlight. Awaking from her sleep of ages, her "sunny fountains" and her "golden sands" have aroused renewed and increasing interest. Obstacles which once seemed insurmountable are disappearing before the march of civilization.

Mr. George R. Stetson, a very eminent authority, says: "There is nothing in the physical geography, or in the climate of the continent, or in the hostility of the natives, or any part of discovered Africa which will suffice to bar out the indomitable European or prevent him from taking peaceable or forcible possession of the country for his own and the world's advantage, or which will prevent Africa from joining in the great march of modern civilization and commercial development." Intrepid explorers are now treading its interminable forests, or scaling its lofty mountains, or winding along its historic rivers, or treating with its mighty rulers, and thereby are obtaining a better knowledge of its wonderful resources.

Representatives of the strongest civilized nations on earth have already planted the standards of their respective governments, and are operating and co-operating, as the case may be, in the interest of the peculiar geographical, topographical, and climatological character and conditions of this the most interesting, wealthy, and romantic of all the continents of the earth.

In Africa we have all the elements out of which to construct such a civilization that will evoke the admiration of the entire civilized world. In ancient history, its place in prophecy, its place in the commercial world, its place in literature and art and science, has already attracted the attention of the great powers of the earth. Christian philanthropists, scientists, diplomats, statesmen, explorers, and missionaries find in its vast mountains, deserts, plains, and rivers, its teeming millions of diverse peoples, its multiform types of civilization, object-lessons of the most momentous import.

Africa is an inexhaustible subject. It has been in the thought of scientific men ever since the dawn of history. More than forty centuries of its strange history look down upon us to-day. It has taken an active part in the greatest drama of the world's history. On this great continent, Israel's matchless leader and lawgiver received that training which made him the most conspicuous character upon the pages of either sacred or profane history.

Here was established the first form of political government. Here the world's great Redeemer found an asylum from the rage of the cruel Herod. Here, in the dim past, the arts and sciences were patronized, and philosophers and sages and wise men were conversant with the literature that has come down to us with little change after the lapse of more than four thousand years. We are surprised and astounded that this great continent, which once had the post of honor in the great procession toward a higher and a better civilization, and once mistress, she

> Of vast domain, the land and sea,
> Paid tribute to the light that shone
> From glittering hall and stately throne.

And to break these chains which error and superstition has forged, and to rescue the teeming millions of her children for Christ and the gospel, is the imperative work of our Christianity.

The Christian world owes to Africa its highest and best forms and types of Christian civilization. To throw railroads and telegraph lines over its vast area; to launch steamboats and other vessels upon her great rivers and lakes; to draw from their hidden resources her fabulous treasures; to utilize her wonderful natural wealth; to transform her vast feudal and tribal relations into well organized forms of political governments, are among the great civil movements necessary to African redemption. But by far the greatest work is the spreading of the Gospel of the Son of God throughout her borders. Blessed Gospel! God's chosen means for the redemption of a lost and ruined world! It will win some of its most magnificent victories in this great land

Christianity is not contented with a mission here and there along the coasts of the "Dark Continent." It must push its victories from ocean to ocean There ought to be, and there must be, an unbroken line of Christian workers stretching from the Cape of Good Hope to Egypt; thence to Sierra Leone and Liberia; thence onward victoriously and gloriously to the Soudan and the Congo State; thence to her historic islands, and moving forward with increasing momentum it must make her great desert blossom as the rose.

Is not America providentially related to the salvation of Africa? Is it not eminently fitting that our own beloved country should be thoroughly identified in this great work? Are we not specially obligated to pay back to Africa the debt which we owe to her stolen sons?

I believe in Africa. I believe we are here to-day to consider some of the most vital questions that were ever submitted to human hearts and human judgments. This question of planning for the salvation of hundreds millions is too big for any but a true Christian heart. The desire to save one soul gives more happiness than the possession of millions of wealth. To be able to put our heart in touch with the great, tender, loving heart of the Master is the climax of earthly joy.

As sinners saved by Gospel grace, we represent here to-day more concentrated spiritual power and light and love and unquestioning faith in the world's redemption than was represented in the "upper room" at Jerusalem on the day of Pentecost. Let us look for another Pentecost, here and now! and from this, our Pentecost, let us go forth full-panoplied to take the world for Jesus.

The attention that has been paid to Africa during the last two decades by Christian philanthropists, scientists, explorers, missionaries, diplomatists, and others is without a single parallel in the world's history.

The marvelous revelations as to the character of its multiform types of civilization, its untold commercial resources, and its unlimited and unequaled avenues for scientific and geographical investigation, have brought the "Dark Continent" to a place in public attention occupied probably by no other on earth. As in ancient times all roads led to Rome, so in these days of the world's best progress we may hopefully say that all eyes are turned toward Africa.

We see now as never before the feasibility and the practicability of all the civilized nations taking part in the conquest of the "Dark Continent" in the name of science, commerce, and the religion of Christ." We are coming now into touch with the work as never before. To have the hand-touch of those whose feet have trod the soil, whose eyes have looked upon the people, and to hear from their own lips the story of their own experiences, sacrifices, and travels, is an inspiration. But to hear from the lips of the natives of the Dark Continent the story of their marvelous transformation into Christian citizenship and the fellowship of the saints thrills the heart to sing "Praise God from whom all blessings flow."

In my humble judgment, our own native land is providentially prepared to play a most conspicuous part in the redemption of Africa. It does not require the ken of a seer to notice the great chain of providential events which are so full of hopeful promises with regard to this important field. America, the land of our birth, was consecrated to the cause of civil and religious liberty by the Pilgrim fathers who laid the foundation of the splendid institutions which are the proud boast of every loyal American. It will go without saying that no country upon the face of the globe exceeds ours in its aggressive and progressive missionary spirit and in its disposition to carry the gospel of peace and good will to the very ends of the earth. Christian people of other nations may have preceded those of our land in entering foreign fields and instituting plans for the salvation of the people, but none have surpassed, and few equalled, the great zeal and religious enthusiasm of American Christians to propagate the faith of the gospel among the heathen.

Another important link in the providential chain is the American Negro. The presence of seven and a half millions of Afro-Americans in this country is a matter of no little significance. More than one-fourth of these millions have been brought under the direct influences of the Christian religion. That they are a loyal, order-loving and law-abiding class, no one conversant with their history will deny.

In matters pertaining to their social, moral, intellectual and industrial development, and in their knowledge of true morality and the Christian religion, they will compare favorably with any other class of people on the American continent. Our white fellow-citizens, who know them best, being the judges.

Notwithstanding it has been suggested that there has been a "seeming lack of interest in African missionary work shown by the colored people of this country," I am not prepared either to affirm or deny that this lack is either seeming or real. I am certain, however, that there are very gratifying evidences of increasing interest on their part.

The Pittsburg *Christian Advocate* says: "Thirty years of freedom, education and development is not much in the way of growing strong and reliable missionaries to plant and lead a church among heathen peoples. Possibly providence is holding them back for more thorough preparation and experience before they shall enter upon this great work of carrying the gospel to the tribes of the Dark Continent, out of which their own ancestors came. At all events, they do not yet seem ready for that work. But it is evident that there is among them a growing interest in the subject. They are investigating and discussing. In this they are being aided and encouraged, and by no agency more than by the 'Stewart Missionary Foundation for Africa in Gammon Theological Seminary.'"

Brother Stewart's plan possesses four distinct and important characteristics. It is wise, far-reaching, strategic, and providential. No one will doubt its wisdom, because it proposes to help in the evangelization of the world, and any movement which looks toward hastening the day of peace bears upon its face the impress of wisdom.

R. S. RUST, D.D., LL.D.

Honorary Secretary of the Freedmen's Aid and Southern Education Society of the Methodist Episcopal Church; Secretary from the Foundation of the Society in 1866 to 1888

R. S. RUST, D.D., LL.D.
Honorary Secretary of the Freedmen's Aid and Southern Education Society of
the Methodist Episcopal Church; Secretary from the Foundation of the Society in
1866 to 1888

The Needs of Africans as Men

BY
REV. R. S. RUST, D.D.
HON. SECRETARY FREEDMEN'S AID AND SOUTHERN EDUCATION
SOCIETY

Dr. Rust, the chairman, in concluding the exercises of Sunday afternoon, said:

Only one session more of this congress of scholars, philanthropists, and clergymen remains. It is a remarkable assembly of distinguished persons convened for the philanthropic purpose of awakening a deeper interest among our students and people in behalf of the evangelization of the Dark Continent.

I have been present at every session of the congress, and have been profoundly impressed by the spirit, ability, and eloquence of the speakers and by the earnest attention and enthusiasm of the audiences which filled to its utmost capacity the great assembly room. It is not often that a convention furnishes its attendants such rare entertainment of elevated thought, patriotic sentiment, and holy inspiration. It resembles the inspiring gatherings of the old-time abolitionists in the early history of the anti-slavery struggle, which I was accustomed to attend in my boyhood, when such heroic souls as William Lloyd Garrison, George Thompson the English philanthropist; Wendell Phillips, Orange Scott, Joshua Leavitt, Alvan Stewart, Gerritt Smith, John G. Whittier, Theodore D. Weld, George Storrs, James G. Birney, Daniel Wise, C. C. Burleigh, Henry B. Stanton, Frederick Douglass, Amos A. Phelps, Sarah and Angelina Grimke, Lucy Stone, Abby Kelly, and Lydia Maria Childs thrilled and moved their audiences with their inspiring eloquence to the highest enthusiasm and heroic effort for the freedom of the enslaved millions of our land. It is my earnest prayer that this congress, and similar ones to be holden in the near future, may be as successful in awakening an interest that shall redeem Africa, as the old anti-slavery gatherings were in awakening and creating a public sentiment that resulted in the emancipation of the slaves.

It is not the purpose of this movement to encourage a stampede of our colored population to Africa. This would be a disastrous experiment to our colored people, to the United States, and to Africa itself. Unskilled labor is far more remunerative in this country than in that. The United States gives the great body of the colored people a warmer welcome and higher wages than any other land can offer. Africa is already burdened with its ignorant and thriftless native population. It needs skilled labor, true patriotism, and broad Christian scholarship. It is the aim of this enterprise to turn the attention of some of our best students to the necessities of their native land, to the grand opportunities of doing good offered them there, and to the vital importance of a most thorough preparation for the sublime work of aiding in laying the foundation of an empire by establishing a system of agencies for the redemption of the benighted people of the land of their ancestors.

Dr. Rust gave an emphatic approval to these great primal truths of the Fatherhood of God and the brotherhood of man, and the unity of the whole human race, which has branched out into five divisions and has scattered itself all over the world, as recognized in the addresses of the speakers, as taught by the best thinkers of the age, and corroborated by the oracles of God, "For God hath made of one blood all nations of men to dwell upon all the face of the earth"; and in our supplications, we are taught to address our Father in heaven, the Father of us all, by creation, preservation, and redemption. "In the beginning God created the heavens and the earth," and not until He reached the creation of man did he take counsel in his work. Then in sublime conference with the Trinity, He said: "Let us make man in our image and likeness." "In the image of God created He man." In all the wondrous work of creation the making of man is God's crowning act, and whoever has his image has infallible credentials of his high origin and sonship. Man is our universal representative head and from him all peoples sprung. God never made a superior race nor an inferior one; and there is nothing in the heavens above, nor in the earth beneath, that can substantiate any such doctrine, "For God hath made of one blood all nations of men to dwell upon all the face of the earth."

The Doctor asserted as a sequence from these great truths, the unity of the race, and the brotherhood of man, that the whole human family, from the divine model, had been created substantially alike, in body, soul, and spirit, and that in spite of the differences produced by birth, character, food, and culture, there should be furnished for all an opportunity for broad and thorough training and culture. Each child that enters the world has a claim for the full development of all the powers with which, by his creator, he has been endowed. There should be no discrimination in their education and preparation for the race of life. Those anticipating mission work in Africa should be models, highly educated and fully consecrated to Christ and their work. The heathen world has suffered severely from missionaries of moderate ability and limited attainments. Those who go to Africa as missionaries should be, on account of their character and qualifications, in great demand at home.

This enterprise is an argument in favor of high, broad Christian culture. Education is too often considered an accomplishment of the scholar rather than an indispensable requisite for all in the important duties of life. It is deemed essential to the candidate of a profession, while it is reckoned among the non-essentials to the candidate of usefulness and immortality. Just as if the impartial Governor of the universe had bestowed intellect to irradiate the limited segment of a profession, and not to illumine the vast sphere of universal manhood. God has not created a race for the lower walks and toils of life, while those designed for the learned professions and offices of trust, have been endowed with powers of a nobler nature and a vaster scope. We make a fearful mistake if we think that man needs no other education than what will barely fit him for a life of drudgery. His claim for an education comes from his nature, and not merely from his calling. He is to be educated because God created him for this high purpose, and not because he is to be devoted to any particular profession or employment.

If there ever was a cause worthy to be cherished with especial care, it certainly must be that of educating our youth for useful lives and immortality. It would be a libel on human nature to assert that a deep interest may be awakened on every other subject but that of education, which surpasses all others in the magnitude of the interests at stake and the blessings it dispenses. More arguments and weightier may be adduced in favor of thorough Christian education for all than for almost any other interest connected with the welfare of man. The body, the intellect, the soul, time, and eternity advocate the claims of this noble cause. Some enterprises are sustained by considerations drawn from *this* world, others enter eternity and seize upon motives calculated to stir the very souls of men. But this enterprise, unlike almost every other, is supported by everything *valuable* and *weighty* on earth, as well as *moving* and *thrilling* in heaven. There is not a single errand of mercy upon which Christian or philanthropist may enter, but may be aided by education. There is not an evil that inflicts its curse upon humanity that can be removed without its assistance.

The Negro in His Relations to the Church

BY
H. K. CARROLL, LL.D.
EDITOR NEW YORK *Independent*

The Negro is a religious being wherever you find him and under whatever conditions. In his own continent, where civilizing influences have hardly begun to lift him above the state of savage degradation in which he has so long remained, his religious instincts are dominant. They find expression often in superstitions, idolatrous and cruel rites and observances; but it is a mistake to suppose that even in this primitive and unenlightened condition he is bound down to his fetich, and never looks above the curious and sometimes loathsome object of his worship. He does dream of a *Nyangmo* who sends sunshine and rain, who veils his face with clouds and adorns himself with stars; he believes in the *hibari,* or Spirits of the Lake, and he has conceptions of beings of exalted power who affect the destiny of men. The Negro is a religious being, and he is equally a reasonable being; and when the claims of a more rational, worthy, and spiritual religion are presented to him, he is as ready to cast away this fetich as our remote ancestors, the savage Britons, were to give up their horrid Druidism. Bishop Crowther, the learned, dignified, and respected prelate of the Church of England, was a native African slave. What religion and education did for him, they have done for others in that benighted continent, proving the truth of the Scriptures, that God made of one blood all the nations of the earth and that Christ is equally the Savior of all races.

The Negro of the United States has no religion but the Christian religion. He is not a heathen like our native Indian. He worships but one God, who is a just and merciful God, desiring that all men should be free from sin, and should come to a knowledge of the way of life through Jesus Christ. He is still more or less superstitious; he still has some faith in the power of charms; there is still some trace of heathenish practices in him; but our own race has not altogether outgrown childish thoughts about unlucky days and the way to avoid the evil they bring, and how "mascots" produce success. We cannot condemn the Negro for his superstition without taking blame upon ourselves for the tenacity with which we cling to belief in signs and times and things, lucky and unlucky.

The Negro of the United States is a Christian, not an atheist or a doubter. He gives no countenance to secularist or freethinking organizations; nor does he prefer abnormal types of religion, such as Mormonism and Spiritualism. Moreover, he is not a Rationalist, or a Theosophist, or an Ethical Culturist. He does not turn aside to follow the erratic turns of little coteries of religionists. Neither does he show a preference for the Roman form of Christianity. The splendid ceremonies of Catholic worship might be supposed to have a strong attraction for him; but it is not so. The actual membership of Negro Catholic churches does not exceed fifteen thousand, and yet the Catholic church is not weak in Louisiana, or Maryland, or the District of Columbia. Thirty-one represents the total of Catholic Negro churches. This is not a great result for over a century of Catholic endeavor.

The Negro is not only a Christian, he is an Evangelical Christian. He is a devout Baptist and an enthusiastic Methodist. He loves these denominations, and seems to find in them an atmosphere more congenial to his warm, sunny nature, and fuller scope for his religious activity than in other communions. Perhaps this is due to his long association with them and his training. There is no reason to believe that he might not have been as intense a Presbyterian as he is a Baptist, or as true a Congregationalist as he is a Methodist, if these denominations had been able to come as near to him in the days of slavery as did the Baptists and Methodists. It was fortunate for him that while he was the slave of the white master, that master was a Christian and instructed him in the Christian faith. The school was practically closed to him; but the church was open, and thus he came into personal freedom and into the rights of citizenship an illiterate, but a Christian, with that measure of culture in things spiritual and moral that the Christian faith, voluntarily accepted, necessarily involves.

According to the Census of 1890, there are 7,470,000 Negroes in the country. This includes all who have any computable fraction of Negro blood in their veins. Of these, all except 581,000 are in the old slave territory, now embraced in sixteen States and the District of Columbia. In other words, notwithstanding the migration of Negroes to the North and West, 91 per cent. of them are still in the South, on the soil where the Emancipation Proclamation reached them in 1862 and made them forever free from involuntary bond-age. The Negro churches of the South, therefore, form a large and important factor in the Christianity of that section. In ten of those States the number of Negro communicants ranges between 106,000 and 341,000, and in four of them it exceeds the total of white communicants. Thus, in Alabama, Georgia, Mississippi, and South Carolina, there are more colored than white communicants, although in Mississippi and South Carolina only does the Negro population exceed the white. This shows that, in point of church membership, the Negro is quite as devoted as his white brother. Indeed, the proportion of colored people who are connected with the church, throughout the United States, is larger than that which obtains among the white people. About one in every three whites is a church member On this basis there should be 2,410,000 colored members. The actual number is 2,674,000, or an excess of 264,000 beyond the proportion that obtains among the whites.

The aggregate of colored communicants in the United States, so far as it could be ascertained by the careful methods of the Census, is, in round numbers, 2,674,000. This includes all colored denominations and all colored congregations in mixed denominations, so far as they could be ascertained; but it does not take account of colored communicants in mixed congregations. The number omitted, however, cannot be very large. The States in which the Negro communicants are most numerous are as follows:

Georgia	341,433
South Carolina	317,020
Alabama	297,161
North Carolina	290,755
Virginia	238,617
Mississippi	224,404
Texas	186,038
Tennessee	131,015
Louisiana	108,872
Arkansas	106,445
Kentucky	92,768
Florida	64,337
Total	2,398,865

In these twelve States are found 2,398,865 communicants, leaving about 275,000 to the rest of the States and territories of the Union.

As to denominational connection, the Negro is predominantly Baptist. More than half of all Negro communicants are of this faith, the exact number being 1,403,559. Most of these are Regular Baptists, there being less than 20,000 in the Freewill, Primitive, and Two-Seed-in-the-Spirit branches. It is significant that the

Negro prefers the progressive and missionary type of the Baptist faith, and does not believe in the Hardshell, Old School, or Antimissionary wing. Not less Calvinistic than the most Calvinistic of the Regular Baptists, he is also strict in his practice and thoroughly denominational in his spirit, and takes no little satisfaction in winning Negro members of other bodies to the Baptist faith.

The number of Negro Methodists is 1,190,638, or about 213,000 less than the aggregate of colored Baptists. The Methodists are divided into more branches than the Baptists, those having the Episcopal system embracing the great majority of church members. The Presbyterians have about 30,000, the Disciples of Christ 18,578, and the Protestant Episcopal and Reformed Episcopal bodies somewhat less than 5,000. The Baptists are organized into associations and have State conventions; the Methodists and Presbyterians into annual conferences and presbyteries. A large measure of superintendence is characteristic of the Methodist bodies, the system of Episcopal and sub-Episcopal supervision resulting, apparently, in more intelligent endeavor, greater concert of action, and better discipline.

The increase in the number of colored communicants since Emancipation has been marvelous. How many of the slaves were church members is not and cannot be known certainly. Such statistics as we have must be regarded as imperfect, particularly of the colored Baptists. There were of colored Methodists, at the outbreak of the war, about 275,000, as nearly as I can ascertain. According to this there has been an increase in thirty years of over 900,000 Negro Methodists. This is truly enormous. In the Methodist Episcopal Church alone are more colored communicants, mainly in the South, than the Methodist Episcopal Church, South, reported in 1865, and the two leading African branches have had a marvelous growth. The number of colored Baptists in 1860 probably did not exceed 250,000. We do not know, of course, how many colored communicants there were who were not organized into churches and reported in denominational statistics. But according to the figures we have, there was an increase in thirty years of more than 1,150,000 colored communicants. I know of no parallel to this development in the history of the Christian Church, when all the circumstances are considered.

The Negro, considering the little wealth he had at command when slavery ceased, has achieved wonders in the accumulation of church property. The value of the churches he owns is $26,626,000, the number of edifices being 23,770. Making due allowance for the generous help which the whites have given, it still appears that the Negro has not been unwilling to make large sacrifices for the sake of religion, and that his industry, thrift and business capacity have been made to contribute to his successful endeavors to provide himself with suitable accommodations for public worship.

JOSEPH E. ROY, D.D.
Field Secretary of the American Missionary Association; President of the World's Fair Congress on Africa, Chicago

Africa and America Illustrated; Their Mutual Relation of History and of Service

BY
J. E. ROY, D.D.
DISTRICT SECRETARY AMERICAN MISSIONARY ASSOCIATION

Map of Africa and America.

* The terms in italics indicate the names of the slides.

Here is my subject, the mutual relation of these two great continents. In the self-consciousness of us of the North American division, we are apt to think and speak of it as all of America. Here we have the whole, including its full nest of the West India islands, which Columbus picked up first, and where, soon after, Africa and America made acquaintance. You observe how that sweep of indentation in the contour of the triple America, on its eastern side, is matched by the immense swell on the West side of Africa, as if also to fit their histories into one another, as if drawn together by a strange affinity. Indeed, in his incomparable work, "The Discovery of America," Prof. John Fisk makes much of the fact that "the fates of the continents, America and Africa, with their red men and black men, became linked together from the early time when Prince Henry of Portugal was making his exploring expedition that prepared the way for the great discovery of Columbus." While Columbus was searching for the Indies by a westward, or the Spanish route, the Portuguese were searching for them by an eastward route, and as Columbus on his line discovered America, the Portuguese in theirs are making discovery after discovery along the western coast of Africa, and soon the New World is entering with Africa into the fellowship of woe.

Ravenstein's Map of Africa. This view shows the great river basins, those of the Nile, the Zambesi, the Orange, the Congo, the Niger. These reveal the great extent of Africa's rivers and their valleys, her immense resources for production and for inland commerce. We have here indications of her variety of climate, of her interior and mountain ranges and plateau sweeps that break the rivers into falls and cataracts as they push on down to the coasts. We have here a country three times as large as Europe, extending from north to south five thousand miles, and from east to west four thousand six hundred. Here are two hundred millions of people.

Columbus Discovers America. Observe that while he discovers here the Indians, as seen in the picture, he finds no black men in America. How did they ever come here? This question is answered by four views of the African slave trade,--(1) Catching Slaves at the Night Assault, taken from Stanley; (2) The Slave Market, also from Stanley; (3) The Slave Gang, in wooden yokes marching to the coast; (4) The Middle Passage.

Before the annual meeting of the American Missionary Association, in 1859, Rev. Dr. George B. Cheever, from Harper's Cyclopedia of Commerce, made the following statements as to the slave trade. For it every year twelve vessels were fitted out by three cities each, Boston and Baltimore being of the number, and from other places enough to make forty slave ships, owned mostly by northern men. Each made two trips a year, at a total cost of three million dollars. The receipts being twenty million dollars, left for profit seventeen million dollars. One voyage of the fleet would bring in twenty-four thousand slaves, of whom four thousand were lost by death. The two trips a year would make the total importation forty thousand. These were mainly taken to Cuba, but fifteen thousand were for the United States the preceding year. A slave ship was landed after the war broke out, in a distant part of the South, and there the slaves were held till after the war. It has been estimated by Hon. John M. Langston and by Col. Keating, of the *Memphis Appeal,* that up to 1825 forty million slaves had been imported to the West Indies and to the American Continent.

Map of the West Indies:--To this beautiful land the first importation was brought, to San Salvador, then to Hayti, then to Cuba. As early as 1503 this satanic commerce began. And that "open sore of the world," as Livingston names it, is still a running sore. Mackay reported two thousand slaves going by his place every year from Uganda to the coast, and two thousand from Unyoro. In 1883 a slaver was caught with one hundred and eighty-five victims on board to be set free. Emin Pasha, in May, 1882, reports that for six days following the track of an Arab chief, Ben Chalid, who had a caravan of twelve hundred starving captives, he saw fifty-one corpses by the way, and three hundred and ninety-three of the gang had their necks broken as they became unable to continue the march.

Next after the West Indies, Brazil took up the horrid traffic, and then North America, receiving her first cargo at Jamestown, Va., in 1620. And, notwithstanding the law abolishing the slave trade in 1808, it was really kept up in a surreptitious and an occasional way until the war of the slave-holders' rebellion.

A Slave Market at New Orleans:--Here is a symbol of our domestic slave trade. Up and down the corner of that three-story building you see the sign "Slaves for Sale." It stands to this day with its old sign in sight, and is now owned by a colored man who runs it as a hotel. When the young Abraham Lincoln had made sale in that city of the produce he had taken down from Illinois on a flat boat, he went with his associates into one of those slave marts. There he witnessed the process of examination and of sale, and as he was leaving he turned to his friend, quivering with indignation and said: "Hanks, if ever I get a chance to hit that thing, I'll hit it hard, by the ever living God." Perhaps it was in this very building where he registered in heaven that solemn oath. And didn't he hit it hard when God's time had come?

An Old Slave Bell:--This bell was on exhibition at the Fair in New Orleans of 1884-85, standing by the side of the old Liberty Bell from Philadelphia When the slave bell was made the master had cast into the amalgam one thousand silver dollars to make it ring the better.

Declaration of Independence:--Following that introduction of slavery into our country, there came on, in one hundred and fifty years, in the advanced nations, an era of revolution for liberty. In the United States, where with glaring inconsistency, slavery had been let to fester in the body politic, that uprising wrested independence from the mother country as shown by this signing of the declaration.

Old Liberty Bell :--At that time this bell was rung bearing its scripture message, "Proclaim liberty throughout all the land unto all the inhabitants thereof." As already suggested that old messenger went down to New Orleans to finish its proclamation, and the wonder was that the people of that region should bring and set up by the side of this National symbol, their Dagon of the slave bell. In France that era accomplished a revolution in the government, and by 1794 the emancipation of all slaves in the French dominions. In Hayti, by the development of the spirit of manhood in the servile race, the yoke of bondage was thrown off, and the first Black Republic of the world was set up.

Toussaint L' Ouverture Reading Raynal :--This black slave is reading that work on freedom which had prophesied that some black man would be raised up to bring emancipation and had inspired Toussaint with the idea that he was that man. This proved to be true. He became the statesman, liberator, general of the new Republic.

The Capture of Toussaint by the Strategy of French Officers :--He goes to Paris a prisoner, and there dies, as subsequently his persecutor, Napoleon, went a prisoner to Helena also to die.

Port Au Prince, Capital of Hayti, which Langston said was the Garden of Eden: But the tide of liberty-sentiment must be made to rise still higher before the English islands of that America can come on to abolition. And so there were raised up Clarkson and Wilberforce, whose pictures come before us, the one the moral reformer, the other the political reformer; the one the agitator to develop moral sentiment, the other the statesman to mold that sentiment into law; the one Wendell Phillips, the other Charles Sumner. And then, August 1, 1834, came

Emancipation in Jamaica and in all the English Islands :--The emancipated people, as seen in the picture, instead of rising to massacre their masters, are seen burying their chains in the earth and spending the livelong night in praises to God and rejoicing and dancing. And here we present entrancing views of cities and scenery in those islands.

Port Royal, Kingston, Valley in the Blue Mountains of Jamaica, Trinidad Island, Volcanic Crater in Dominica Island, and Premises of the Mission of the A. M. A.: In these islands have come on a population at least of ten millions with their freedom and their republicanism, Cuba having been the last to receive the boon of emancipation, and now being in the throes of revolution for a republican government. This is a part of the grand result secured by Providence in overruling the horrid system of the slave trade and of slavery. As when the Israelites had spoiled the Egyptians, going out free, so these captives had taken on the advanced ideas of liberty and had come to this high estate of personal freedom and of civilized government.

Following this secondary era of revolution, England abolished her slave trade. At one time, when effort was made in Parliament to ameliorate somewhat the horrors of the middle passage by letting in a little more air, a noble lord besought the members "not to meddle with the alarming question." But now that mother country, 1787, goes, on to provide for the miserable victims of the slave trade, on the coast of their native land, those colonies and cities of refuge for their safety and for their training into civilization and character. Those colonies are:

Sierra Leone and Lagos, as appear upon the screen :--They have come on to be vastly important centers of enlightenment for that coast and its interior, having advanced schools and churches and civilized modes of business life; and in 1821, at the instance of the American Colonization Society, on that same coast, the colony of

Liberia was set up to become the first and model Black Republic of the Dark Continent :--But still the accursed thing clings to the standard republic of America, gnawing at her vitals, falsifying the genius of her institutions, and making a Dark Continent of the very land of boasted enlightenment, as seen by this

Map of Illiteracy, black and white, in our land :--That illiteracy is indicated by the dark shading of the map south of Mason and Dixon's line, and also by the figures of the percentage of such illiteracy in all the States and territories of the Union. At the end of the war, among the Negroes, that illiteracy was about 100 per cent. By the Census of 1880 it had been reduced to 70 per cent., and by the Census of 1890 to 56 per cent., so grand had been the success of mission and public schools among them. By the last Census the white people of the South had reduced their illiteracy from 20 to 14 per cent. But we must take into account the growth of the Negro population, which, by the last Census, was seven and a half million. Now their 56 per cent. of that population will make us a gain of about four millions, the same number we had of colored illiterates at the end of the war. Coming on through the era of the anti-slavery agitation, we find that the conscience of the North has been under such a process of training, that it is ready to meet the slave power when it raises the arm of rebellion.

[Then followed in order, with appropriate words by the speaker, slides on "Firing on Fort Sumter," "Assault on Fort Wagner," "Battles of Lookout Mountain and Missionary Ridge," "Capture of Atlanta and Sherman's March to the Sea," "Reading of the Emancipation Proclamation," "The Surrender of Lee," "The Flag and the Eagle," "My Country 'tis of Thee," "The Wounded Scout," "A Monument to Abraham Lincoln," "George Peabody," "Daniel Hand," "Frederick

Douglass," "General O. O. Howard," and many institutions of high grade among the colored people.]

From this specimen exhibit of the primary and the higher educational work going on in the South, we turn to the service which America, in reparation, has been rendering back to Africa. We strike in upon the west coast.

We give you first the *Dark Continent* in its blackness. Next we present *Ravenstein's Map of African Religions.* Here we see the great belt across the continent of the north for Mohammedanism, and for paganism across the tropical regions. Around the rim of the continent we see the white spots where missions are clustering, with occasional shooting into the interior. We bring you next the *Partition of Africa.* Here we find 10/12 of the entire area appropriated by the governments of Europe. We must see in Providence the good to result from this yoking of those civilized nations into the business of redeeming Africa from her barbarism. But where is the sphere of the United States? It does not cover an acre of ground in Africa. We do not wish any soil there. But our sphere of influence, as we would have it, is the whole of the vast continent, a moral possession. As we have no landed aspirations, this gives us the better opportunity and the larger obligation to occupy our sphere of moral influence.

As to missions, we start in at Sierra Leone, with its city, with our Bishop Turner, who visits there the work of the African M. E. Church, and with our good friend, *Mr. Orishetukeh Faduma,* who, having been graduated from college in England, has had his four years in the Divinity School of Yale, and who, now under appointment of the American Board to return to Africa as soon as the finances will allow, is serving under the A. M. A. in North Carolina, and who has delighted us in this Congress with his two profound dissertations upon Africana. Dropping down a little upon the coast, we present you, as yet within Sierra Leone, the old *Mendi Mission* of the A. M. A., which, after many years of sturdy service, was transferred to the missionary society of the United Brethren, whose only foreign mission was that at Shengay, adjoining the Mendi. We present you the *School Building* of that mission, presided over by Mr. Wilberforce, a native of the region, who was educated in the U. B. College at Dayton, Ohio. We bring you also their Bishop Flickinger, who has been to the field many times without losing his life; also Mr. Gomer, a colored man from this country, who for twenty years served as superintendent of that mission. His death was at an advanced age, and the mission has not lost any other missionary who went from this country, and but one native worker in these twenty years. Here is *Mr. Albert Jowett,* a son of a prince at Mendi, a graduate of Fisk and a student of Chicago Seminary, who is to return to labor with his people.

We bring you next the American Episcopal mission at Cape Palmas, Liberia, with its mission buildings and its colored bishop, *the Rt. Rev. Samuel D. Ferguson.* Next we present you four young men from the Vey tribe in back of Liberia, who, having been educated at the Lincoln University in Pennsylvania (Presbyterian), have given themselves to Gospel work among their people, two returning to Africa, where they are doing custom work, and two remaining in this country to help us in evangelizing America. And here, too, is another native, *Momolu Massaquoi,* a prince, who, educated at the Central, Tennessee, College, was prominent at the Congress on Africa at the time of the World's Fair, and who has returned to introduce Christian civilization into the affairs of his own realm. And here, too, before we leave Liberia we must present you *Bishop Gilbert Haven,* who, having made an official visit to that country, contracted a disease which finally took his life. The colored people of the South know no greater friend than he. He was practically the founder of the Clark University with its immense plat of land. His was a soul all courage and all devotion to his understanding of the word of righteousness. And here comes *Bishop Burns,* the first colored man to be ordained to that office by the Methodist Episcopal Church. For fifteen years before his death he magnified his great office among the people of Liberia. He was followed by another colored bishop.

Dropping down to the mouth of the Niger, we give you a map of its immense valley and fine portrait of *Bishop Crowther,* a native, who, in boyhood, was a slave and who, educated in London, was permitted to build up, in the lower valley of the Niger, a system of churches and schools which has transformed that district of cannibals into a fair region of enlightenment. Here, too, we present you his son, *Archdeacon Crowther,* who, with two new bishops, is holding up the work of his father. And here at the Gaboon, under the equator, is Rev. William Walker, who, after forty years there, is still living at eighty-four years of age in this country. Clearly, all who go to Africa do not die early.

Coming now to the mouth of the Congo we ascend it for one hundred miles to Matadi, where the ocean steamer is halted by the series of cataracts which extends inland two hundred and fifty miles. The new railway is now completed and running for thirty-five miles, and in two years is to be carried through to Stanley Pool, beyond which, in the valley of the Congo, are eight thousand miles of navigable water. We bring you here Bishop Taylor, also *Bishop Taylor aad his*

Conference; also *Miss Georgia Patton, M.D.,* who, as a graduate of the Mehary Medical College, went out to that land to use the healing art, as the Saviour did, for spiritual results. Here also we give you *Miss Gordon* and *Miss Ferguson, M.D.,* Baptist ladies, who are doing their Christly work in the lower valley of the Congo. And here is the little steamer, Henry Reed, plying above Stanley Pool as a missionary messenger. Here too is Mr. George Grenfell, of Bolobo on the Congo, astride his noble ox which he has ridden for a thousand miles, a man of science who has been employed by the Congo Government for delimiting some of its possessions. And this only as a by-play to his missionary work.

Calling off at Benguela, we go inland two hundred miles to the Bihe mission of the American Board and present you some of its buildings and its missionaries, and its scholars and adherents. From St. Paul de Loanda we may take a real train and shoot straight east for two hundred miles into the heart of the continent.

Now whisking around the Cape of Good Hope, we come to Natal. We present you, as connected with South Africa, *Dr. Robert Moffatt and wife,* their son-in-law *David Livingston,* and *Revs. Drs. Josiah Tyler and A. Grout,* who had each been in that service for forty years before returning to their native land for the spending of the remnant of their days. Surely again we exclaim, all missionaries to Africa do not die early! We present you also the *Zulu Mission, Its Members, Male and Female,* a beautiful sight. Next we show you *Rev. M. W. Pinkerton,* who, having had eleven years of delightful service in Zululand, lost his life by the fever while endeavoring to locate the East Central African Mission. The workers die, but God carries on the work. Here are *Mr. and Mrs. Ransom,* who have fallen into the work of Mr. Pinkerton in Natal. He was a graduate of Chicago Seminary, whose faculty and students are raising each year some five hundred dollars toward his support. And finally, here are the members of the *Mission of East Central Africa,* except the colored members who were not in that region when the picture was taken. The Rev. B. F. Ousley and wife and Miss Nancy Jones, graduates of Fisk University, have given some eight or nine years to that mission with conspicuous success.

We bring you here the dissolving set, *"No Cross, No Crown."* (1) A beautiful young lady, standing out, seems to be meditating whether she will take up the cross of this sort of work. (2) The cross appears. Will she take it? (3) She accepts the cross, and in peace of mind sits down at its foot, leaning against it, and meantime, falling asleep, has a dream. Will that dream come true? (4) An angel appearing from above, descends and places the crown upon her head. Crowned at last.

With the representation of the *Afro-American Bishop Holley* we close. For twenty-eight years he has represented the American Episcopal Church in Hayti. He must be a good preacher, for, a few years ago, being in London, he was invited to preach in Westminster Abbey. As he was offering the appropriate prayer for the day, he interposed a petition of his own:--

"Oh, thou Saviour, Christ, Son of the Living God, who, when thou wast spurned by the Jews of the race of Shem, and when thou wast delivered up by the Romans of the race of Japheth, on the day of thy crucifixion, hadst thy cross borne up the side of Golgotha by Simon the Cyrenian, of the race of Ham; oh, thou precious Saviour, remember that despised, forlorn, rejected race, whose son bore thy cross, when thou comest in the power and glory of thy kingdom to dispense thy crowns of everlasting glory."

Surely the Lord, the Christ, will answer that prayer of Simon the Cyrenian from Africa, and remember that despised, forlorn, rejected race whose son bore his cross. Surely our Lord will remember that land which gave him refuge in the day of his infant exile. And surely now, as Gen. Garfield said to the Jubilee singers at Chautauqua, while Ethiopia is stretching out her hands unto God, God is stretching out his hand unto Ethiopia.

Minutes
OF THE
CONGRESS ON AFRICA
HELD IN
ATLANTA, GA., DECEMBER 13-15, 1895

FIRST DAY--FRIDAY, DECEMBER 13

MORNING SESSION

LOYD STREET METHODIST EPISCOPAL CHURCH

The Congress on Africa began its session at 9:30 a.m. in the Loyd Street M. E. Church, with President Wilbur P. Thirkield, D.D., of Gammon Theological Seminary, as President of the Congress. The Missionary Hymn, "From Greenland's Icy Mountain," and two choruses were rendered by the Seminary Choir; after which, the Rev. R.S. Rust, D.D., LL.D., Honorary Corresponding Secretary of the Freedmen's Aid and Southern Education Society, Cincinnati, read the Scriptures, Psalms lxvii and lxviii, and led the audience in prayer. Seated upon the platform were the Rev. Bishop I. W. Joyce, LL.D., of Chattanooga, Tenn.; the Rev. Bishop W. W. Duncan D.D., Spartanburg, S. C.; The Rev. Drs. R. S. Rust, Cincinnati, O.; Joseph E. Roy, Chicago, Ill.; President E. M. Cravath, D.D., Fisk University, Nashville, Tenn.; President John Braden, D.D., Central Tennessee College, Nashville, Tenn.; President J. D. Chavis, B.D.,Bennett College, Greensboro, N. C.; Mr. Heli Chatelain, Mr. Cyrus C. Adams, Editor New York *Sun*; the Hon. W. Y. Atkinson, Governor of Georgia; the Hon. John H. Smyth, LL.D.

On motion of Prof. E. L. Parks, D.D., J. W. E. Bowen was elected Secretary of the Congress.

President Thirkield then delivered the opening remarks, explaining the history, purpose and plan of work of the Stewart Missionary Foundation for Africa under the auspices of which this Congress is held. He then read the following telegram from the Secretary of the World's Fair Congress on Africa, as follows:

To President W. P. Thirkield, D.D., Gammon Theological Seminary, Atlanta, Ga.

"May Atlanta's Congress advance Africa's annexation to Christ's kingdom."

FREDERIC PERRY NOBLE

Bishop I. W. Joyce, LL.D., was then introduced as Chairman of the morning session, who, in very fitting terms at this point, introduced His Excellency, the Hon. W. Y. Atkinson, Governor of Georgia, who, in the name of the Commonwealth, delivered the address of welcome. The Governor's address was received with great enthusiasm and a rising vote of thanks with the Chautauqua salute was tendered him for his sincere and manly words.

The Rev. Bishop W. W. Duncan, D.D., of the Methodist Episcopal Church, South, was called and extended words of greeting.

Dr. Thirkield read a letter to the Congress from the Hon. E. W. Blyden, LL.D, who was detained in London by sickness. See letter of greeting.

The following addresses were then delivered: "A Bird's-eye View of African Tribes and Languages," by Heli Chatelain, African Traveler and Phililogist; "The African in Africa and the African in America," by the Hon. John H. Smyth, LL.D, ex-Minister to Liberia.

The Rev. Ross Taylor of New York, was necessarily absent. In place of his paper one on "Self-supporting Missions" by the Rev. Wm. Taylor, D.D., Bishop of Africa of the Methodist Episcopal Church, was subsequently forwarded, and is published.

In the absence of the paper from Dr. Blyden, the Rev. Josiah Tyler, D.D., forty years a missionary among the Zulus, spoke on "Missionary Experiences in Africa," and subsequently wrote a summary of his address for publication.

The discussion was opened by the Rev. C. S. Smith, D.D., Secretary of the Sunday-school Union of the African Methodist Episcopal Church.

Prof. J. C. Murray, D.D., read to the Congress the following letter of regrets and congratulations from the Rev. W. F. Stewart, A.M., who established the

Foundation, and who, by reason of sickness, was prevented from attending the Congress:

SEA BREEZE, FLA., October 12, 1895.

Bro. J. C. Murray, D.D., Gammon Theological Seminary, Atlanta, Ga.

DEAR BROTHER: In view of the state of my health and the advice of my physician, we will have to give up our visit to Atlanta. Mrs. Stewart will feel the disappointment even more than myself. By your kindness I shall hope to receive whatever reports are made of the addresses, etc. Has the thought been entertained of publishing the addresses, papers, and proceedings in a pamphlet for distribution and preservation?

Though not in body, I will be with you in spirit, and expect that the blessing of the Great Missionary--the Lord Jesus--will crown the Congress with success.

Your brother in Christ,

W. F. STEWART

On motion of Prof. E. L. Parks, D.D., the Secretary was instructed to send a telegram of greeting and sympathy to the Rev. and Mrs. W. F. Stewart, Sea Breeze, Fla.

Notices were given by Dr. Thirkield, and the Congress adjourned after the benediction by the Rev. Dr. Palmore, editor St. Louis *Christian Advocate,* Methodist Episcopal Church South.

AFTERNOON SESSION

LOYD STREET METHODIST EPISCOPAL CHURCH

The Congress reconvened at 2:30 P. M., Bishop I. W. Joyce, LL.D., in the Chair.

The Rev. E. W. S. Hammond, D.D., editor *Southwestern Christian Advocate,* New Orleans, La., conducted the devotional service by reading selections from the 12th chapter of Isaiah, and after the singing of suitable hymns by the Seminary choir, led in prayer.

Bishop Joyce then introduced the Rev. Orishetukeh Faduma, B.D., of West Africa, who addressed the Congress upon "The Religious Beliefs of the Yoruba People, Africa."

In the absence of Bishop H. M, Turner, D.D., of the African Methodist Episcopal Church, his paper on "The American Negro and his Fatherland" was read by the Rev. W. G. Alexander," D.D., pastor of Bethel African Methodist Episcopal Church. Atlanta.

After which, the Chairman introduced Prof. J. W. E. Bowen, of Gammon Theological Seminary, who delivered an address upon "The Comparative Status of the Negro at the Close of the War and of To-day."

The Secretary then read the telegram ordered to be sent to the Rev. and Mrs. W. F. Stewart, as follows:

ATLANTA, GA., December 14, 1895.

To the Rev. Wm. F. Stewart, Sea Breeze, Fla.

The Congress on Africa salutes you. Marked success. Enthusiastic, overflowing audiences. Ethiopia stretches forth her hand.

J. W. E. BOWEN, Secretary of the Congress.

Notices were given by Dr. Thirkield, and the benediction was pronounced by Bishop Joyce, and the Congress adjourned.

EVENING SESSION

BETHEL AFRICAN METHODIST EPISCOPAL CHURCH

The Congress on Africa reconvened at 7:30 P. M., with Bishop W. J. Gaines, D. D., of the African Methodist Episcopal Church, in the Chair.

The devotional exercises were conducted by the Rev. Wm. McMorris, of Vicksburg, Miss.

A paper on "The American Negro in the Twentienth Century," contributed by H. K. Carroll, LL.D., Editor New York *Independent* and Superintendent of the United States Census of Churches, was read by Professor E. L. Parks, D. D., of the Seminary.

Mr. Cyrus C. Adams, Editor of the New York *Sun,* then delivered his famous illustrated lecture on "New Things We Have Learned about Africa." The lecture was profusely illustrated with large and accurate maps and geographical data from the earliest discoveries to the present time.

The notices were read by President Thirkield, and after the benediction by Bishop Gaines, the Congress adjourned.

SECOND DAY--SATURDAY, DECEMBER 14

MORNING SESSION

LOYD STREET METHODIST EPISCOPAL CHURCH

The second day's sessions of the Congress witnessed still larger audiences than those of the first. Through the public press, notably the Atlanta *Constitution* and the *Journal,* not only the city, but the entire State and surrounding States were alive with interest in the proceedings of the Congress. Representatives came from all sections of the South, North and the far Northwest.

President Thirkield introduced the Rev. Bishop W. W. Duncan, D. D., of the Methodist Episcopal Church, South, as Chairman of the morning session.

President L. M. Dunton, D. D., of Claflin University, Orangeburg, S. C., led the devotions with a Scripture selection from Acts 1, and then with prayer.

Music was rendered by the Seminary choir.

Bishop Duncan introduced the Rev. Thomas G. Addison, D. D., special delegate from the American Colonization Society, who delivered an address upon "The Present Policy of the Colonization Society."

The next speaker was the Rev. Alexander Crummell, D. D., "Rector Emeritus" of St. Luke's Episcopal Church, Washington, D. C., author of "Africa and America," and a missionary for twenty years in Africa. His subject was "The Absolute Need of an Indigenous Missionary Agency for the Evangelization of Africa." His second address was not delivered owing to his delay in reaching the city. It is, however, published with the other addresses. The subject was: "Civilization as a Collateral and Indispensable Instrumentality in Planting the Christian Church in Africa."

The next speaker was Mr. T. Thomas Fortune, Editor of the New York *Age;* subject, "The Nationalization of Africa."

Then followed an address on the subject, "Occult Africa," by the Rev. J. W. Hamilton, D.D., of Boston, Mass., Corresponding Secretary of the Freedmen's

Aid and Southern Education Society, Cincinnati, Ohio, of the Methodist Episcopal Church.

The next speaker was Miss Alice Bacon, Secretary of the Hampton Folk-Lore Society, in Hampton Industrial and Normal Institute. Her subject was "The Study of Folk-Lore."

The closing address of the morning was delivered by Mr. Cyrus C. Adams, Editor of the New York *Sun,* on "Some Results of the African Movement."

The discussion was led by President E. M. Cravath, D. D., of Fisk University, Nashville, Tenn.

Annnouncements were read by President Thirkield.

Bishop Duncan then said: "I was born among you. Don't think of yourselves as 'colored people,' but think about yourselves as those whom God has called to be men. I never put in my definition of 'man' the idea of color. Be men, and I assure you that lines of longitude and latitude will not measure the respect given to you. I welcome this hour. Determine that you will solve your own problem by being true to the estate to which you are called in these latter days."

The choir then sang the Doxology, and the benediction was pronounced by Bishop Duncan.

AFTERNOON SESSION

MOODY TABERNACLE

The afternoon session was held in the Moody Tabernacle. In the absence of the Hon. W. J. Northen, ex-Governor of Georgia, who was to preside, the Rev. Bishop I. W. Joyce, LL.D., of Chattanooga, Tenn., presided.

The devotional service was conducted by President D. C. John, D.D., of Clark University, who read the Scriptures and led in prayer.

President Thirkield read letter of regrets from ex-Governor W.J. Northen explaining his inability to be present.

A song service was led by the seminary choir, which sang many of the jubilee songs of the Negroes, and also two of the prize hymns composed by students of the seminary for the Stewart Missionary Foundation for Africa.

Another unique feature of the Tabernacle meeting was the presence in a body of the students and teachers from Spellman Seminary, Atlanta Baptist University, Atlanta Seminary, and Clark University.

The first address was on the subject, "Success and Drawbacks of Missionary Work in Africa," by the Rev. Orishetukeh Faduma, B.D., West Africa.

The next address was on the subject, "My Life in Africa," by Miss Etna Holderness, of the Bassa tribe, Africa.

Then followed Mrs. M. French-Sheldon, F.R.G.S., African Traveler, and Author of "From Sultan to Sultan," on "Practical Issues of an African Experience." Mrs. Sheldon exhibited, during her address, a large number of articles of African skill and industry, and also curios from Africa that she had gathered.

After announcements the benediction was pronounced by the Rev. J. S. Flipper, D.D., of Atlanta.

EVENING SESSION

MOODY TABERNACLE

The sixth session of the Congress was held on Saturday evening, December 14th, in the Moody Tabernacle, with Professor E. L. Parks, D.D., of Gammon Theological Seminary, as chairman.

The Rev. A. M. Trotter, Presiding Elder in the Mississippi Conference, read the scriptures and made the opening prayer.

The first paper presented was on, "Health Conditions and Hygiene in Central Africa," by R. W. Felkin, M.D., F. R. S. E., F. R. G. S., ex-missionary to Uganda, Africa.

Then followed a paper on "The Negro in His Relations to the Church," by H. K. Carroll, LL D., Editor of *The Independent,* New York, and Superintendent of the United States Census of Churches. This paper was read by the Rev. Geo. W. Arnold, B.D., Presiding Elder of the Atlanta District, Atlanta Conference.

An address was then delivered by the Rev. J. C. Hartzell, D.D., Corresponding Secretary of the Freedmen's Aid and Southern Education Society, Cincinnati, O. Subject: "Africa in America and beyond the Seas."

The closing address was made by Mrs. M. French Sheldon, F.R.G.S., African Traveler, and Author of "From Sultan to Sultan." Her address was illustrated with many original and instructive views of African scenes, peoples, and countries.

The following resolutions were presented by the Rev. E. W. S. Hammond, D.D., and the Rev. M. C. B. Mason, D.D , and were unanimously agreed to.

"WHEREAS, The great Cotton States and International Exposition has furnished the Negroes of this country with a rare opportunity for the exhibition of their trades and skill in handicraft; and

WHEREAS, This great Exposition now being held in this city is accomplishing great good in bringing to our Southland people of the various States of the Union, and which, we believe, will contribute largely towards the growth of a better sentiment and the obliteration of sectional strife and confusion; and

WHEREAS, The Commissioners of the Exposition have merited the respect of the colored citizens of the State of Georgia and elsewhere by generously inviting them to take part in the Exposition, by encouraging them in a display of their skill and handicraft and genius, and by the erection of a suitable and commodious structure, the well-known and magnificent Negro Building, set apart especially for this purpose; and

WHEREAS, We are highly pleased, helped and instructed by the marvelous display made by our institutions of learning and industrial schools, and also by those displays made by individuals of the race, we rejoice in the fact so triumphantly established that these exhibits have won encomiums from the thousands of visitors who have been in attendance, without regard to race or color, from His Excellency, the President of the United States, and the honorable Governor of the noble State whose citizens we are, to the humblest farmer. Therefore,

Resolved, That this Congress on Africa gives its indorsement to the work of the State Commissioners and the Commissioners of the States who have labored so earnestly, faithfully and persistently in accomplishing these splendid results, which stands as magnificent object lessons of the capacity and ability of the Afro-American.

Resolved further, That we therefore cheerfully commend these exhibits to our people, and join with our honored Chief Commissioner, I. Garland Penn, and the eminent gentlemen with him, in extending an invitation to all our people to attend the Exposition and behold the great results which speak so eloquently for the race.

Resolved, That we haste this generous invitation to the Negro to take such a conspicuous part in the Cotton States Exposition as the harbinger of a better era for the Negro, which we pray may eventuate in his full and complete recognition as an important factor in the solution in all of our great national problems."

The doxology was sung by the choir, and the benediction pronounced by the Rev. Geo. W. Arnold, B.D.

THIRD DAY--SUNDAY, DEC. 15

MORNING SERVICE

LOYD STREET METHODIST EPISCOPAL CHURCH

The Sabbath opened bright and clear and the announcement that Bishop Joyce would preach was sufficient to draw an immense audience in the morning.

Professor J. C. Murray, D.D., of Gammon Theological Seminary, had charge of the service

The Rev. J. B. Middleton, D.D., of the South Carolina Conference, read the "Missionary Hymn for Africa," written by the Rev. Joseph Wheeler, of the Conference, in the contest of the churches for the Stewart Missionary Foundation for Africa.

After singing by the choir, Professor J. C. Murray, D.D., led in a fervent prayer for the Spirit's blessing upon the service and for the largest results of the Congress upon Africa, and also for God's special blessing upon the establisher of the Foundation, the Rev. W. F. Stewart and his wife.

The Bishop then announced the Missionary Hymn, "From Greenland's Icy Mountain" and after the singing, read the morning lessons from Psalms cxlix and cl.

Announcements were made by Dr. Murray.

The sermon was preached by the Rev. Bishop I. W. Joyce, LL.D. His text was 1 John iv, 7th verse. It should be said at this point that the Bishop came to the congress from a long tour of episcopal work in the Northwest. An abstract of the sermon would not do him justice. He contributed largely to the success of the Congress, both by his sermon and by his tact and wisdom in presiding at several of its sessions.

The closing prayer was made by the Rev. George Standing.

After the doxology by the choir, the Rev. J. A. Brown, Presiding Elder in the South Carolina Conference, pronounced the benediction.

AFTERNOON SERVICE
LOYD STREET METHODIST EPISCOPAL CHURCH

The Rev. R. S. Rust, D.D., presided.

Devotional service was conducted by the Rev. S. J. Harris, pastor of the church. The choir rendered a selection.

Mr. Heli Chatelain, African Traveler, Philologist and Author of "Folk-Tales of Angola," delivered an address upon "African Slavery : Its Status; the Anti-Slavery Movement in Europe; What Can and Ought to be Done by Americans for the Relief of African Slaves."

At the close of Mr. Chatelain's valuable address, Bishop Joyce spoke words of commendation for the valuable service Mr. Chatelain had rendered this Congress and the cause of Africa by his travels, researches, and literary and philanthropic plans. He then submitted the following resolutions, which were adopted unanimously by a rising vote:

We have heard with growing satisfaction the address of our brother, Mr. Heli Chatelain, on "The Status of African Slavery and the Anti-Slavery Movement in Europe," and also of his purpose to form a society for the study of the subject with the object in view of the ultimate suppression and extirpation of slavery and the slave trade in Africa; therefore,

Resolved, That we, as a Congress assembled to discuss and consider the interests and wellfare of Africa, do hereby express our sympathy with our brother, Mr. Heli Chatelain, in his great purpose and work, and wish him every possible success in his great and humane as well as Christly mission, and as we have means and opportunity we will co-operate with him.

The next paper was on the subject: "The Outlook for African Missions in the Twentieth Century," by Mr. Frederic Perry Noble, Secretary of the World's Congress on Africa at the Columbian Exposition, Chicago, Ill. This paper was read by the Rev. Joseph E. Roy, D.D., of Chicago, Ill.

Then followed an address upon "Africa in its Relation to Christian Civilization," by the Rev. E. W. S. Hammond, D.D., Editor of the *Southwestern Christian Advocate,* New Orleans, La.

The Chairman, the Rev. R. S. Rust, D.D., LL.D., Honorary Secretary of the Freedmen's Aid and Southern Education Society, and for thirty years closely connected with work of educating the colored people, then spoke upon "The Needs of Africans as Men."

The session closed with the benediction by Dr. Rust.

EVENING SERVICE

BETHEL AFRICAN METHODIST EPISCOPAL CHURCH

The final session of the Congress opened with President W. P. Thirkield, D.D., of Gammon Thological Seminary, as chairman.

The Seminary choir led the song service with many of the original hymns of the Negroes. Not since the days of the famous "Jubilee Singers" and the plaintive "Tennesseeans" has the songs of Negro melodies been so effectively rendered. Those historic heart-songs were wrung out of the deepest heart of a woe-stricken people. Of those that were sung, special mention may be made of "Steal Away," "Swing Low Sweet Chariot," "He Rose from the Dead," "We Shall Walk Through the Valley," and the two Prize Missionary Hymns of the "Stewart Missionary Foundation for Africa." Under the leadership of Instructor Schilling, who directed the singing, and Mrs. J. W. E. Bowen, who presided at the instrument, the vast audience joined with the trained choir of the seminary and gave to these songs their old name, "the songs of the soul." This feature of the Congress was an element equally enjoyed by all the visitors.

The opening prayer was made by the Rev. B. F. Witherspoon, Presiding Elder of the South Carolina Conference. Seated upon the platform were the distinguished visitors who had taken part in the Congress, and many others who had come from many States.

The audience packed the aisles long before the service opened, and soon after it opened the doorways, vestibules, and even the sidewalks in front of the church were banked with a mass of anxious humanity. It was the crowning audience that had visited the Congress.

The first address was delivered by the Rev. M. C. B. Mason, D.D., Assistant Corresponding Secretary Freedmen's Aid and Southern Education Society. His subject was "The Methodist Episcopal Church and the Evangelization of Africa."

The closing address was delivered by the Rev. Joseph E. Roy, D.D., Chairman of the World's Congress on Africa at the Columbian Exposition, Chicago, Ill., on "Africa and America." The lecture was illustrated with numerous and interesting views of the Negro in Africa, in the West Indies, and in America, illustrating almost every phase of his old life and his modern life.

President Thirkield then closed the Congress with fitting words upon the labor involved, plans of the Stewart Missionary Foundation, and the success of the movement. He announced also that the Seminary had decided to publish the proceedings of the Congress in book form, and that already there were eight hundred subscribers to the same. In the name of the faculty and Seminary and the people of Atlanta, and in the name of the generous founder of the Foundation under whose auspices this Congress was held, he thanked the speakers who had contributed to its success, and the churches that had generously opened their doors to the sessions of the Congress, and also the newspapers, the Atlanta *Constitution* and the *Journal,* which had given favorable comment upon the Congress from its inception and had widened the sphere of its influence and power by liberal and accurate publication of its sessions.

The Doxology was then sung, the benediction pronounced by the Rev. I. W. Joyce, LL.D., of the Methodist Episcopal Church.

Thus closed the first Congress on Africa held in the South,of which the Atlanta *Constitution* said: "What was probably the most distinguished gathering of learned men of both colors that has ever assembled together in the history of the South met yesterday morning when the African Congress began the first session of its deliberations on the history, life and progress of the Christianization of the African. * * * * * There certainly has not been gathered in any other city a more august body of colored divines and men of brains and eloquence in their race since the days of slavery."

J. W. E. BOWEN,
Secretary of the Congress

Prize Hymns Written By American Negroes

AWARDED FIRST PRIZE OF HYMNS FROM THE SEMINARY IN 1894

Original Hymn--(Tune, "Autumn")

A HYMN OF SYMPATHY AND PRAYER FOR AFRICA

BY ALEXANDER P. CAMPHOR, A.M. B.D., CLASS '95

Far across the mighty ocean
Is a land of palmy plains,
But that land is not enlightened;
It is one where darkness reigns,
There the heathen in his blindness,
Knoweth not the blessed word,
Nor of Jesus Christ, the Savior,
Precious Lord, our only Lord.

Africa, 'tis named, that country,
Far away from this bright shore,
Far removed from light and knowledge,
Far remote from Christian lore;
There, for many, many ages,
Ling'ring still in blackest night,
Africa, dark land of hist'ry,
Void of light, is void of light.

How can we remain contented
In illuminated homes,
While our brother gropes in darkness,
And in heathenism roams ?
Should not his complete salvation
Be our earnest, prayerful plea,

Till that long-neglected country
Shall be free, yes, wholly free ?

Africa, thou ebon country,
How we long to see thee free !
E'er shall we, for thy redemption
Work and pray, till thou shalt be
Free from every degredation,
That has cursed thy sunny land,
This the constant supplication
Of our band, our Christian band.

Awarded First Prize of Hymns from the Churches in 1895
Original Hymn--(Tune, "Webb")
MISSIONARY HYMN FOR AFRICA
BY THE REV. JOSEPH WHEELER, HARRISBURG, PA.

O, Africa, in darkness
Thy land shall all be bright;
Thy people shall be favored
With hallowed Gospel light.
The coming years will bring thee
Great blessings yet undreamed;
Thy people shall be numbered
Among the earth's redeemed.

The ancient seers have spoken
The word at God's command,
They told the sacred story
Of Ethiop's outstretched hand;
They cry to God in pity,
Send, Christians, to their need,
O, labor for the Master!
Sow now the precious seed!

Arise, O Afric's children,
Enter your fatherland,
Take ye the Gospel banner,
Go forth at God's command;
Remember, Christ is with you,
His arm will you defend,
Remember Jesus' promise:
I'm with you to the end.

O, God of grace and mercy,
Look from thy throne above,
On Africa whose millions
Have never known Thy love;
Grant that the Spirit's power

On them may now descend;
Grant Thou our prayer in mercy,
As at Thy throne we bend.

APPENDIX A

Table of Bible translations (the Whole Bible or Portions), by Robert Needham Cust, LL.D., Author of Modern Languages of Africa, Bible Translations and Notes on Missionary Subjects:

NORTHERN REGION

1	Koptic (3) D. (dead)	4	Kabáil
2	Arabic	5	Shilha (1) D., Riff
3	Nuba	6	Shilha (2) D., Shlu

WESTERN REGION

1	Jolof or Wolof	15	Igára
2	Mande or Mandingo	16	Idzo
3	Susu	17	Ibo
4	Bullom	18	Nupé
5	Temne	19	Hausa
6	Mende	20	Efik
7	Grebo	21	Dualla
8	Ashanti (1) D., Fanti	22	Pongwe
9	Ashanti (2) D., Akwápem	23	Benga
10	Akra or Ga	24	Kelé
11	Ewé (1) D., Anlo	25	Teke
12	Ewé (2) D., Popo or Dahómi	26	Kongo
13	Yáriba	27	Angolan or Ki-Mbundu
14	Igbira	28	U-mbundu

SOUTHERN REGION

1	Hereró	6	Pedi
2	Nama or Hottentot	7	Zulu
3	Chuána	8	Gwamba
4	Súto	9	Sheitswa, or Tonga, or Siga
5	Xosa (Káfir)		

EASTERN REGION

1	Nyanja	14	Tavéta
2	Kondi	15	Kamba
3	Wanda, or Nyikinsa	16	Galla (1) D., Shoa
4	Zulu, D., Ngoni	17	Galla (2) D., Ittu
5	Yao	18	Galla (3) D., Barrarretta
6	Makúa	19	Amháric
7	Swahili	20	Tigré
8	Bondei	21	Tigrinna
9	Kagúru	22	Giz or Ethiopic
10	Gogo	23	Bogos or Bilin
11	Ganda	24	Agua, D., Falásha Kara
12	Nyika	25	Luba
13	Giriáma		

ABSTRACT

Northern	6
Western	28
Southern	9

Eastern	25
Total	68

N. B.--Translations are reported to be in preparation in other languages, but the greatest reserve has to be maintained until a copy is in print.

APPENDIX B
ALPHABETICAL LIST OF MISSIONS

BY ROBERT NEEDHAM CUST, LL.D.
Author of Modern Languages of Africa, Bible Translations, and Notes on Missionary Subjects

No.	Name of Missions.	Region.	Nationality of Senders.	Protestant or Church of Rome.
1	African Missions of Lyons	Northern Western	France.	R
2	Arnot's Mission	West'n & East'n	Great Britain.	P
3	Baptist Society, America	Western	United States N. A.	P
4	(1) North	Western	United States N. A.	P
5	(2) South	Western	United States N. A.	P
6	(3) Colored	Western	United States N. A.	P
7	Baptist Society, English	Western	Great Britain.	P
8	Basle Mission	Western	Switzerland.	P
9	Bavarian Protestant Mission	Eastern	Germany.	P
10	Benedictine Congregation	Eastern	Germany.	R
11	Berlin Missionary Society	Southern Eastern	Germany.	P
12	Bible Society, American	Northern	United States N. A.	P
13	Bible Society, British	Northern Western Southern Eastern	Great Britain.	P
14	(Congregational.) Board of Foreign Missions, Am'n	Western Southern	United States N. A.	P
15	Capuchin	Northern Eastern	International.	R

16	Christian Doctrine, Brothers of	Northern Western	France.	R
17	Church Missionary Society	Northern Western Eastern	Great Britain.	P
18	Colonial Missionary Society	Southern	Great Britain.	P
19	Cowley Fathers	Southern	Great Britain.	P
20	Dominicans	Southern	Great Britain.	R
21	Dutch Reformed Church	Southern Eastern	Cape Colony.	P
22	Episcopal Church, American	Western	United States N. A.	P
23	Episcopal Church, English	Western Southern Eastern	Great Britain.	P
24	Established Church, Scotland	Eastern	Great Britain.	P
*25 * Probably the "International Missionary Alliance." Western, U. S. A., P. (Undenominational).	Evangelical Alliance, American	Western	United States N. A.	P
26	Evangelical Lutheran, American	Western	United States N. A.	P
27	Finnish	Southern	Finland, Russia.	P

28	Franciscans	Northern Eastern	International.	R
29	Free Church of Scotland	Southern Eastern	Great Britain.	P
30	Friends Mission	Southern	Great Britain.	P

31	German East Africa Mission	Eastern	Germany.	P
32	Gordon College	Northern	Great Britain.	P
33	Holy Ghost and Heart of Mary	Western Southern Eastern	France.	R
34	Hermannsburg Mission	Southern	Germany.	P
35	Issoudon Mission	Southern	France.	R
36	Jesuits	Northern Western Southern Eastern	International.	R
37	Jews' London Society	Northern	Great Britain.	P
38	Jews' Parochial Mission	Northern	Great Britain.	P
39	Kaiserswerth Deaconesses	Northern	Germany.	P
40	Kongo-Balólo Mission	Western	Great Britain.	P
41	Lady Huntingdon's Connexion	Western	Great Britain.	P
42	Lady of Africa	Northern Eastern	France.	R
43	Lazarists	Northern Eastern	International.	R
44	London Miss'ry Soc'y, Cong'al.	Southern Eastern	Great Britain.	P
45	Mahometan Mission	Southern	Cape Colony.	P
46	Marists	Southern	France.	R
47	Methodist Episcopal, American.	Western	United States N. A.	P
	Methodist Episcopal, African	Western	United States N. A.	P
48	Moravian Mission	Southern Eastern	Germany.	P
49	Menkirchen Mission	Eastern	Germany.	P
50	North Africa Mission	Northern	Great Britain.	P
51	North German Mission	Western	Germany.	P
52	Norwegian Mission	Southern	Norway.	P
53	Oblats of Mary	Southern	France.	R
54	Oblats of Francis of Sales	Southern	France.	R
55	United Brethren	Western	United States N. A.	P

56	Pallotin Congregation	Western	Germany.	R
57	Paris Evangelical Mission	Northern Western Southern	France.	P
58	Portuguese Priests	Western Eastern	Portugal,	R
59	Presbyterian Church, American (North)	Western	United States N. A.	P
60	Presbyterian Church, American (South)	Western	United States N. A.	P
61	Presbyterian, United, American	Northern	United States N. A.	P
62	Presbyterian, United, Scotch	Northern Western Southern	Great Britain.	P
63	Primitive Methodist	Southern Eastern	Great Britain.	P
64	Rhenish Mission	Western	Germany.	P

65	Sahara, Brothers of	Northern Eastern	France.	R
66	Schent lez Bruxelles Missions	Western	Belgium.	R
67	Spanish Priests	Northern Western	Spain.	R
68	Sudan Mission, American	Western	United States N. A.	P
69	Swedish Church	Southern	Sweden.	P
70	Swedish Evangelical Mission	Western Eastern	Sweden.	P
71	French-Swiss Mission	Eastern	Switzerland.	P
72	Taylor, Wm., Bishop Methodist Episcopal Church	Eastern Western	United States N. A.	P
73	United Methodist Church Miss.	Western Eastern	Great Britain.	P
74	Universities' Missions	Eastern	Great Britain.	P
75	Verona Institute	Northern	Italy.	R
76	Wesleyan Missionary Society	Northern Western	Great Britain.	P

		Southern		
77	West Indies Episcopal	Western	Great Britain.	P
78	Whatley School and Hospital	Northern	Great Britain.	P
79	Young People's Foreign Missionary Society	Eastern	United States N. A.	P
80	Trappists	Southern Western	France.	R

A view in the Reading Room of the Library of Gammon Theological Seminary

An interior view in Library of Seminary and Depository of Stewart Foundation Collection